THE **BLACK LORDS** OF **SUMMER**

Ashley Mallett is a former spin bowler who played 38 Test matches for Australia from 1968 to 1980. He took 693 first class wickets at an average of 26, including 132 Test wickets, with an innings best of 8/59 against Pakistan at the Adelaide Oval in December 1972. Mallett is a cricket writer, TV commentator and coach, and was involved in a film documentary of the 1868 Australian Cricket Team, *The First Eleven*. *The Black Lords of Summer* is his twenty-second book and he is currently coaching at the elite level throughout the world.

Also by Ashley Mallett

Rowdy
Spin Out
100 Cricket Tips
Bradman's Band
Eleven: The Greatest Eleven of the 20th Century
Trumper: The Illustrated Biography
Clarrie Grimmett: The Bradman of Spin

Master Sportsman Series
Cricket: *Don Bradman, Doug Walters, Geoff Lawson, Kim Hughes,
    Rod Marsh, The Chappell Bros, Dennis Lillee, Allan Border*
Soccer: *John Kosmina*
Tennis: *Evonne Cawley*
Australian Rules Football: *Mark Williams, Wayne Johnston,
    Robert Flower, Tim Watson*

THE **BLACK LORDS** OF **SUMMER**

ASHLEY MALLETT

THE STORY OF THE 1868 ABORIGINAL TOUR OF ENGLAND AND BEYOND

University of Queensland Press

First published 2002 by University of Queensland Press
Box 6042, St Lucia, Queensland 4067 Australia

www.uqp.uq.edu.au

Typeset by University of Queensland Press
Printed in Australia by McPherson's Printing Group

Distributed in the USA and Canada by
International Specialized Book Services, Inc.,
5824 N.E. Hassalo Street, Portland, Oregon 97213–3640

 Sponsored by the Queensland Office
Queensland of Arts and Cultural Development.
Government
Arts Queensland

  Promotion of this book was financially
assisted by the South Australian Government
through Arts SA.

Government of
South Australia   **A R T S A**

Cataloguing in Publication Data
National Library of Australia

Mallett, Ashley, 1945–   .
    The black lords of summer: the story of the 1868
    Aboriginal tour of England and beyond.

    1. Cricket — Tournaments — England — History. 2.
    Aboriginal Australian cricket players — Victoria. 3.
    Cricket players — Australia. I. Title.

Bibliography.
Includes index.

796.358650994

ISBN 0 7022 3262 9

Cover painting by Dave Thomas. Limited editions of this painting are
available for purchase through artofcricket@capint.com.au

ACKNOWLEDGMENTS

DAVID DUNBAR-NASMITH's widow, Elizabeth, sent me photostat copies of parts of Brown's journal, the original of which is kept at the Dunbar-Nasmith family home at Rothes in Morayshire. David Dunbar-Nasmith died a year before my research took me in his direction. My thanks to Elizabeth for her help.

The letter to *The Times* brought an array of people, such as Peter Lovesey, with his tips and pointers to *Bell's Life*, Janet Gilford from Witham, Keith Booth of the Surrey County Cricket Club, David Poole of York, Jonathon Martin and Philip A. McHoul. Some of these people, especially Peter Lovesey, Janet Gilford and Keith Booth went out of their way to help. Philip Jones and Kate Alport of the South Australian Museum (archives) helped with interpretation and explanation of Aboriginal terms, meanings and place names. Their input helped me get a handle on the culture of the Aboriginal groups from where the players came and sense of family the Aboriginal players had in Australia. Thanks also to the Reverend Bill Edwards of Adelaide for his paper on 'The fate of an Aboriginal cricketer: where did Dick-a-Dick die?' (*Australian Aboriginal Studies*, 1999). Christina Hindhaugh, writer and researcher, was helpful in lending me copies of newspaper cuttings and jottings about the 1868 tour. Christina was the driving force behind the story of the 1868 Australians being told in the documentary film. Warwick Torrens helped in relation to the Queensland Cricket Association letter which sounded the death knell for Eddie Gilbert's career. David Frith, the well-known cricket author and long-time editor of *Wisden Cricket Monthly*, was superb in his help and encouragement. He directed me towards specific articles and books and the 1930 Cricket article by Major C. B. H. Pridham I found at the Lord's Cricket Ground Library. There curator Stephen Green and his assistant Michael Walton could not have been more helpful. My thanks to Sir Alec Bedser for his information on the gas holders at The Oval and to Jan Leishman of *The Spectator*,

Hamilton. The State libraries of South Australia and New South Wales, the South Australia Mortlock Reference Library and the Mitchell Library in Sydney all provided excellent sources for my research. I thank Julie McKenzie, a librarian and researcher of Bellevue Heights for her input and encouragement. Julie helped me find Faith Thomas (nee Coulthard), the first female Aboriginal Test cricketer. Thanks also to Faith and to Jason Gillespie, the first acknowledged Aboriginal (male) Test player and his father Neil.

To Rick Shafter and Rodney Cavalier, to Mick Dodson, Margaret Walters (Sydney University), the late Charles Perkins, ATSIC field officer John Tatten and Grant Sarra, ATSIC media officer Mark Heward and John Maquire — thank you all. I sought a particular article written for the Journal of Labor History and pertinent to the legal aspects of the 1868 tour. Associate Professor Wendy Brady of the Aboriginal Research and Resource Centre, University of New South Wales, was most helpful. Wendy alerted me to a thesis written by Genevieve Blades on Australian Aborigines in Cricket and Pedestrianism: Culture and Conflict, 1880–1910. The 1868 Australians had an enormous impact on what was to come for Aboriginal cricketers and thus Genevieve's study was of importance to this story. Bernard Whimpress, the South Australian Cricket Association Museum curator, provided encouragement and help. Bernard wrote *Passport to Nowhere: Aborigines in Australian Cricket, 1850–1939*, and found some enlightening material, much of which confirmed my own research. Thanks also to the custodians of the Melbourne Cricket Ground Museum and Library for allowing me to study George Graham's ledger of the 1868 tour, a most revealing document and extraordinary for what was not included in the columns. James McCaughey allowed me to take a long look at the 1868 England tour score-book, which he had been nervously storing at his home office in Middle Park for months during his work on the documentary film. The idea of publishing the book in the United Kingdom dawned on me and UQP put me in touch with Ernest Hecht of Souvenir Press. So the book was to be published in Australia and in England in the year of 2002, timed to get the start of the 2002 English cricket season. Thanks to Christine for reading the copy and for her patience. Thanks to her and to my son, Ben, for their advice on how I might possibly get through the opening few paragraphs to introduce Charles Lawrence.

INTRODUCTION

THIS work is ostensibly about the 1868 Aboriginal cricketers tour of England — Australian cricket's first official overseas tour. However, it is more than a cricket story. It has led me along the most fascinating literary journey of my writing experience. It has been a journey of tears and laughter, because, as you will see, as you turn the pages, I actually become part of the story, this never-ending tale of heartache and hope. I fell into this book. In 1999 I was speaking to John McGuire, the man who captained the 1988 re-enactment of the Aboriginal tour of England. The team, managed by rugby star Mark Ella, played at many of the venues of the original 1868 team. Maguire had played for my old Perth club, Mt Lawley. As an opener, he amassed some 500-plus runs per season, but he never played for Western Australia. Why? He smiled the sort of smile you might expect from a man who has suffered injustice. I thought aloud and offered a Test cap for the Aboriginal community to have on loan until such time as they produced a male Test cricketer. I knew that a female — Faith Thomas — had played for Australia many years ago, but never had an Aboriginal player worn the baggy green cap for our Test XI. Well, none that we knew about.

Maguire spoke about a well-known theatre identity, director James McCaughey, who was producing a documentary-film on the 1868 Australians. Maybe my cap offer could be worked somehow into the film? Eventually McCaughey and I got together. We discussed the offer of the cap and how it might work in the film. Not long after the news came that Jason Gillespie's paternal great-grandfather was Aboriginal. Gillespie became the first officially acknowledged Aboriginal (male) Test cricketer. Whew! I'd saved my Test cap, but as a writer and researcher I had committed my services to the making of the documentary. I would help with the script and with some of the narration. I became fascinated with the subject. James McCaughey's professionalism was also greatly impressive. A few months later I spoke passionately about the 1868 Australians with Laurie Muller of the University of Queensland Press.

Laurie didn't hold back: 'Let's write the book!' His enthusiasm was infectious. I saw the importance of this story far beyond the realm of cricket and I knew it would take an enormous amount of energy and persistence. I agreed immediately. What a challenge. I pointed out that historian and expert on Aboriginal anthropology Professor John Mulvaney had written a book on the 1868 Australians back in 1967. Then in 1988 Mulvaney had joined forces with Melbourne historian Rex Harcourt and in collaboration they produced an updated version of the story. *Cricket Walkabout: The Australian Aborigines in England* (Macmillan) is a thoroughly well researched book. However, I believed that the story needed greater depth and colour about the culture clash between the team's captain, Charles Lawrence, a white man, and the Aboriginal cricketers, most of whom hailed from the western districts of Victoria (the Wimmera) in the shadow of the awesome Gariwerd (Grampian mountains). How Lawrence from one old and established culture came to lead people from the most ancient culture on earth on Australian cricket's first overseas tour is a fascinating tale.

It has been important to detail where the Aboriginal cricketers came from and the injustices brought upon their people by the invading Europeans who became the occupying force. This story is an important historical event, for it had (and has) enormous sociological implications for all Australians. The 'protection' of Aborigines was hastened in the wake of the 1868 tour, especially as a result of the death of King Cole in the early stages of the tour, and that so-called protection led to children being taken from their families and placed in foster care.

Charles Lawrence came out to Australia with the first England team in 1861/62. He stayed and became Australia's first professional coach, supplementing his income with a stint as a publican in Sydney. Lawrence certainly wanted to enhance the cricket of the Aboriginal players from the Wimmera and other parts. But his greatest motive was to make money, and lots of it. His reason for taking the men to

England to play cricket was to make a financial killing out of their skill at hurling a boomerang and throwing a spear. Lawrence drilled them at cricket, but he figured that they were of such entertainment value that he could make money by showing them off in England as 'curiosities'.

Lawrence treated his men well. There is no suggestion that he or any other member of the team management maltreated the players in a physical sense. When King Cole died, Lawrence was the only member of the side to attend the burial, but there was a reason for other members of the team being absent.

As my research progressed I was able to date every one of the 47 matches played by the Aboriginal team. Their first match was at The Oval, the great England ground with its famous gas-holders and the place where Bradman played his last Test innings. When in England in June 2000, I was at a ground called Mote Park to coach some Kent County Cricket Club spinners and found that I had stumbled upon a ground on which the 1868 Australians had played one of their early matches. One of the players, Redcap, had in fact killed a squirrel with one hurl of his boomerang as it scurried up a giant oak. At Nottingham I was helped by Nottingham County Cricket Club historian Peter Wynn-Thomas, a cricket lover if ever there was one and author of many books, including a series produced by the Association of Cricket Statisticians and Historians on famous cricketers, including George Parr, W. G. Grace, Harold Larwood and Frank Tarrant. So few good photographs of the 1868 Australians exist that I toyed with the idea of placing an advertisement in *The Times* of London in the hope that someone might come forward with a photo hitherto unseen. It was possible, for Clarrie Grimmett was just about to deliver his first ball at the nets at Lord's in 1930 when a man approached him and handed him a brown envelope containing a photo of the 1868 Aboriginal team that had never been seen in the public forum. A lengthy article about the 1868 Australians had recently appeared in *The Cricketer*, a splendid English cricket magazine begun by no less a personage than Sir Pelham Warner. The article was the catalyst and Grimmett was the bowler of the moment, so he got the precious photograph. An advertisement of the size I would have needed to make my point would have cost about 1000 pounds, so I wrote a Letter to the Editor instead. That did the trick.

The letter was published in *The Times* on 12 June 2000 and I received a tremendous amount of mail and offers to help with the research. It was quite overwhelming and extraordinarily helpful. I received a letter from a well-known and long-established English author, Peter Vansittart. Peter agreed to read through the section of my first draft that traced the route Lawrence took when he walked along the banks of the Thames to London Bridge on his way to Lord's. It was vital that the details were accurate. Vansittart, as a boy, knew C. J. Kortright, who played for Essex from 1895 to 1907 and was regarded as the fastest bowler of the day.

I spent a day at Lord's in the library, looking up all manner of material that might be helpful to this book. Curator Stephen Green is another with a passion for the game and he was most helpful, even digging out two old 1868 scorecards of the Aboriginal matches. The original cards stand alongside Dick-a-Dick's leangle or 'killer boomerang', which he used (along with a parrying shield) to dodge cricket balls hurled at him by excited members at Lord's and elsewhere. In 2001 I got to hold the Dick-a-Dick leangle. Usually Stephen Green is adamant about priceless objects staying 'safe' behind the glass. *The Ashes* urn itself stands proudly only two paces from Dick-a-Dick's leangle. On the morning of a re-enactment match between the MCC and our Aboriginal youth team the war-club suddenly appeared and we got a close look at the intricate carving and the message written on pig-skin stuck to the side of the weapon by the old South Australian and Test all-rounder George Giffen, once known as the W. G. Grace of Australian cricket. Matt Peacock of the ABC was filming the occasion. Adam Walker, who is related to another 1868 team member, Johnny Cuzens, held the war-club and the cameras captured the moment, for Walker is almost certainly the first Aboriginal person to hold the killer boomerang since Dick-a-Dick left it in England in 1868.

This extraordinary literary journey brought me in touch with a wonderful array of people. David Berry from the New South Wales State Library searched and sifted for passenger lists of various ships. Alas there was none to be found for the wool-clipper *Parramatta*.

Certainly not for the *Parramatta* that left Sydney on 8 February 1868 bound for England with the Aboriginal cricketers on board. Often lists would name only the first-class passengers and provide the overall number of second-class and steerage passengers. Coincidentally there is no list for the return of the *Dunbar Castle*, which brought the cricketers back home from England and berthed in Sydney on 4 February 1869.

The *Parramatta* returned to Sydney in December 1868, bringing home two of the 1868 Australians, Sundown and Jim Crow. Their premature return was due to illness. Duncan Brown was a passenger on board the *Parramatta* for that journey. He kept a journal of his travels and he was an excellent sketcher. Yet in all his drawings and jottings, Brown did not once mention either of the two Aboriginal cricketers on board. Brown's journal fell into the safe hands of Rear Admiral David Dunbar-Nasmith, a naval officer in the British Navy who won a DFC for recovering valuable cryptographic material from an Italian submarine sinking off Malta in 1942. Dunbar-Nasmith was intrigued by naval history and collected old ships logs, among them Duncan Brown's journal. The journal tells us much about life aboard the *Parramatta* and is important in that context, even though it doesn't mention the two Aboriginal cricketers returning home from England.

Politicians have unwittingly fired my determination to have this story told for I have long been unimpressed with this nation's performance in accepting a version of history written by the conquerers of a peace-loving race. Our history books are full of misnomers, misconceptions and blatant omissions.

More than 10,000 years ago the Aborigines hit upon aerodynamic technology in making the boomerang. This technology stumps scientists today and may yet prove the technology we need to travel to the stars. The Aboriginal people are highly adaptable. They have proved their resilience and their survival instincts for more than 100,000 years in the harshest land on the planet. In 1992 former prime minister Paul Keating said:

> ... the starting point might be to recognise that the problem starts with us non-Aboriginal Australians. It begins, I think, with the act of

recognition. Recognition that it was we who did the dispossessing. We took the traditional lands and smashed the traditional way of life. We brought the diseases. The alcohol. We committed the murders. We took the children from the mothers. We practised discrimination and exclusion …

His successor, John Howard, had a different view. On Australia Day 1997, he said that Australia 'should not be perpetually apologising for the sins of the past'. Historian Geoffrey Blainey has described the trend towards recognising the truth of the nation's past as the 'black armband interpretation of Australian history'. The Governor-General of Australia from 1996 to 2001, Sir William Deane, said that the 'past is never really gone' for 'it is absorbed into the present and the future … it shapes what we are and what we do'. Sir William lamented that if Australia could not achieve reconciliation with the Aboriginal people by the year 2001, 'we'll enter the second century of our nation as a diminished people'. Justice Marcus Einfield said that he would 'rather wear a black armband than a white blindfold to shut out the truth'.

In 1878 Dave Gregory led the second Australian cricket team to England. The world was then an ignorant place and many Englishmen, even those well-schooled, thought that the team would comprise men as dark as the historic 1868 Aboriginal team. Allan Gibson Steel, who later became an England Test captain, was playing his first first-class summer for Lancashire and he was getting wickets galore. He finished the summer with 164 wickets at an average of 9.43 with his right-arm medium pacers and 537 runs. Steel had just learnt that he had won selection for The Gentlemen against the Australians, to be played at Lord's in a few days time. That day Steel was sitting with Fred Spofforth, the demon Australian fast bowler. Steel takes up the story:

… they [the English public] fully expected to find members of Gregory's team black as the Aboriginals. We remember the late Reverend Arthur Wood 'putting his foot in it' on this subject before some of the Australians. One day in the pavilion at Lord's, I was sitting beside Spofforth watching a game in which neither of us was taking part. Mr Wood, coming up, accosted me: 'Well, Mr Steel, so I hear you are going to play against the niggers on Monday.' His face was a picture when Spofforth was introduced to him as the 'demon nigger bowler'.[1]

Spofforth became one of the great bowlers in Test history. Four years after Gregory's tour Spofforth took 7/46 and 7/44 to help Australia win by just 7 runs in The Oval Test of 1882, the only one played that summer. *The Sporting Times* carried a mock obituary notice stating that the body of English cricket would be cremated and the Ashes taken to Australia. Spofforth was the catalyst in the birth of a great sports legend, but the words of the Reverend Wood burned deep in the Aboriginal psyche. Ignorance is one thing, blatant racism is another. Wood's words that day at Lord's in 1878 were symptomatic of the prevailing attitude among the clergy towards the Indigenous people of Australia. This book may help the Aboriginal spirit rise from the ashes of a despair created by the white man's prejudice and past injustices.

CHAPTER ONE

THE gum trees of the Wimmera stand defiantly against the unforgiving cold. They are one of the great survivors of Planet Earth. A cold day in the Wimmera penetrates to the bone. Such was the cold that Friday, 14 August 1864, when the three Duff children left the warmth of their shepherd's hut to cut brush in the lush thickets below the towering gums. The Duff children — Isaac, 9, Jane, 7, and Frank, 3 — left Spring Hill Station, west of Natimuk in the western district of Victoria, late in the afternoon. Their mission was to cut brush for the making of brooms.

A scurrying animal caught Frank's eye and he escaped Jane's clasp and darted into the thicket. By the time Jane, the unacknowledged leader of the group, discovered that Frank was missing, darkness had almost fallen. Frank had wandered deep into the scrub, which seemed to get thicker with each step. There were small pockets of clear ground in that maze of tea tree and acacia, with kangaroo grass reaching up in clumps.

Frank was found in one such clearing. He sat and cried and Jane comforted him, all the while ensuring that her older brother, Isaac, was by her side.

When the children failed to return to the shepherd's hut that night, their father conducted his own search. He rode his horse frantically through the scrub calling their names. An agonising Saturday passed. By Sunday, 16 August, thirty men were combing the bush. They linked hands and walked the scrub in a grid pattern. No clues were found until eventually Alexander Wilson discovered tracks, which he followed for fifteen miles. By Thursday the tracks were washed out by heavy rain. The gods, it seemed, were not with the Duff family: they had now been lost in the deadly winter cold of the Victorian bush for six days. Time was running out for any chance of the children's survival. In utter despair, Duff senior played his last hand. He called in the Aboriginal trackers.

They turned up late on Friday night — a week, almost to the hour, since the day the children set out to cut brush in the Wimmera scrub. Almost without exception, the people of the Wimmera feared the worst.

At first light on Saturday (22 August), Wilson, Duff senior, his stepson Keena and the three Aboriginal trackers renewed the search. The trackers studied the ground, finding minute cracks in twigs and disturbances in the ground: telltale signs of what a child's shoe might do in relation to panic and disorientation. Within hours of their being called in, the trackers had found the very clearing in which the Duff children had spent their first cold and scary night in the bush.

An hour before sunset the three trackers wandered through tall kangaroo grass to find the children huddled together and asleep in a clump of trees. In the midst of the euphoria about the children being found safe and well, the Aboriginal trackers, whose mastery in reading the children's tracks had saved their lives, were given scant attention. They were allegedly given money — amounts which varied in reports from a few shillings to twenty pounds, five pounds of which was supposedly spent in the local pub. A local squatter, Dugan Smith, was said to have donated five pounds and Mr Duff gave ten pounds. Without the expertise of the Aboriginal trackers the Duff children would have perished. However, the story of the lost children became folklore and it was Jane Duff who was to be acknowledged the folk hero of the colony. Brothers Isaac and Frank Duff were apparently sustained by their seven-year-old sister. The legend of Jane Duff's bravery in the bush was embellished and enriched by the story-telling craft of the fictional pen. *The Illustrated Australian News* of 24 September 1864 told a thankful community: 'The painful account of the loss and subsequent discovery of the three children near Horsham, in the Western District, is perhaps the most remarkable in the history of such cases in the colony.'

In 1866 the British public learnt the story, dramatised in *The Australian Babes in the Wood*, a rhyme narrative for the young. A year later the Victorian Education Department immortalised the saga for Australian school children as part of the Grade Four Reader.

Where were the Aboriginal trackers in all of this? Did they share in the glory of having actually saved the Duff children? Records do not show it to be so. They were paid for their efforts and thanked, but acknowledgment was never forthcoming. The three trackers remained unsung. They rate hardly a mention in the newspaper reports.

Sketches of the children depict the children in the foreground with one of the white 'rescuers'. The Aboriginal trackers were either omitted or relegated to the background. Even S. T. Gill, a prolific and skilled artist of the period, in the *Australian Sketchbook* (1864) drew the children's father on horseback, his hands raised, about to fall to the ground in prayer in relief at the children being found alive. The children are huddled in a clearing, the two boys asleep and Jane watching over them like a vigilant mother. The Aboriginal trackers are well in the background.

Noted author William Strutt, who was born in Devon, England, in 1825 and came to Australia in 1850, wrote a fictional version of the Duff story. Isaac, Jane and Frank 'became' Roderick, Bella and David. His illustration ignores the Aboriginal connection in the saga, an exclusion in keeping with colonial Australian sensibilities.

But the irony was that two of the three trackers in the lost kids saga were to become famous in their own right. They — Dick-a-Dick and Redcap — were members of the 1868 Aboriginal Cricket Tour of England. Dick-a-Dick one time recalled the saga in 1868, when his own fame was emerging, and said that the Duff children would not have survived another night in the bush. Was it irony or a double standard that allowed an entire community to weep for the lost Duff children when the families of the original inhabitants such as Dick-a-Dick and Redcap, whose cultural knowledge had saved the children, were the victims of racial genocide. It was a shameful imbalance that began with the European invasion of the Great South Land in 1788.

Neither Dick-a-Dick nor Redcap did famously well in England, if we are to take the figures for batting and bowling on that tour as the only criteria. However, Dick-a-Dick became a legend of the tour. In purely cricketing terms Dick-a-Dick was no great shakes. He scored only 356 runs at an average of 5.26 and he took 5 wickets at 19.2. Dick-a-Dick became the 1868 tour's 'Artful Dodger', for he had an amazing capacity to duck and dodge. For a shilling, people paid for the chance to hit him with a cricket ball from a distance of ten paces. He armed himself with a parrying shield, which was about the width of a cricket bat, and a leangle or killer boomerang, a weapon shaped like the letter L and used to inflict injury on someone behind a shield. The parrying shield was used by Dick-a-Dick to fend off missiles above the waist and the leangle to protect his legs and feet. He arched his back and twisted like a contortionist, always exciting an appreciative crowd.

The challenge to hit Dick-a-Dick was there for any spectator before play, during any break in play and after the match. Men who fancied their chances would lay down their top hats and tails, roll up their sleeves and chuck the cricket ball with gusto. Dick-a-Dick was only ever hit once on tour and that happened in September, when one got through Dick-a-Dick's guard and struck him a glancing blow on the left shoulder.

Dick-a-Dick hailed from the Wimmera, or the Western District of Victoria. He knew the country like the back of his hand. His traditional name was Junggunjinanuke.

Redcap's greatest claim to fame on the 1868 tour was that he played in all 47 matches — an amazing feat of endurance. He scored 630 runs at 8.46 and he took 54 wickets at 10.7. But he was not a star of the tour, rather a bit player with the constitution of an ox.

The 1868 Aboriginal Cricket Team was not the first visit of Aboriginal people to England. Australia's first Governor, Arthur Phillip, returned to England in 1793 with two Indigenous Australians — Bennelong and Yemmerawannie. That was four years after Phillip first set eyes on Bennelong.

On 25 November 1789 two men — Benallon (later known as Bennelong) and Colbey — were captured, some might say kidnapped, and brought to Government House in Sydney Town. The two men were washed, shaved and clothed. They were restrained by an iron shackle on one leg and each was left in the care of the convict keeper. On 12 December 1789 Colbey loosened the rope from his iron shackle and escaped. During his confinement Bennelong learned to speak English and he acquired a taste for European food and alcohol. He escaped from Government House in May 1790. That September Governor Phillip learned that Bennelong and Colbey were at Manly Cove. He wished to establish friendlier relations with the Indigenous people, so he rowed across to Manly Cove to meet them. The instant he set foot ashore a volley of spears soared towards him. He was seriously wounded by a spear hurled by a man named Wileemarin. The colony surgeon, William Balmain, successfully extracted the spear from Phillip's leg and, although he suffered great pain from the wound, Phillip made a full recovery. But the incident played on Phillip's mind: As chief of the new colony, he was trying to make friends with the Indigenous people, and in return they stole from the settlement and attacked the inhabitants. Was he being played for a fool? On 9 December 1790, M'Entire, Governor Phillip's game-keeper, was speared while hunting in Botany Bay. Phillip sprang into punitive action, calling for a swift retaliatory strike against the Bidjigal people of Botany Bay. Phillip ordered that six Bidjigal men were to be captured and brought back to Sydney Town, where some were to be publicly executed and the rest, after observing the fate of their brothers, were to be released. If six men could not be captured, six men were to be shot. The punitive party spent a fruitless week scouring the Botany Bay area, but they could not capture one solitary person, nor did they manage to get within range to shoot one. They returned to Phillip empty-handed on 16 December 1790. Out-smarted and having lost face, Phillip launched a second expedition to find the Botany Bay Aborigines, but when the Redcoats arrived the camp had long been abandoned. Phillip was understandably annoyed, but he had great respect for the Aboriginal people. On 10 December 1792 he boarded the *Atlantic* to return to England. He was said to have been exhausted and unwell, but not so ill as to forget his precious cargo. Accompanying him were Bennelong and Yemmer-rawannie.

The two Aboriginal men were said to have boarded the ship 'voluntarily' and 'cheerfully'. However, it seems certain that in Phillip's mind he was taking home a collection, a few 'curiosities' in the form of two natives, several dingoes and four kangaroos. We know little of the manner in which Bennelong and Yemmerrawannie were treated in England, how often they were made to stand about to be gawked at, weighed, measured, prodded, poked and discussed.

(A Tasmanian cricketer, the first Aboriginal cricketer in Australia, was a man named Shinal (sometimes called Shiney) who played for Hobart Town in 1835. When Shinal died, his severed head was sent to a resident doctor in an Irish museum as a 'specimen' to be preserved. The head was returned for proper burial in 1992 — 157 years later and only because a small group of Aborigines with links to the Indigenous people of Tasmania agitated for its return.)

Bennelong and Yemmerawannie met King George III on numerous occasions. Yemmerawannie succumbed to a chest ailment and died long before Bennelong returned to Australia on the same ship as Captain John Hunter, arriving in Sydney Cove on 7 September 1795. Hunter was sworn in as Governor on 11 September four days after Bennelong 'threw off his fine clothes and restraints of civilised life, as alike inconvenient and distasteful and in spite of persuasions to the contrary, reverted to his old habits and haunts'.[1]

The English might have stopped and gawked at the 1868 Australian cricket team, but in contrast to the players' shabby treatment at home, they were warmly received by the English. Ironically the name of Bennelong lives on in a federal seat in Sydney, held by the prime minister, John Howard.

This is the prime minister who could not bring himself to say "sorry" for the injustices inflicted upon Australia's Indigenous people by the European settlers. Certainly young Australians growing up in the 1940s, 1950s and 1960s were handed a sanitised version of history. They learned little of the massacres of the Aboriginal people, who died in their thousands as white settlers sought ever more land on which to grow their crops and graze their cattle and sheep. Aboriginal resisters hit back in retaliation for murder and rape, but their spears were no match for the white man's warfare and bureaucratic suppression.

Aborigines began playing cricket in Australia at the missions or on the sheep stations. Most of the 1868 team came from the Western District of Victoria. The white men on the stations would play cricket as a relief from their station duties and shearing. Often they were a few players short and they noted how brilliant the Aboriginal workers were in retrieving and throwing; they were swift and agile and had powerful throwing arms. The pastoralists liked the idea of the Aborigines playing cricket, for in so doing they were conforming to the European way of life. Some colonialists wanted cricket to replace a vital part of Aboriginal culture, the corroboree.

Before the invaders came the people of the Wimmera lived in harmony with the land. The land is their mother, source and giver of all life. There were a number of language groups in the Wimmera, the main two being the Djab Wurrung and the Jardwadjali. The two main tribes of the region were the Madimadi and the Wutjubaluk. Near Edenhope the Jardwadjali language was commonplace, whereas in the area near Hamilton Djab Wurrung was the main language. However, each language group in the area could understand the other. The Djab Wurrung (pronounced 'Chap wurrung') and the Jardwadjali (pronounced 'yardwa-jarli') language groups embraced the Gariwerd-Grampian Ranges and the surrounding plains and wetlands, such as the Toolondo Reservoir, Lake Lonsdale and Lake Bolac. The coming of the white man was to provoke inevitable conflict, for no matter how well-intentioned the pastoralists were, their presence was a threat to the environment which up until that time had been successfully managed by a people who lived in harmony with nature. Then came Major Thomas Mitchell, the New South Wales Surveyor-General, and his expeditionary force. The Aborigines looked upon Major Mitchell's 1838 wheel tracks as the prints of the white man, the hoof marks of the bullocks as the footprints of the white woman. Europeans perceived the Aborigines as more like apes than humans and did not acknowledge their ownership of or connection with the land.

European cattle herds and sheep flocks trampled the lush pasture, destroying fragile plants such as the much-sought murnong or native yam daisy that sustained the Aboriginal people. The grass was flattened by the new animals and less grass was available for traditional game such as kangaroo, wombat and emu. Seeking better pasture, the animals left the region, leaving the Aboriginal people to either spear sheep or cattle and risk being shot or accept handouts from the invaders. The Europeans hunted kangaroos because they competed with the sheep and cattle for pasture fodder. Hundreds of thousands of kangaroos were slaughtered. By the 1860s the landholders reckoned that the land was still too heavily stocked with natural fauna. A report in the Hamilton *Spectator* claimed that some 150,000 kangaroos were slaughtered on two stations in the Warrnambool area within a few years. In one day's kangaroo shoot in 1867 some 6000 kangaroos were destroyed.

This was Dick-a-Dick's land and Redcap's land. It was land stolen from the Aborigines. Given that the invader stole the land, raped the women, killed the men and brought the deadly white men's diseases, it seems incongrous that such a people could play cricket which was a game supposedly free of anything sordid and a great character builder. Perhaps the Aborigines of the Wimmera saw in cricket what they couldn't see in the white man: integrity and honour.

They embraced the game. They played for stations in the Hamilton, Edenhope and Warrnambool areas and while their technique was rough and ready, they had natural ability. Among them were players of whom it was said had the eye of the hawk and the strength of an ox and could run like a hare. There are no definite dates of when these pioneer Aboriginal cricketers were born. We can only surmise that they took up their first stance on this earth at about the end of what is known as the 'frontier period', so at various times in the 1840s. At the time the Aborigines began playing cricket, Victoria did not have the Aboriginal Protection Act in force. This Act (which was enacted in 1869), one year after the famous 1868 tour, effectively restricted Aboriginal people in so many ways that the so-called 'protection' amounted to no less than genocide. Many of the players were fortunate in that the stations for which they worked were on their own stolen lands, so they were able to live and work on their traditional piece of earth. However, they lived not as equals but as serfs, doing the white man's bidding. The Aborigines of the 1840s taught their children as their parents had taught them and their parents before them. They retained the old ways, however desperate their situation.

By 1845 an estimated 70 per cent of the Djab Wurrung and 80 per cent of the Jardwadjali were dead. From a conservatively estimated pre-contact population of 2050 Djab Wurrung and 2200 Jardwadjali, only 615 Djab Wurrung and 455 Jardwadjali remained alive. A quarter of those people who died are thought to have been killed by rifle attack. The rest died as a result of introduced diseases, poisoned flour, arsenic-laced woollen blankets, and starvation due to a shortage of traditional foodstuffs.

Once lords of all they surveyed, the Aboriginal people of Western Victoria were reduced within a decade to the status of beggars in their own land. The frontier period was over.[2]

Dick-a-Dick and Redcap were very much tribal men. They learned the old ways and they were soon to show the world how they could adapt to the ways of the Europeans. Both men were probably born between the years 1845 and 1850, which puts their ages at the early twenties by the start of the 1868 tour. Their parents had suffered at the hands of the white men. Demeaning laws and decrees came to pass:

> In 1858 a Government Select Committee recommended the formation of reserves for the various Aboriginal groups on their traditional hunting ranges, where they could combine agriculture and grazing of livestock. Three reserves were established in Western Victoria. None, however, were on the traditional hunting ranges of either the Djab Wurrung or the Jardwadjali. Instead the Djab Wurrung and the Jardwadjali were catered for by a second system of protection. A number of landholders were appointed as local guardians to provide foodstuffs, clothing and other needs to Aboriginal people in their neighbourhoods. Only a few hundred Djab Wurrung or Jardwadjali were left by 1860. In this decade, the last attempts were made to perform traditional ceremonies or entertainments such as corroboree dances.[3]

The Aboriginal people of the Ice Age hunted giant marsupial game, such as the hippopotamus-sized, two-tonne Diprodoton, a wombat the size of a horse called a Phascolonus and the giant kangaroo, the Macropus titan. Archaeologists have found evidence that the Aborigines changed with the times. They improvised and adapted to the changing climate and the vast diversity of the Australian continent. The early Aboriginal people used silcrete from central Victoria or the Mallee and rhyolite from the Rocklands region as the raw material for their stone-age axes. But 5000 years ago the Aborigines switched their focus to a new material for their cutting tools — quartz and quartzite.

The Aborigines were a patient people. It took 1000 years to perfect a technique for making small thin blades from quartz. Another millenium and the Aborigines discovered near 'magical' qualities in a flint-hard volcanic rock called greenstone. It was extremely hard and had a fine grain, a perfect combination for the craftsman, limited by the scope and quality of his tools, to fashion an axe-head. The greenstone axe became a symbol of power and strength, a highly prized item in any Aboriginal community.

Before contact with the Europeans, the Wimmera was a land of plenty. The streams provided a rich bounty and the Indigenous people knew ways to easily extract the rich food sources. They built fish and eel traps, damming the waterway with stacked stones, cleverly fashioned so that the fish found an ever-narrowing avenue which led to a narrow exit where the fish hunter waited, ready to pounce. The Aboriginal people of Western Victoria moved in family bands of twenty or more, sometimes as many as a hundred. They revisited specific places, exploiting the seasonal food supplies and allowing nature to replenish the next season's harvest. Where they found plentiful water and an ongoing supply of food and game, they would set up camp, constructing strong huts called wuurns. The wuurn was constructed with strong limbs of gum trees, set in such a way that they resembled a dome or barrel cut in half. Each limb was lashed to the next and the space between was filled with smaller limbs. Sheets of bark, thatch and sods of earth were placed over the tree branches to provide a family with a hut that gave protection from wind and rain and whose outer wall could not be penetrated by spears. Bands of up to a thousand people were believed to have gathered for special occasions in two important wetlands of the Djab Wurrung and Jardwadjali territory — Lake Bolac in the east and Lake Lonsdale in the west. Great numbers also gathered for the festival of eels. It was noted that in the early part of every summer the Aborigines would gather, forming a village that stretched each side of the creek leading into Lake Bolac, a village stretching almost 40 kilometres, from Lake Bolac to its junction with the Hopkins River. The annual migration of eels provided great fun and feasting. Tonnes of eels poured downstream and were easily harvested from the clever stone traps. The area became a maze of artifically constructed channels. The people dug and maintained these channels with primitive implements, one of which was believed to have been a wooden shovel, crudely carved from the thick bark of a gum tree. These eel channels often covered a distance of up to 4 kilometres. Sadly farmers have ploughed over most of the eel traps.

> The most elaborate system known was as Lake Condah, where different sets of stone fish traps came into operation at each major fluctuation in water level. The most remarkable 'discovery', resulting in careful re-evaluation of written records in conjunction with field survey, concerns eel fishing.
>
> One of the most important sites is at Toolondo … In a complex of artificial channels which once connected swamps, including two systems separated by a rise, a total length of 3.75 kilometres was dug. Some sections are narrow drains but almost a kilometre consisted of a drain more than two metres wide and a metre deep.[4]

Families passed down their own patch of turf. For the Djab Wurrung and Jardwadjali people a specific hill, or waterhole or area of their yam daisy delicacy was an inherited ownership. The concept of descent ownership was akin to that of a Scottish clan. Within the clan, the male who stood out as a leader was acknowledged as clan head, or *gnern neetch*. Clan members are forbidden to marry within their own clan; thus the people had an in-built protection against a downward genetic spiral. They needed to find a partner born under an opposite symbol to themselves. Anthropologists learned that the Indigenous people divided themselves into *moieties*. Half the clans took on the totemic symbol of the white cockatoo and were called *gruejidj*. The other half assumed the totem of the black cockatoo and were known as *gamadj*. When a *gruejidj* man fell in love with a *gamadj* woman there was a sanctioned match.

Family and extension of family was important. There was a communal atmosphere which was ongoing. The elders passed down the stories from the Dreamtime as everyone sat around a communal log fire. Those talks forged lasting friendships and an unbreakable bond. There were great corroborees at Lake Lonsdale, where various groups gathered and settled legal conflicts, acted out traditional stories, and competed in throwing the boomerang and spear.

The great gatherings were the perfect place to market a new tool, such as a greenstone axe. It was also a place of fun, a place to play. Archaeological evidence of a large ceremonial ring burnt into the earth on the eastern shoreline of Lake Lonsdale tends to support the theory that the various bands and tribes were alerted to a big ceremony at the lake by a specific smoke signal.

There is growing evidence that a game the Aborigines had been playing for centuries was a primitive form of the game we know today as Australian Rules Football. Most historians laud Tom Wills and his cousin H. C. A. Harrison for the 'invention' of the game. However, the Aborigines of the Wimmera should not be denied due acknowledgment in this matter. The Aborigines used rolled-up possum skins and fashioned a round ball. The fur was always on the outside, a complete reversal of the animal-skin water containers. A Wimmera pioneer James Dawson noted the skill of a group of young Djab Wurrung men at play.

> One of the favourite games is football, in which fifty or as many as one hundred players engage at a time. The ball is about the size of an orange, and is made of opossum-skin, with the fur side outwards … The players are divided into two sides and ranged in opposing lines, which are always of a different "class" — white cockatoo against black cockatoo …
>
> Each side endeavors to keep possession of the ball, which is tossed a short distance by hand, and then kicked in any direction. The side which kicks it oftenest and furthest gains the game. The person who sends it highest is considered the best player, and has the honour of burying it in the ground until the next day.[5]

Tom Wills was an excellent footballer and brilliant all-round cricketer. He played inter-colonial cricket for Victoria. Wills' introduction to 'kick and catch' football was when his family had a squatting run, 'Lexington', near Ararat. His earliest playmates were Djab Wurrung children. He loved the excitement of the kick and the mark and he later revisited the possum-skin football of his youth and took the embryo of Australia's most exciting football code into the white man's world.

Tom Wills became an intriging man of Australian sport and was destined to play a vital role in the lead-up to the 1868 Aboriginal Cricket Tour of England.

CHAPTER TWO

THE captain of the 1868 Australian cricket tour was Charles Lawrence. He also coached the team. However, to get both roles Lawrence had to perform much thrust and parry, for his greatest rival was Tom Wills, a man Lawrence met in Ireland. In 1854 Lawrence, an Englishman, arranged for a side from Liverpool to play a combined team of the Military and Civilians of Ireland. Tom Wills not only turned out for Liverpool but bowled like a demon and took all ten Irish wickets. Little could Wills and Lawrence have known of the extraordinary part they were both to play in the historic 1868 Aboriginal Cricket Tour of England. The Wills–Lawrence connection is one of the most intriguing liaisons in Australian sport.

Thomas Wentworth Spencer Wills was born 8 August 1835 at Molongo Plains, New South Wales. In 1852 his father, Horace Spencer Wills, sent young Tom, then aged 15, to England to be educated at Rugby School. Tom captained Rugby School at both cricket and football. He played for Cambridge against Oxford in 1856, despite the fact that he was never a student at either university. His first-class debut was for the Gentlemen of Kent in 1854, the same season in which he took all ten wickets against Lawrence's Ireland. Wills played three matches for Kent (1855–56) and sixteen games for Victoria from 1856–57 to 1875–76.

Once his headmaster at Rugby asked Tom what he thought of the novel *Tom Brown's Schooldays* and asked whether it was 'a realistic look at life at the school'. Tom said it was, and then proceeded to inform the head that Rugby needed a more competitive spirit in its football, indeed its sport in general. The headmaster was taken aback, not quite knowing whether he was dealing with an upstart or a young man of considerable pluck and vision.

Just days after Tom had arrived at the school, he was given a subtle warning by the cleaner: trouble was imminent. School bullies had a habit of seeking out the newcomers and giving them a thrashing, and the new boy would suffer in silence or fall in a heap. But Tom knew how to fight. Among his best friends while he was growing up in Melbourne were some Aboriginal lads, and his activities with his black companions were to prove extremely useful. A flare heralded the attack from the bullies, which began just after 10 pm. There was a sort of collective battle cry of 'at 'em lads!' and half a dozen boys rushed towards Tom. To their surprise, Tom was waiting for them, holding in one hand a pronged spear and in the other a killer boomerang. His would-be attackers stopped dead in their tracks. Their hesitation was the prompt for Tom to let forth with a blood-curdling war-cry. The bullies made a rapid retreat. They knew then and for evermore that young Tom Wills was not a person to tangle with. The headmaster also noted that Wills had 'an unruly, extravagant handshake'.

Wills developed into a fiery fast bowler. He returned to Australia in 1856 and became a stalwart of inter-colonial cricket. In all first-class matches Wills took 121 wickets at 10.09, his most impressive inter-colonial figures being his 6/26 and 4/40 for Victoria against New South Wales in 1857, his 7/44 against New South Wales in 1869 and his double of 7/48 and 6/44 against Tasmania in 1870–71. He was a big, heavy-bearded man with a strong constitution and said to be fond of a drink or two. Representing Victoria Wills was the leading Australian wicket-taker in 1856–57 (10 wickets at 6.50), 1857–58 (26 wickets at 5.03) and 1858–59 (11 wickets at 4.45).

In 1859 Queensland became a separate colony. Wills' father envis-aged great business and lifestyle opportunities in the new colony so he sold his Geelong home and took his family and a few trusted employees north. Twenty-five people in all made the trek to Queens-land, along with 10,000 head of sheep. They reached Cullinlaringo Station at Nogoa, some 200 miles from Rockhampton on 3 October 1861. The trek had taken ten months and the party had to negotiate some very rugged terrain. They found the local Aboriginal people not as tolerant as those they had encountered in Victoria. There were lots of reasons why the Queensland Aborigines were aggressive in those northern parts.

White settlers killed some 10,000 blacks in Queensland between 1824 and 1908. Considered 'wild animals', 'vermin', 'scarcely human', 'hideous to humanity', 'loathesome' and 'a nuisance', they were fair game for white 'sportsmen'.[1]

The Wills family were, in effect, walking into a hostile environment. Horace Wills may have had every intention of treating his Aboriginal workers with fairness and humanity, but seven weeks after the Wills' caravan arrived to put down roots in Queensland, tragedy struck. It was a hot day — noon on 7 October 1861. The attack was planned to perfection. The Cullinlaringo Station hands were having an afternoon snooze after a big lunch. In a quick, announced ambush, a group of Aboriginal men swept into camp. Horace Wills managed to get off one shot before he was clubbed to death. He died along with all the station hands and every family member — 19 in all. It was the largest massacre of whites by Aboriginal people in history.

Young Tom Wills had a lucky escape from death. Two days before the massacre Horace Wills had sent his son to fix a dray which had broken down two days' journey from the main homestead. His father had unknowingly saved Tom Wills' life. Tom stayed on and for two more years managed Cullinlaringo Station. He had always got on extremely well with Aboriginal people. That he continued those good relations after the massacre provides us with an insight into his character. Did he know of any family members or station hands at Cullinlaringo Station who had ill-treated the local Aboriginal people? Maybe he knew of rapes and beatings. Brutality and oppression in its most evil forms continued long after the Cullinlaringo massacre, long after the 1868 tour.

In 1883, the British High Commissioner, Arthur Hamilton Gordon, wrote privately to his friend, William Gladstone, Prime Minister of England.

'The habit of regarding the natives as vermin, to be cleared off the face of the earth, has given the average Queenslander a tone of brutality and cruelty in dealing with the blacks which is very difficult to anyone who does not know it, as I do, to realize. I have heard men of culture and refinement, of the greatest humanity and kindness to their fellow whites, and who when you meet them here at home you would pronounce to be incapable of such deeds, talk, not only of wholesale butchery (for the iniquity of that may sometimes be disguised from themselves) but of the individual murder of natives, exactly as they would talk of a day's sport or having to kill a troublesome animal.'[2]

Charles Lawrence was sailing to Australia with the first England cricket team, H. H. Stephenson's Eleven, at about the time of the Cullinlaringo Station massacre, but it would be some time before he and Wills met up again. By the time Wills decided to return to Melbourne, Lawrence was successfully running a hotel in Manly and coaching New South Wales cricketers. Wills' cricket career continued for Victoria and he turned out against George Parr's England Eleven in 1863–64, the second touring party to tour Australia from the old country. Before he had left Melbourne bound for Queensland, Wills, at the age of 22, had become a member of the Melbourne Cricket Club. He was also club coach. In Keith Dunstan's celebrated book on the Melbourne Cricket Ground, *The Paddock that Grew*, he claims that Wills was the MCC Secretary from 1857. In 1857–58 Wills wrote a letter to *Bell's Life* suggesting that the Melbourne Cricket Club form a football team to ensure that their cricketers would be fit for the summer. Wills thought that Australian grounds were far too hard for the fierce tackling required in rugby football, so new rules had to be found. The Irish brand of football, Gaelic, took his fancy, so too the thought of a combination of the skills of Gaelic football and rugby. Wills also knew of the game the Aboriginal people had been playing for centuries, a type of football using a round wad of tightly wrapped possum skins.

A great deal of cricket was played by local enthusiasts in the Hamilton–Edenhope region. Thomas Gibson Hamilton of Bringalbert Station began instructing the local Aboriginal workers in cricket in 1864. William Reginal Hayman (1842–1899) became the driving force behind the formation of the Edenhope Cricket Club. Founding members included two members of the historic 1868 team, Peter and Bullocky. Tom Wills was to become their coach.

Aboriginal men started playing cricket on the stations rather by chance. They made up the numbers. They would sit on the fence watching the cricket on Saturdays. Occasionally they would fetch a long hit and return it on the full to the wicket-keeper, a distance often in excess of 100 metres. Their skills were noted.

Aboriginal workers on the stations were given nicknames. Their traditional names were difficult to spell or pronounce, so Arrahmu-nijarrimun became 'Peter', Bullchanach became 'Bullocky'. Station workers also went by such names as Sugar, Waddy and Tarpot. Some thought these nicknames were further evidence of the white man's contempt and lack of respect for Aboriginal people.

Johnny Mullagh, who was the star turn of the 1868 team, had the traditional name of Unaarrimin. He transferred from Pine Hills Station to work for John Fitzgerald at Mullagh Station and the man who was formerly known as 'Black Johnny' took on the name of the Station and became Johnny Mullagh. Mullagh spent most of his life on the two properties, which covered an area in excess of 40,000 hectares.

Tom Hamilton was a stimulus for cricket on the stations in those formative years. He coached and encouraged Peter and Bullocky at Bringalbert Station, just as did the likes of John Fitzgerald at Mullagh and Charles Officer at Mount Talbot Station. Officer paid his Aboriginal workers the same rate of pay as his white workers, and under his tutelage a number of Aboriginal players became prominent. They included Bullocky, who moved from Bringalbert, Billy Officer, Harry Rose, Sugar, Neddy (Jim Crow) and Stockkeeper.

An adventurer, Tom Hamilton, encouraged the Aboriginal workers to play cricket with flair, to take risks with both bat and ball. They loved Hamilton; perhaps they could identify with his sense of adventure and they could recognise the 'warrior' in him. Four years after the 1868 Aboriginal tour of England, Tom Hamilton drove horses across Australia. He followed the new overland telegraph route through the McDonnell Ranges and on to Darwin: a 3000-kilometre trek. A year later, in 1873, he died of malaria in Queensland. He was 29. However, his early work with Aboriginal cricket ensured him a place in Australian sports folklore.

By the year 1865 station cricket had become so popular that a match was arranged between the Aborigines and the Europeans.

It was played on rough ground near the Bringalbert Station woolshed and the Aborigines were victorious. The following stations were among those involved in the match; known individual participants are included in brackets. Benayo (D. McLeod and W. O. Groom); Bringalbert (T. Hamilton); Brippack (A. A. Cowell); Hynam (T. Smith); Lake Wallace South (W. R. Hayman); Morat, also known as Rose Banks (W. Douglas). Pine Hills (David Edgar) and Mullagh (J. C. Fitzgerald) presumably participated, while other possible affiliates were Mount Talbot, Miga Lake, Fulham and Struan. All were properties in the area, mostly in the Edenhope–Harrow region.[3]

The match fired the imagination of Tom Hamilton and Edenhope Cricket Club's William Hayman. They envisaged great possibilities for Aboriginal cricketers and it is believed that these two men collaborated to bring the players together to train on the shores of Lake Wallace at Edenhope. Tom Wills was earmarked to coach the Aboriginal players, but before Wills was engaged they were to play a few matches. Initially they struggled to gel as a team and their technique was found wanting. James Edgar's influence on the new style of bowling soon had the Aboriginal players bowling over-arm. It was accurate and fast and they could achieve lots of bounce. Having been soundly beaten by Edenhope in an earlier game, the Aboriginal team played a return game against them at Bringalbert on 24 January 1866, easily exacting their revenge on the club with a victory of an innings and 13 runs. The Aboriginal team scored 75 and Edenhope scored 36 and 26.

In March 1866 the Aboriginal team challenged Hamilton and had a big win: Aborigines 64 and 52; Hamilton 36 and 30. Johnny Mullagh got five second-innings wickets bowling the round-arm style, his arm slightly higher than the shoulder on this occasion. A sports meeting followed the cricket and Mullagh again starred, clearing the bar of the high jump at 5 feet 3 inches and hurling a cricket ball 110 yards. A dinner was held for the players after the match, but only three members of the defeated Hamilton team turned up, much to the dismay of officials. Later the losing team was castigated by the local newspaper, the *Hamilton Spectator*, for its lack of sportsmanship.

Charles Officer then challenged the Aborigines to a game against his beloved Upper Glenelg club. This time Mullagh top-scored with

31, but the Europeans out-batted them in both innings and won convincingly by nine wickets. Despite the loss, many people saw huge potential in the Aboriginal cricketers. Some, such as Dr W. T. Molloy, were genuinely interested in their welfare but most, it seemed, saw only the opportunity to make money. William Hayman sent photographs of the Aboriginal players to the Melbourne Cricket Club in the hope that a match might eventually be staged at the MCG between an Aboriginal team and the Club. A refreshment pavilion provider, Rowland Newbury, lodged an application to cater for such a fixture and he offered twenty-five pounds for the right to provide for the hungry, thirsty spectators.

It was about August 1866 that Tom Wills was due to set off for Lake Wallace to coach the players. Wills thought that the match with the MCC was to be played in November, but it had to be put back two months as the players were required at the stations in November. It was shearing time. Many of the team's players, including the talented Mullagh, were top-flight shearers and even those who did not shear were required as roustabouts. A new date was set for the match: Boxing Day, 1866. Wills did not arrive at Lake Wallace until 20 November 1866, so he was forced to provide a crash course in cricket for his Aboriginal team. They played a few lead-up games, losing the first match, but beating Lake Wallace with 8/170, Mullagh hitting 81 not out and dismissing their 16-man-strong opponents. Lake Wallace managed only 34. Mullagh took six wickets and Wills eight. Against an Edenhope XVI, they scored 164, winning by an innings and 69 runs. Selection was tough for Wills, but he finally settled on the following combination: Billy Officer, Sugar, Jellico, Cuzens, Neddy, Mullagh, Bullocky, Tarpot, Sundown and Peter. The team was named days in advance of the match, but changes had to be made. Sugar died from 'unknown causes' just before the game and Neddy (Jim Crow) was omitted from the final line-up. They were replaced by Dick-a-Dick and by Paddy, a player who had a propensity to slog at any ball within reach.

Wills was a hero to every sports lover in Melbourne. He was a prolific sportsman. He co-umpired the first Australian Rules Football match between Scotch College and Melbourne Grammar School on 7 August 1858 and he played many of the early matches at Richmond

Paddock. Along with his cousin W. C. A. Harrison, Wills drew up the rules for the Melbourne Football Club. By 1876 Wills had played more than 200 games, mainly with Geelong, and was five times 'Champion of the Colony'. The early signs of mental instability were evident, and there were growing concerns about his drinking. He later became a hopeless drunk and in 1880 he took his own life, stabbing himself to death with either a pair of scissors or a ceremonial sword, depending upon which source you access. Another version of Wills' suicide has it that a neighbour spied Wills in his Sunday best feeding the chooks, saying, 'Eat up. This is the last meal you'll be getting from old Tom.'[4] Wills had been launching into tirades leading up to that day, talking in melancholy tones about how he was going to do himself in. On the fatal day, Wills grabbed a kitchen knife and, holding his de facto wife off with one hand, inflicted three stab wounds to the chest, one of which, it seems, pierced his heart. Only four people turned up at his funeral.

But in December 1866 Tom Wills was a hard-drinking, hard-playing cricketer with a coaching mission to transform the raw and talented Aboriginal players into a crack outfit. A few days before the big Boxing Day match of 1866, the players' general talent and attitude at the nets so impressed the MCC members that they hurriedly set about strengthening their team. However, many of their best men were in Sydney playing an inter-colonial game against New South Wales, also set down for Boxing Day. A Melbourne cricketer, James, a good spinner of his day, was brought into the MCC squad. Melbourne was abuzz with excitement. This was a much talked-about contest. Refreshment tents dotted the grassy banks surrounding the MCG playing surface, as they did during the big England–Victoria matches of 1861–62 and 1863–64. Reports of the Aboriginal team making good progress under the guidance of coach Tom Wills at their training camp at Lake Wallace filtered through to the people of Melbourne. Five of the MCC players were considered good enough to play for Victoria in inter-colonial cricket and the MCC was perhaps always going to be too strong for the inexperienced Aboriginal players. Johnny Mullagh was nursing an injured finger, but he was confirmed to be fit enough to take his place, and Johnny Cuzens looked in fiery form at the St Kilda nets before the game.

The big day finally arrived and some 8000 people turned up to watch the game. MCC batted first. Cuzens bowled like the wind, taking 6 wickets to help Tom Wills (2 wickets) and Mullagh (2 wickets) bowl MCC out for 101. The crowd roared their delight at the Aboriginal team's fielding performance, their athleticism delighting all and sundry. They dashed in towards the ball — ever on the move, as is the modern trend today. Their balance matched their speed and little got past them. They could dash in, balance on the balls of their feet, then dart either to the right or the left, depending on the direction from which the ball was arriving. Cuzens starred at point, Tarpot was long-stop, Billy Officer was long leg or cover, Peter was short-leg, Dick-a-Dick was mid-on, Jellico was cover or long leg, Sundown was long slip, Paddy was third man and the skipper, Wills, fielded either short slip or point. The players wore different coloured hat-bands so that spectators could easily identify them. Cards with the player's name and his 'colour' were sold around the ground.

When Ben Wardill came to the crease, reported a contemporary newspaper, the Aboriginal players became very excited, 'the darkies taking off their hats and giving the hurrah in fine British style!'[5] Ben Wardill was born in Liverpool, England, in 1842. He settled in Melbourne in 1861 and kept wicket for the MCC and Victoria. Wardill became secretary of the MCC in 1879 and managed three Australian Cricket Team tours of England in 1886, 1899 and 1902. When Horan was brilliantly caught by Billy Officer at long leg the crowd went wild, inspiring Tarpot to further entertain them with a double somersault, which nearly brought the house down. The crowd rose from a paltry 500 at the start of play on the second day to about 4000 by mid-afternoon. Jellico had gone for a duck the previous evening, and the rest of the team did not fare much better. The side was dismissed for 39, Mullagh revealing his artistry with a compact 16. This was a very courageous knock, given that his middle finger was split, the flesh laid bare to the bone. Batting a second time the Aboriginal team fared better, scoring 87, Mullagh a superb 33. He stood tall and drove crisply and also hit hard to leg. By every account, Mullagh played with a straight bat and made great use of the wrists, 'working' the ball into the gaps. The MCC, 164 and 120, defeated the Australians, 185 and 45, by 54 runs.

The Aboriginal players showed they were up with their opponents in bowling and fielding, although they did not have a slow man to compare with either Hadfield or James. It was their batting that needed to show the most improvement. Apart from Mullagh, the batsmen struggled to cope. Bullocky, the team's wicket-keeper, and Cuzens showed they might well help Mullagh in future contests for they batted in conservative vein, not merely slogging at every ball. However, Paddy, Tarpot and Sundown fell easy victims.

Next day a hurriedly-put-together match billed as The Natives v. The World was played with a number of MCC players bolstering the Aboriginal outfit. The Natives XI, led by Tom Wills, consisted (in batting order) of Bennett, Mortimer, Orr, Cuzens, Bullocky, Wallace, Wills, Tarpot, Dick-a-Dick, Gorman and Watty. The World XI players were Horan, Wilson, Kelly, Sewell, James, Fowler, Ashton, Reid, Jacomb, Hamilton and Plummer. The World scored 132, Cuzens taking 6/36, Wills 2/48 and Watty 1/14. The Natives replied with 65 and 5/22 when time ran out for the day. James, the MCC spinner, took 8/20, the players, especially the Aboriginal players, having great trouble coping with James' flight and spin. Again it was the fielding which stood out. Without Mullagh, the team's batting was a bit short of the mark.

Day Three was devoted entirely to sports. Tarpot, Jellico and Mullagh excelled, with Tarpot's extraordinary feat of running the 100 yards dash backwards in 14 seconds bringing the crowd to its feet. Jellico revealed his keen sense of humour. He was the crowd favourite:

> When a spectator addressed him in broken English, Jellico was reported as saying in response, 'What for you talk to me in no good Inglis. I speak him as good Inglis belonging you.' Turning to Tarpot, he observed, 'Big one fool that fellow. He did not know him Inglis one dam.'[6]

The team relaxed at the Fitzroy Bowling Club on 31 December and they had to be convinced that this was not a ploy to have them return to the old under-arm style of bowling. Dick-a-Dick, Jellico and Tarpot showed excellent skill at lawn bowls.

William Hayman was well pleased with the Aboriginal players' progress. He was principally seen as the Aborigines 'protector', but subsequent events in 1867 proved beyond reasonable doubt that

Hayman was keener on making money that he was on the welfare of the players. Tom Wills saw the peril in exploiting the players for financial gain. The seeds of doubt over Wills' professional commitment were sown early, for the coach of any tour venture would also need to be in full agreement about the need to make the venture pay a handsome dividend.

In January 1867 both Cuzens and Bullocky played for Victoria against Tasmania in an intercolonial fixture. Cuzens took two wickets, but both Cuzens and Bullocky failed miserably with the bat. Johnny Mullagh had been selected in the original line-up but he had to withdraw and Bullocky got his chance. Bullocky usually kept wicket and opened the batting. Ironically injury and circumstance worked against Mullagh and he didn't get the chance to play for Victoria until 1879, when he took the field against Lord Harris's Englishmen at the MCG, eleven years after the historic 1868 tour.

One man who was particularly interested in the Boxing Day match at the MCG was Captain W. (William) E. B. Gurnett, or W. E. Broughton-Gurnett, who was later regarded as being rather dubious in a business context. He seemed a man of means, although the Sydney directories and newspapers of the day are revealing if only for the complete absence of any mention of the captain's name, let alone his doings, up until the time he approached manager Hayman and coach Wills with a plan to take the Aboriginal players on a tour of Sydney, then beyond the seas.

> Gurnett proposed a 12-month cricket tour to Sydney and England, during which he would finance the team's wages, expenses and clothing, together with those of the captain and manager. In return, each Aboriginal would receive a 50 pounds bonus, and Wills a larger sum; the fortunate Hayman would take a percentage of the profits. Gurnett undertook to make all shipping and other business arrangements. Youthful and gullible, Hayman and professional sportsman Wills gladly signed the proffered contract, while the 12 dark cricketers affixed their marks ...[7]

Captain Gurnett turned out to be a right rogue. If he had any money, none was forthcoming. Gurnett would have seen the enormous profits H. H. Stephenson (1861–62) and George Parr (1863–64) made for their respective England tours of Australia. Hayman and

Wills were no doubt excited about the possibilities of the Aboriginal cricketers moving about the countryside as a 'wandering eleven'. Gurnett's offer probably only served to galvanise Hayman and Wills' collective mindset. Instinct rather than any brilliant business acumen told them that they must act swiftly to take advantage of the popular momentum established at the MCG in December 1866.

Wills took his side to the country areas of Victoria. They played and beat the Corio Club at Geelong, then 15 men of Collingwood's Prince of Wales Club. On 18–19 January 1867 the Aboriginal team played a Bendigo XI, a side which included 15-year-old William Evans Midwinter. The young Midwinter took four wickets, but his greatest claim to fame was to come in the years ahead. He played in the first Test Match, against England, at the MCG in 1876–77, toured England in 1878, the second Australian Tour, and again in 1884. He also played for Gloucestershire and toured Australia with the 1881–82 England team. W. G. Grace talked him into playing for Gloucestershire when he was in England with the 1878 Aussie team. Midwinter is the only cricketer to have represented England in Australia and Australia in England in Tests. Charles Lawrence, of course, came to Australia with the first England Xl and then he led the 1868 Aboriginal side to England; however, he never played in a Test. On 8–9 February 1867 the team played County of Bourke at the MCG and, thanks to Johnny Cuzens, who hit a bold 49 and took four wickets, the Aboriginal team won comfortably. The win came despite Mullagh missing the match through injury.

Tarpot also missed playing. He had a severe chest cold and Dick-a-Dick had measles, a dreaded disease among the Aboriginal population. After the side lost at Ballarat, the press alluded to the side being 'underdone' and suggested that Wills provide a great deal more tuition in the basic skills of the game before the team even thought of taking on the English at their own game. However, Gurnett was keen to keep the momentum going. He introduced the players to the Victorian Governor during the MCG match. Then on 12 February 1867, two days before the team was to leave with Wills for the Sydney leg of their tour, the Central Board for the Protection of Aborigines met in Melbourne in an attempt to prevent the players touring.

The Chief Secretary of Victoria was asked in a written communication to do his utmost to have the government intervene, effectively stopping the tour. In 1858 the Victorian Government had set aside reserves for Aboriginal people to one day reside there on their tribal lands. In 1860 the Central Board for the Protection of Aborigines was established by the Governor's Decree. R. Brough-Smith was the Board secretary. The Board in 1867 was something of a toothless tiger, for it had no statutory power; statutory authority did not visit the Board until 1869 — one year after the 1868 tour of England. However, through Brough-Smith, the Board recorded its concern for the welfare of the cricketers. The Board urged that unless the promoters of the intended tour of Sydney, then England, left a sufficient guarantee — a sum deposited that would ensure the team's safe return home — the governor should stop the tour.

> The Chief Secretary replied by return post, in an essentially negative vein. He regretted that neither the governor nor the Government 'have any legal power to compel persons who are taking the Aboriginals to England to give any such guarantee as is proposed. If the Central Board can suggest any legal course by which their object can be accomplished the Chief Secretary will be glad to adopt it.'[8]

Once the Board possessed statutory power in 1869, the Aborigines of Victoria were officially at the mercy of the government administration. They were then dependent on the whim of the Board collective.

> The Act determined where Aborigines could reside, the distribution of money granted by Parliament, and their children's education. It was paternalist as well as protective. The Act remained on the statute books until it was amended as the Aborigines Act 1886, when 'half-caste' male Aborigines under the age of 35 years and 'half-caste' females, unless married to, and living with an Aborigine, were expected to be absorbed by the white community.[9]

Figures of 1000 pounds and 500 pounds were bandied about as 'bonds' put up by Gurnett to appease the Board; however, no money was forthcoming. Gurnett must have spun a convincing yarn, for the Aboriginal players turned up in Sydney a few days later for a match against the Albert Club in Redfern. The match started on 21 February 1867. Before the big match, the team played at Manly Beach, and won, but more significantly for their future cricket careers, the men stayed at Charles Lawrence's Pier Hotel in Manly. It was their first meeting with Lawrence. And Lawrence made an immediate impact on the team. He had charisma and he was shrewd. He envisaged making big money on this team.

A win at Manly was followed by two successive victories to make it three in a row, but the euphoria of that hat-trick of wins had hardly subsided when there was a dramatic turn of events at the start of the Redfern game against the Albert Club. Sensationally both coach Tom Wills and the manager William Hayman 'were arrested at the suit of Mr Jarrat (Gurnett) for alleged breach of contract … Messrs O'Brien (Tattersall's) and Lawrence (the cricketer) became security for them, and they were at once released, and the game proceeded.'[10]

This incident was the beginning of the end for Tom Wills as the coach of the Aboriginal team. Lawrence had seen his chance and while he didn't quite seize the opportunity to put Wills away he had worked towards gaining the confidence of the Aboriginal players and he had shown great cunning in providing a guarantee for Wills and Hayman.

The Aboriginal team travelled to Wollongong for the match against Illawarra, which was scheduled to be played on 5–6 April 1867. This match is significant in that it was the first occasion on which Wills and Lawrence played together for the Aboriginal team. The Aboriginal team batted first, hitting 116. Mullagh batted stylishly for a top score of 45 and Wills remained unbeaten on 27. Lawrence opened the batting but fell for just 5. However, their score was too great for the Illawarra team, which managed only 20. Wills and Lawrence both bowled like men possessed, as if one was trying to outdo the other. They each collected five wickets. The newspapers were strangely quiet about the introduction of a new player (Lawrence) in the saga of the Sydney tour. The tour had been hampered by reports and whispers and innuendo of Gurnett being perhaps not quite the well-heeled gentleman he purported to be. As early as February 1867 the newspapers announced that the team would return to Victoria, cutting short its Sydney tour and abandoning all hope of a trip to Queensland and then on to England. Hayman blamed Gurnett. Gurnett wrote a pathetic letter to the *Sydney Morning Herald*, citing illness, yet remarkably he remained upbeat about an England tour, saying that he would, with the help of a friend, come good with the necessary funds to allow the England tour to go ahead. Hayman also wrote to the *Herald* putting his case, refuting Gurnett's remarks and pointing out that Gurnett had not paid him one penny towards the costs of the tour, nor had the coach Tom Wills received any money for the agreed weekly allowance. Nor indeed had the players themselves received the agreed 50 pounds. The team would play a few more matches to try and raise the fare back to Melbourne, but effectively the team was stranded in Sydney. Lawrence saw his chance and like the true opportunist he was he helped in the arrangement of matches.

Lawrence and Wills again played in a match together, against the Cumberland County XI in Parramatta, and between them they scored 57 runs and took 17 wickets, but the side lost. Lawrence arranged a 'benefit' match against a New South Wales XI at the Albert Club Ground, Redfern, where he had persuaded the club to waive all fees. Bad weather made conditions tough and ruined the chance of a bumper crowd. Thus gate receipts fell way below expectations. Lawrence and Wills again took the bulk of the wickets and restricted the New South Wales XI to the paltry scores of 99 and 43, but the Aboriginal team struggled even more on the treacherous pitch and lost the match by 15 runs. Hayman contributed 400 pounds to ensure that everyone in the touring party could return home, but the human cost of this 1867 Sydney tour was horrific. Sugar had died suddenly before the Boxing Day match at the MCG and Watty, a replacement, died on the road journey home. Jellico, a young man with a brilliant wit, and Paddy died from pneumonia soon after the side returned to Victoria. Watty was within 25 kilometres of Edenhope when he died. An inquest failed to find the true cause of death, although the rumour was that the demon drink had accounted for him. The *Australasian* correspondent wrote a scathing piece on the ill-fated Sydney tour as the team wended its way back to Melbourne, a dejected group:

> It has been a most unfortunate affair from the day they entered into agreement with one Gurnett — E. Brougham Gurnett Esq. I beg his pardon. What an injured innocent he is by his own showing! Unfortunately for him, people in Melbourne are disposed to believe what Mr

Hayman says in the matter, and it would require Mr Gurnett's presence in Melbourne to remove a very unfavorable impression there is abroad respecting him. I think the secretary of the MCC would be glad to see him. I think one or two of those who won prizes on the MCC ground would be glad to see him. I think many of his 'friends' in this city would be glad of a call.[11]

Another newspaper article concluded, 'It was inked a most unfortunate day when the agreement was signed.'[12]

Mounted Constable Thomas Kennedy alleged in a letter to his superior in Portland that Watty had indeed died from the consequences of over indulging in alcohol, adding that others in the team were also continually drunk.

Tom Wills was seen as a bad influence on the Aboriginal players because of his less-than-sober habits. The way was open for Charles Lawrence to take over the day-to-day management of the players. Despite the hardship, the criticism and the tragedy of player deaths, an England tour was very much on the mind of Charles Lawrence when he left his hotel business in Manly and took up an appointment in the winter of 1867 to coach the Aboriginal players at Lake Wallace. There were, of course, obstacles to clear. Gurnett's credibility was shot to pieces, and his tour contract needed careful vetting. The Central Board for the Protection of Aborigines in Victoria was gaining strength and was close to winning statutory power. After the abortive Sydney tour, the Board was unlikely to entertain another attempt to take the Aborigines out of Victoria. A fresh injection of capital was also needed. Two men came to the party: George Smith, a Sydney man with a love of racehorses and the hard cash to buy what he wanted, and George Graham, Smith's cousin. Smith played for Manly when Lawrence hosted the Aboriginal team at the Pier Hotel. The pieces were starting to fit. Lawrence now had the support of Hayman, who was still seething over Gurnett's deception and Wills' supposed bouts of drinking, and both Smith and Graham. Wills was effectively shoved aside.

Lawrence took over and the tour 'backers' began to plan for the tour to England. Lawrence drilled his men in all the batting, bowling and fielding skills. They practised on the shores of Lake Wallace, an idyllic scene to set the stage for the big adventure. Lawrence encouraged them to continue to practise their traditional skills: throwing the boomerang and hurling the spear. He could see the enormous drawing power of tribal displays on the cricket grounds of England. But first, the side needed to play the game of cricket to a standard that would warrant a chance against the Englishmen. It would take lots of hard work and a great deal of patience by Lawrence to have the men ready in time for the hectic 1867–68 Australian summer, then an even more demanding 1868 northern summer. Lawrence arranged a number of practice matches. On 28 August 1867, Lawrence took a good, long look at his players in a match at Edenhope. Mullagh, Cuzens, Tarpot, Peter, Dick-a-Dick, Jim Crow (sometimes called Neddy), S. Harry, Harry Rose and C. Rose (probably the King Cole of the 1868 team and brother of Harry Rose, who is a relative of Lionel Rose the great Australian boxer) played in one side, while their opponents included Redcap, Sundown, Stock-keeper, Store-keeper and Gorman. The teams were a mismatch, but Lawrence had probably already settled on his England squad. As coach, Lawrence managed to do what good leaders do: he created an atmosphere of trust and he empowered his players. The blacks enjoyed more freedom of expression than ever before and they rewarded that trust and empowerment with unconditional loyalty.

Lawrence, Hayman, Smith and Graham formed the executive committee for the 1868 tour. It was planned that the team play in the leading regions of Victoria and New South Wales, then sail to China, en-route to England. On Monday, 16 September 1867, Lawrence and Hayman and thirteen Aboriginal men, a cook and a coachman left Lake Wallace aboard a large American wagon drawn by four horses. A man in a separate horse and cart travelled with the troupe, carrying a tent and camp supplies:

> It rained very heavily when we started with lightning and thunder, which continued until dark. We camped as the wagon got bogged. This was between Harrow and Edenhope. It was impossible to release the wagon, so the blacks soon made a fire and cut down trees to make a shelter from the rain. After we had something to eat we then got bark off the trees and made ourselves pretty comfortable for the night.[13]

The party woke at dawn. It was still wet and cold and the men toiled for an hour to extract the wagon from the mud. It had sunk to the depth of the wheel hubs overnight. The wagon was unloaded completely, then with expert use of ropes and lots of huffing and puffing, the wagon was set free and moved to firm ground. Lawrence noticed a large number of water fowl in the nearby swamps, but they had no time to arrange a shooting party. They decided to forge ahead, but along the way they managed to shoot a few birds, which they later roasted over a fire when they made camp, in a clearing near the town of Harrow.

> We drove until 6 o'clock for camp which was most enjoyable round a big camp fire, with plenty of logs for seats and any amount of mutton chops cooked on the gridiron and tea out of a little billie. We didn't require either milk or sugar as we had such good appetites that these extras were never thought of … we were a happy family indulging in all sorts of funny talk of our homeward anticipations … and the fairytales I used to tell them, which pleased them very much, and also the match to be played at Warrnambool.[14]

It was not until Saturday, 21 September that the party reached Trainor's Hotel, near Hamilton, where they were entertained by the host. Some Hamilton cricketers met them at the hotel and invited them to play a game of football that Saturday afternoon. However, Lawrence did not take up the offer, for they refused to play his men at cricket, 'not wishing to regain the laurels they lost two years since'.[15] Lawrence and his men continued their journey after only a brief stay at Trainor's Hotel. That night the party camped at Germantown. Again they sat around a huge camp fire sipping tea after a hearty meal of roast mutton. Lawrence loved to tell the Aboriginal men stories, fairytales and fables. That night Lawrence noticed Johnny Cuzens looking quizzically at a picture of Jesus Christ. Dick-a-Dick peered over Cuzens' shoulder and asked, 'Do you know who that little piccaninny is … for they kill him.'

'What for?' Cuzens asked.

'I don't know, for he is Jesus Christ.'

'Who is he?'

'I don't know.'

Johnny then called Dick-a-Dick to account. 'I think you are telling lies, Dick. Why should they kill a little baby like that …'[16]

Later Johnny Cuzens approached Lawrence and asked him if what Dick-a-Dick had told him about Jesus was true. Lawrence assured Cuzens that he would explain the story of Jesus to the whole party during their get-togethers round the camp fire. He did so almost immediately for the dinner bell rang and everyone gathered around for the evening meal.

Lawrence spent one night at a hotel. He explained that he was 'knocked up' from the bush experience, and Hayman continued on with the Aboriginal players. Lawrence rejoined the group after a good night's rest and was sitting next to Cuzens who had taken the reins because the regular coachman was sick. As they passed near Caramut, Cuzens had the horses in full trot, negotiating a steep incline. The coach lurched and Cuzens was thrown out of the vehicle. He landed on his head and Lawrence feared the worst. But Cuzens had rolled himself into a ball and the wheels only touched his legs, tearing his clothes but not his flesh. The horses were immediately stopped by a couple of the Aboriginal men who were walking ahead to relieve the horses. Apparently the coach had lurched when the wheels came in contact with a large stone on the track. Asked how he felt after the accident, Cuzens rubbed his chin gingerly and said: 'I think my head hurt a little.'

That night everyone was in a jovial mood. They all congratulated Cuzens on his miraculous escape and as Charles began his regular stories, Cuzens implored him to tell the group some more about the baby Jesus. They said it was the best of the fairytales. This didn't suit Lawrence who wanted the men to think of the story as the truth. So he said to them:

> Now, I want you to believe in the baby in the manger. For he grew up to be a man and was the son of God, Jesus Christ. God gave his son's life to save all of ours if we believe in him and try our best to be kind and good to each other. Then when we die we shall go to him in heaven. This I want you all to believe for I will not deceive you. When we go to church in Warrnambool I feel sure you will all like it …'[17]

That night Dick-a-Dick and Lawrence armed themselves and

went hunting for a bird or two to roast on the camp fire. They returned to camp to discover that a stranger was in their midst — a black man. The man explained that he could play cricket and was keen to join the troupe. Lawrence invited him to stay for supper and spend the night with the party. However, he sensed that the men did not take to the stranger, so he advised his men to load their guns and if the camp was 'rushed' to fire in the air and give the customary war-cry. The men made Lawrence a comfortable spot in the fork of a gum tree, but sleep evaded him. Suddenly a terrible noise, like stampeding cattle, was heard. From his tree-top vantage point, Lawrence called to his men to ready themselves. White men on horses burst into the camp, threatening to pull the camp to pieces and kill them all. Lawrence gave the signal to fire and the players, camp cook and coachman all pointed to the heavens and fired. The men on horses fled at a gallop. When the men had gone, the black stranger confessed that he had run away from a sheep station and that the men on horses were after him. Lawrence gave him a cricket trial in the morning, but he considered him insufficiently skilled to join the band of cricketers. He gave the man some money and advised him to return to the station.

The troupe finally arrived at Warrnambool on Tuesday, 24 September — eight days after they had set out from Lake Wallace. They stayed at the Victoria Hotel, where their host, Adam Murray, attended upon them every consideration. The Aboriginal team wore white flannel trousers and red military shirts with a blue flannel sash sewn on from right shoulder to the left hip. They had blue elastic belts, with matching neckties, white linen collars and French merino under-shirts. They could be identified by the different coloured caps they wore. Mullagh's was scarlet, Harry Rose's was Victoria plaid, Cuzens' was purple, Dick-a-Dick's was yellow, Sundown's was check, Redcap's was black, Mosquito's was dark blue, Peter's was green, Jim Crow or Neddy's was pink, Bullocky's was chocolate, King Cole or Charley's was magenta, Twopenny's was McGregor plaid and Lawrence's was white. The side thrashed Warrnambool by an innings and 97 runs. The Aborigines and Lawrence turned on a great show with their sports day and on the Sunday Lawrence took his men, as he had promised, to church.

Advertisement in the *Geelong Advertiser* heralding the Aboriginal sports to be held after the match against Corio in Geelong, October 1867.

They seemed to like it and was [sic] very attentive. When the collection plate was presented they gave a little yelp. When they came out I asked them how they liked it and they said, 'Music very nice and him talk a lot and get a lot of money.' 'What do you think he does with it?' 'Keep it … don't he?'[18]

Lawrence explained to the men that the clergyman collected the money and distributed it among the poor. He noted that they seemed both astounded and delighted, assuring him that they would forever place some money in the church plate.

They were due to travel to Geelong to play the Corio club and Lawrence had hoped to fit in extra matches, but bad weather put a dampener on this plan. Tom Wills was a living legend in Geelong, a rather angry living legend by the time Lawrence and his troupe arrived. Poor weather marred the game, but Wills was none too pleased with Hayman, umpire for the match, who gave Wills out LBW to a ball from Lawrence which all other close witnesses swore would have clearly missed the stumps. However, Wills' men led on the first innings by five runs in a very low scoring affair and in dreadful conditions. Twice Lawrence and Wills met and twice their matches were drawn. They were due to play more matches in Victoria, but arrangements had to be changed swiftly when Lawrence read in the newspapers that the Central Board for the Protection of Aborigines was lobbying the Victorian Government to stop the tour. Lawrence feared that their venture would have to be abandoned. In consultation with Smith, Hayman and Graham, Lawrence planned for his men to slip through the net of 'protection' and sail to England from Sydney.

CHAPTER THREE

CHARLES LAWRENCE's life had been one of constant change and enlightenment. His cricket began for him in the most romantic way. He lived just 22 kilometres from Lord's Cricket Ground, to some people the known centre of the universe. June the 22nd, 1840, was special, for today Charles would walk to Lord's to watch his hero, the greatest batsman of the age, Fuller Pilch, in action. The 11-year-old schoolboy quickly dressed in his school garb, a sad coordination of grey knickerbockers, shirt, jacket, socks, shoes and cloth cap. Charles' trek to Lord's began one of the most remarkable journeys in sports history, for he holds a unique place in the scheme of all things cricket. His mother doted on Charles. He was spoilt, a fact he later readily admitted, but he was not game enough to admit to his intention to wag school and walk on his own to Lord's. Charles had hidden his cricket bat and a small cache of food by the wicker gate. He hurried from the house and when far enough away to avoid prying family eyes, he checked his supplies: an apple, a small block of cheese, a chunk of bread. He carried his bat over his right shoulder and with his left hand he fumbled in his pocket.

He had saved sixpence, ample means, he thought, to spend a day at Lord's. The shiny coin of the realm felt heavenly between forefinger and thumb. Charles found the London road alive with people flitting to and fro, busily going about their business, far too preoccupied to worry about a boy who had stopped to take a sneak look at his shiny sixpence. It featured the new monarch, Queen Victoria, her handsome image set in immortal profile. In this the third year of her reign her profile appeared on the world's first postage stamp, the 'Penny Black'. The young Queen Victoria had just turned 21 and she held a certain charm for Charles. At school Charles learned of the Queen's extra-ordinary start in life. Charles liked good timing. All the great batsmen of the day possessed such a gift, but good timing was not confined to Fuller Pilch and Company. King George IV, the man Victoria had always called 'Uncle King' was blessed with perfect timing, given that he waited until Victoria's parents and other distinguished guests were at the baptismal font at Kensington Palace that June day in 1819 before he informed his audience of anxious royals that the baby princess would be known as 'Alexandrina Victoria', the first name in honor of Alexander I, Tsar of All Russia, who was chosen as Victoria's second godfather despite his not being able to attend the service. Charles also learned that, although Victoria's beloved 'Uncle King' died in 1830 when she was eleven, Victoria honoured the late King by wearing his diadem ('whatever that was') at her Coronation.

Charles was growing up in a nation that was firmly in the grip of great change. The Industrial Revolution was spinning at a feverish rate. Throughout Britain revolutionary change embraced the roads, railways, factories, coal-mines, canals and the minds of the British people. Thomas Telford and John Macadam developed a technique of road-making which rapidly increased both traffic volume and road quality. Fast coaches sped along the roads and highways, replacing the old pack horse. Canals and steam train travel helped reduce the cost of handling raw materials by transporting them direct from the source to the great manufacturing centres such as Manchester. Britain was experiencing the fastest, most efficient road transport since Roman chariots sped along the very length of Watling Street. Even Thomas Lord was clean-bowled by the Industrial Revolution. His beloved Lord's Cricket Ground (Mark II) became part of Regent's Canal in 1813, which meant that a new site had to be found. He found his ideal site at St John's Wood, London.

In 1840 only the well-to-do travelled by coach. Travel by foot was not the hardship we moderns might perceive it to be today, for all things are relative. In the Britain of 1840 women and children were driven like slaves in the factories. While other children Charles' age, and younger, and under-nourished women were working long, desperate hours in appalling conditions in factories throughout Britain just to survive, Charles had not a care in the world. The sun shone, London beckoned and his heart was set on getting to Lord's to watch his hero, Fuller Pilch, bat. He knew nothing of workplace injustice. It was some eight years before Lord Shaftsbury found safe passage of his *Ten Hours Act* through parliament, thus ensuring limited hours and far less exploitation of women and child workers.

Charles was one of eight Lawrence children, who were often left to their own devices, although not through parental neglect. The parents provided their children with ample food, a comfortable home and an average, if not privileged, education. Paradoxically the pampered upbringing did not adversely impact upon Charles. He rapidly developed street-fighter qualities and a sense of fun and adventure.

Charles had heard such glowing reports of Pilch's batting that he simply *had* to risk a beating from the headmaster for taking the day off to visit the famous ground. Pilch was considered the champion of England. He reigned supreme as the best batsman in England from 1830 to the late 1840s. According to Arthur Haygarth, a noted scribe of the period, Pilch's style was:

> … very commanding, extremely forward and he seemed to crush the best bowling by his long forward plunge before it had time to shoot or rise or do mischief by catches.[1]

At the time Charles was approaching London Bridge, Charles Dickens was in Ballechelish in Scotland polishing his newest epic, *Barnaby Rudge.* In *Pickwick Papers* (1836) Dickens writes with charm, if not with technical accuracy, on a cricketing encounter between the fictional All Muggleton versus Dingley Dell. Dickens makes light of the game and shows his eye for detail:

> [Each fieldsman] fixed himself into proper attitude by placing one hand on each knee, and stooping very much as if he were 'making a back' for some beginner at leap-frog. All the regular players do this sort of thing; — indeed it's generally supposed that it is quite impossible to look out properly in any other direction. 'Play', suddenly cried the bowler. The ball flew from his hand straight and swift towards the centre stump of the wicket. The wary Dumpkins was on the alert; it fell upon the tip of the bat and bounded far away over the heads of the scouts, who had just stooped low enough to let it fly over them.[2]

This fictional cricket match between Dingley Dell and All Muggleton is illustrated on the reverse of the current English 10 pound note.

In the 1830s the gentry were eager to bring in outside experts, players who were not only skilled cricketers but who had more than a passing acquaintance with coaching and groundsmanship. Cricket attracted many punters among the rich and famous. Even the less well-to-do got involved by forming syndicates. The 'backers' lured good players for their own gain, for the safest bet is a bet which backs the best man or team or both. As far back as 1811, for a wager involving 500 guineas for each side, winner take all, two Englishmen pitted teams of women at Newington for a three-day match.

> Billed as the 'cricket match extraordinary', two teams of eleven women were pitted against each other at Ball's Pond, Newington on October 3, 1811. Two gambling noblemen made up the teams from Hampshire and Surrey. The players' ages ranged from 14 to 40 and the different parties were distinguished by coloured ribbons: Royal purple for Hampshire and orange and blue for Surrey.[3]

The rich young 'bucks' of the time did not consider there was much 'sport' in a cricket contest unless a bet was involved. Betting was the key to cricket's popularity in the 18th and early 19th centuries. Cricket is a baffling contradiction in that those of us in the Commonwealth of Nations are conditioned to think of cricket as being everything to do with 'fair play' and good sportsmanship, when in reality this is an illusion. Those within cricket guard the game's virtue with a determination that would have gladdened the heart of the most feared turnkey at Newgate Prison, yet we all know that the history of the game includes dishonesty, gamesmanship that bordered on cheating, and the taking of bribes. The bookies at Lord's were known as the 'Marylebone legs'. They moved about the English countryside at the start of the summer 'softening up' prospective players, eventually tempting them with bribes. Hampshire players were particularly targetted in the early days. When in London they often stayed at a pub in Oxford Street, the 'Green Man and Still', and there the 'legs' worked their magic in a convivial theatre. Virtually no famous match in England was played without a wager on the outcome. Cricket history is littered with bets on matches and it was said (although no man had the courage or the evidence to name the culprit) that a famous player accepted 100 pounds in 1838 for 'throwing a match'. The landed gentry often risked thousands of guineas on matches, so there was potential to 'fix' games and corrupt players. Even in those glorious embryonic days of cricket when the men of the Hambledon Club bowled and batted the likes of John Nyren, David Harris, William Beldham and Edward 'Lumpy' Stevens into cricket history, men looked at ways to bend the rules. Sueter, a Hambledon batsman, was believed to be the first batsman in recorded history to leave his crease to get to the pitch of the ball, thus breaking the time-honoured rule of standing firm at the popping-crease.

Thinking changed by the late 18th century, for the likes of William Beldham (and Willam Fennex, the best known single-wicket players of the 1780s) were not content to be anchored to the crease. They both ran down the track or 'gave her the rush'. In later years Victor Trumper and Don Bradman used their feet to destroy a bowler's length. It is not a trend followed by the general run of South African or New Zealand batsmen, save for the brilliant Barry Richards or Martin Crowe. Batting coaches today talk of 'soft' hands to avoid an edge 'carrying' to slip. Talk 'soft' hands to an Australian a few years back and he would tell you to piss on them. The modern player likes to have room in which to free his arms and play his strokes. Not so with the men of Hambledon. They stood transfixed, like statues of stone, anchored to the crease. Nyren writes of the manner in which a batsman should play a length ball a little wide of the off stump:

> This is a puzzler to a short-armed batsman. I recommend the young batsman to have nothing to do with it. The old hand will, of course, do as he pleases: but I should much wish to be informed in what part of the field he can play it with safety and make a run. Beldam would cut at such a ball with a horizontal bat. I once made the remark to him, that I thought it dangerous play: he answered me, 'I always play above the ball.' If he always played above such a ball, it was useless his playing at it at all.[4]

In the early part of the 19th century, lovers of cricket feared that the game was in danger of ruin, for it had become the chief medium for gambling in England. Bookmakers were always at the games, calling the odds as the fortunes of each team ebbed and flowed. Side bets on individuals led to bribery and cheating. With the advent of the Marylebone Cricket Club (MCC) in 1787, many of the landed gentry became part and parcel of the MCC itself. They continued to bet among themselves, but corruption seemed to abate and eventually disappear. MCC members were perceived as men of honour. At the start of the 1835 season, the MCC boasted 600 members, including one duke, two marquises, 11 earls, eight baronets, 23 honorables and some 200 'other' gentlemen. It was not exactly a classless organisation. That the betting continued was apparent, for the rich liked to lure good players to their favoured teams. The 'backers' wanted cricketers of great ability and ones who had the skills to tend the ground and the wickets and ones with some business acumen. And as there was inevitably a pub attached to every cricket ground, a cricketer who could prepare a wicket, maintain a ground and run a pub was every backer's ideal.

Such a calling befell Fuller Pilch when some cricket lovers in Town Malling, in Kent, heard of his prowess. Fuller Pilch — the very name sounds like a high full toss, the kind of delivery so enjoyed by batsmen from the top of the order to the bottom — was born in Norfolk. He sought work in Sheffield as a lad and he learned his cricket in the northern parts of England. As a young man he moved back to his birth county, first to Bury St Edmunds, then to Norwich.

> He took up a post in which Mitford saluted him bizarrely: 'Come forth from thy public house at the bottom of Surrey Hill, Norwich, which thou keepest, with thy sister as thy bar-maid, Fuller Pilch.'[5]

Pilch became a pub owner in Town Malling with an added lure of 100 pounds per annum as ground-keeper.

Matches were played by Town Malling against neighbouring counties or 'England' and proved highly popular. The cricketers of the time wore tall black hats, white duck pantaloons, and highly polished black shoes with shiny brass buckles.

Young Charles Lawrence had his cricket heroes, apart from Fuller Pilch. And while he set out for Lord's for the express purpose of seeing Pilch, he was aware of other cricket 'giants' such as Nicholas Felix, Alfred Mynn, Thomas Box and Samuel Redgrave. Felix was an intriguing character. A small, solid left-hander, he was brilliant on the cut. He was extraordinarily talented: an inventor, an artist and quite proficient in literary and musical pursuits. As a young man Felix inherited a private school in Camberwell. He was born Nicholas

Wanostracht, but changed his name, 'lest his image of scholastic seriousness be tarnished amongst parents'.[6] Felix was the author of a delightful book, *Felix on Cricket* (1845), and one wonders whether it would have sold as well as it did if it had had Felix's original surname in the title.

Rough pitches and the increasing danger of round-arm bowling gave Felix the idea of providing batsmen with greater protection on poor wickets. He invented the first tubular rubber batting gloves. He also created the first cricket bowling machine, the 'Catapulta', and was a clever sketcher and painter in oils. His 1847 painting of William Clarke's All England Eleven is superb.

Alfred Mynn, with whom Felix struck up an improbable alliance, was apparently cut out to do nothing at all with his life but play cricket. The fourth son of a gentleman farmer, Mynn was built like a taller version of Colin Cowdrey. He had a commanding presence and played cricket for most of his young adult life, depending on his father to supplement his income. However, financial worries plagued him when his father died. He tried his hand with his brother in a hop-making business, but soon returned to what he knew best. Lord's rescued him financially with a benefit match. Its success was due to his enormous popularity, for Mynn was a hero to many schoolboys throughout England. Mynn was a member of The South which lost to The North at Lord's on 11 and 12 July 1836, the first such match played in England. He got a duck and 8 not out, but picked up three cheap wickets in The North's second innings, including the wicket of Pilch, bowled for 14. This match saw William Clarke, the man who drove the game in Nottingham, play his first match at Lord's. He was then aged 37. A legend in Nottingham, Clarke later figured prominently in Charles Lawrence's future.

Mynn played the return North–South fixture at Leicester over four days, 22–25 August. In The South's second innings, Mynn batted at the fall of the fifth wicket. He flayed the bowling, led by the redoubtable Samuel Redgate, to score 125 not out, The South eventually winning the match by 218 runs. In 212 big matches for Kent, Sussex and various representative elevens, Mynn scored 4955 runs. His 125 not out remained his highest score, in fact the only century of his career.

Mynn had injured his right leg at practice and wished to wear the 'leggings' or vulcanised rubber padding inserted in long stockings worn under the white duck pantaloons. However, the authorities would have none of it, Lord Frederick Beauclerk 'thought they were acceptable in practice, but unfair to bowlers in a match'.[7] Despite needing a runner to bat, Mynn summoned all of his considerable courage to savage the attack, including that by the brilliant Nottingham fast man Samuel Redgate. Mynn scored an unbeaten 21 in the first innings, the great knock yet to come. But his century came at a price. He was battered on the leg by Redgate, whose breakneck pace caused the ball to fly disconcertingly, either at the throat or scurrying along the tortured turf. Mynn's innings drew great praise from Redgate: 'The better I bowled, the harder he hit me away.'[8]

It was after his epic knock, during The North's second innings, that Mynn complained about the state of his leg to Lord Frederick Beauclerk, the man who had originally dissuaded him from wearing 'leggings'. Beauclerk immediately called for Mynn to be taken for treatment. He was placed on the roof of a stage coach and rushed from Leicester to London, where he first lay in agony at a tavern in St Martin's Lane, then found comfort and treatment in St Bartholomew's Hospital. His leg was narrowly saved from amputation, but he was prevented from playing cricket at all in 1837. It was as a bowler that Mynn shone. He captured 741 wickets (at 10.23 runs apiece), bowling a style which was round-arm and fast. By 1838 his leg had healed and he returned to the game, proving an even deadlier bowler than previously. Mynn was more accurate when he operated off a shorter run. He beat the Yorkshireman James Dearman at single-wicket both at home and away, thrilling the thousands with his all-round mastery. All the time he wore a straw hat with a red ribbon. It was not until 1846 that his chum, Felix, challenged him at single-wicket. Felix lost, but the pair won the crowd over. It was the last match played for the single-wicket championship. As a bowler Mynn could be 'destructive'. He had what Haygarth described as a noble delivery, 'walking majestically up to the crease, though when he first began he used to advance with a run. His bowling very fast and ripping, round-armed and of a good length; and though at first not very straight, he afterwards became as steady as could be wished, rarely delivering a wide.'[9]

Mynn towered over 1.8 metres and weighed 130 kilograms. He had a penchant for cold pork and took a pint of light bitter ale to bed with him every night. Alfred Mynn played a big part in cricket's formative years.

Thomas Box was England's premier wicket-keeper. He was a Sussex man, but won fame for the All England Eleven as a man with 'exceedingly fine style'. According to writers of the day, Box was fortunate to have kept to William Lillywhite, whose bowling was 'slow, but rose well to the bails'.[10] In 1851 Box kept in no less than 41 big matches, a testimony to his stamina and love of cricket. On his retirement Box kept pubs and cricket grounds, overseeing the Hanover Arms and ground in Lewes Road, the Ergemont Hotel in Western Road (Brighton) and later the Brunswick Cricket Ground and Hotel at Hove.

Box died with his boots on. He was working as a ground-keeper at Prince's and dropped dead during the Middlesex versus Nottingham county match of 1876. The match was abandoned as soon as his death became known. During his career behind the stumps, Box played 247 big games, taking 235 catches and effecting 162 stumpings.

Fuller Pilch's nemeses was Samuel Redgate. In *Scores and Biographies* Redgate is described as having been 'fast and ripping, with a good deal of "spin", but the last few years it was slow and feeble, apparently due to ill health. He had also a beautiful easy delivery, and was unexceptional as to fairness.'[11] He was also remarkably successful in getting out Fuller Pilch, when opposed to that celebrity. His first big match at Lord's was on 22 June 1835, exactly five years before the day Charles Lawrence set out to walk to Lord's to see his heroes for the first time. Redgate took up a position as cricket coach at Eton College that very summer of 1840.

Charles scanned the buildings on the North Bank. His mind was elsewhere, but his legs continued to carry him onward, towards London Bridge. Charles' eyes met the battlements of the Tower of London and further on he could just make out a flurry of activity of the waterfront, at Billingsgate Market. Then his gaze fell upon the Monument and he stood transfixed. He knew about this famous landmark. Christopher Wren's grey commemoration of the Great Fire of London in 1666 was a stone pillar some 60 metres high. James Boswell climbed it in 1763 and described it in these words:

In the inside, a turnpike stair runs up all the way. When I was about half way up, I grew frightened. I would have come down again but thought I would despise myself for my timidity. Thus does the spirit of pride get the better of fear. I mounted to the top and got upon the balcony. It was horrid to find myself so monstrous a way up in the air, so far above London and all its spires. I durst not look around me. There is no real danger, as there is a strong rail both on the stair and balcony. But I shuddered, and as every heavy wagon passed down Gracechurch Street, dreaded that the shaking of the earth would make the tremendous pile tumble to the foundation.[12]

Charles could readily identify with Boswell's 'spirit of pride' for the pride he felt in his trek to Lord's to watch Fuller Pilch far outweighed any 'fear' he had for the consequences of his wagging school. He had yet to reach London Bridge when two men in a dogcart happened along. Charles recognised the men as friends of his father's and he recalled seeing them standing by their cart as he passed near Kensington Common. The men asked Charles where he was heading and he told them.

They then asked me if I was playing the wag and I said, 'yes'. They seemed in a fix, what to do, then I heard them say, 'He'll be lost, we had better take him.' So they said, 'jump up, we are going to the match' (they were in a dog cart).

'I fancy you'll get a beating when you get home for playing truant,' one of the men volunteered.[13]

Charles was not, at that precise time, worried in the slightest at the ramifications of wagging school. He was determined to see Fuller Pilch and 'everything else seemed of no consequence'. The dog-cart rumbled along parallel to the Thames. The Tower of London dominated Charles' vista. Sir Thomas More, history records, spent his last night on earth in the tower.

A man, the ex-Chancellor had said, may lose his head, but not his dignity. Awaiting the axe, he pushed aside his beard, commenting that it should not be injured, as it had committed no treason. Usually, the victim, if executed in public, died well.[14]

Now a tourist Mecca, the Tower was then a gloomy place: cold and heartless, like the surrounding stone buildings and battlements. Charles spotted a raven. Jet-black ravens still skulk like shadows of the devil haunting the tortured souls of thousands murdered in the Tower for trivial crimes. Contemporary writer V. S. Pritchett in *London Perceived* does not see past the tragic history of the Tower to present the usual modern romantic view:

> The Tower means murder *now,* torture *now*, stranglings, treacheries, massacre, the solitary cell, the kick of the policeman's boot. The scratchings on the walls of The Tower are the scratchings of Auschwitz.[15]

In 1840 the people feared ending up in either of two places: Newgate Prison or the Tower. Transportation to Sydney ended that year, although the convict transportation to Australia did not stop entirely. In fact, the last transport of British convicts to Perth (Western Australia) arrived on the *Hougomont* at Fremantle on 10 January 1868, bringing the total number of convicts transported to Australia in the years 1788–1868 to 160,500, of which 24,700 were female. Those caught for petty crimes often ended up in Newgate. More serious crimes, especially those of treason, meant a term in the Tower and often the loss of one's head.

Charles marvelled at the sights and sounds of bustling London. So much to see, especially near London bridge, for the eye could take in the Monument, the Tower and St Paul's Cathedral. The dogcart neared London Bridge. There were all manner of carts and coaches and pedestrians busily crossing the Thames that morning. Charles looked down the river and saw dozens of tall ships. There were none of the rotting hulks full of miserable prisoners that so spoilt Dickens' view in the 1830s as he scurried about the roads near the docks, ever searching for character and characters. Dickens found the wretched rotting mill pond, *Jacob's Island*, and he immortalised it in *Oliver Twist*. Suddenly the river's mix of treasures and odours disappeared as the dog-cart reached the North Bank. The tall ships gave way to rows of grey stone and wooden buildings. They seemed all crammed together.

In no time the dogcart skipped past Buckingham Palace, where

Queen Victoria began a modern trend for royals to occupy this fine building, and along the Edgeware Road. Ladies in their finery walked arm in arm with splendidly dressed consorts. The dogcart drew closer towards the famous venue.

All roads, it seemed, led to Lord's. Charles thanked his father's friends for the ride and passed through the entrance gate as if in a dream. The ground looked a treat, lush green. A man in a long brown coat was sweeping the pitch and in the distance a number of boys with dogs on leads were shooing sheep off the arena. Sheep were used to keep the grass neat at Lord's right up until 1850. For many years the Honorable Robert Grimston was on the MCC Committee. He played three matches for Middlesex and played for the MCC at Lord's from 1836 to 1855. It was said that Grimston knew well how to improvise. He used to take two bats to the wicket when confronted by Alfred Mynn — the larger, wider one for Mynn and the more conventional sized one for the other bowlers. Grimston's fetish was for 'sporting' wickets. He put sheep even before the scythe, which Fuller Pilch, a master of the blade, both cricket bat and the scythe, sometimes used to help crop crook wickets at Lord's.

The wicket was nibbled by sheep and often nobbled by Pilch, who, armed with his trusty scythe, wielded the instrument like a flowing cover drive, shaving every blade to minimum height.

I heard them say that Box, Mynn, Felix and Lillywhite and other celebrities were playing, but the only attraction for me was Fuller Pilch. I watched his batting very closely and it left such an impression on my mind that I never forgot it and always tried to imitate him.[17]

When Charles Lawrence walked into Lord's on 22 June 1840 the ground was decidedly rough. After rain the hooves of sheep left their mark. More rain and the ground became a quagmire. The Lord's that Charles first saw was very rural. The original pavilion was destroyed by fire in 1825, and the one that Charles saw was a splendid building with an arched front. It was superseded in 1889 by the grand Lord's pavilion we know so well today.

Awestruck, Charles watched his heroes at practice. For one glorious moment he found himself within arm's reach of Fuller Pilch as the great man strode to a position in front of the pavilion.

Pilch had an upright stance and he held the bat high on the handle. He was renowned for his forward play, smothering the shooters or the fliers and driving the ball, sometimes resorting to Hambleon's Sueter, with his penchant for advancing-down-the-track method of dealing with the slows of the men of guile. Pilch drove with a crisp certainty.

Impressive too was the huge presence of Alfred Mynn. And there was Thomas Box taking the ball with ease, his hands 'giving' as the ball threatened to make a resounding thwack but little or no sound was emitted. His timing was on song that day, Charles concluded. Felix batted briefly and Redgate limbered up. A tall, imposing figure, accompanied by a yapping dog, came onto the hallowed turf and ordered everyone off. The match — Slow Bowlers versus Fast Bowlers — was about to begin. Fuller Pilch was down to bat at number four, following Felix, for Slow Bowlers. Two men fell early. Lillywhite was bowled by Redgate and Cobbett was splendidly caught by Kynaston off Mynn for a duck. Pilch joined the reliable Felix. The little left-hander was shaping confidently. Pilch stood at the crease, erect, like a Grenadier Guard, his left foot pointing straight down the pitch, surely a sign that his toe was pointing in the direction he intended hitting Redgate's first delivery. Charles Lawrence wrote in his journal:

> After a time the game commenced and two or three wickets fell quickly, but I did not take much interest in the game until Pilch's turn came. Then I stood and clapped and shouted with the crowd and looked forward to something marvellous from this great batsman. But the noise had scarcely ceased when I heard someone say, 'oh, he's bowled first ball!' which indeed was the case; the ball having just touched the bail. My heart was in my boots at once and I cried. I then began to realize what I had done and the consequences that awaited me on my return home.[18]

Charles' reaction was typical among those in the crowd, as Fuller Pilch was the crowd favourite. Pilch's batting had been put in poetic terms:

> Another bold tailor, as fine a young man
> as e'er hit a ball and then afterwards ran,
> Is from Bury St Edmunds, and Pilch they him call,
> In a few years 'tis thought he'll be better than all.

At present his batting a little too wild,
Tho' the 'Nonpareil Hitter' he's sometimes been styled;
So free and so fine, with the hand of a master,
Spectators all grieve when he meets a disaster.[19]

Fuller Pilch was born at Horningtoft, in Norfolk, on 17 March 1803. He had two brothers, Nathaniel and William, who both played the game. Fuller Pilch's first match at Lord's was in 1820, the same match that William Ward scored his record 278 for the MCC versus Norfolk. Ward became MP for the City of London and a director of the Bank of England. In 1825 when Thomas Lord was seriously considering developing a large area of Lord's Cricket Ground as a building site, Ward took out his cheque book and handed over 5000 pounds. He sold his lease to James Dark in 1835.

After the dismissal of his hero, a spectator engaged Charles in conversation. 'I see you have one of Dark's bats,' the man said. 'Looks like the old one-piece. They make them better these days.' Then the man explained how the modern bats had a spliced handle to allow more 'give'. Charles' father purchased the bat for his son from Sadd of Cambridge for 8/6d. Dark bats were good, but they tended to jar if you didn't find dead centre. Cane handles were not introduced until 1853.

James Henry Dark ran Lord's from 1835 until 1864 when the MCC purchased the remainder of the lease he had bought from William Ward in 1835 for 2000 pounds and an annual payment of 425 pounds. Ward's lease had 58 years left to run.

Dark knew the area like the back of his hand. He was born in the Edgeware Road in 1795 and by 1805, at the age of 10, he used to earn a few shillings as a fielder for practices at the first Lord's, in Dorset Square. At the age of 39 Dark was listed in the 1851 Census as a 'propietor of houses'. Dark built himself a house in a corner at Lord's. He effectively kept his Lord's commitment in the family. His brother Benjamin Dark was the bat-merchant. He kept a large group of willow trees at the north-west end of Lord's. His son, Benjamin junior, eventually took over the business from his father. Another of James Dark's brothers, Robert, made leg-guards and balls at Lord's. Robert Dark was also a gate keeper, collecting entrance money at the gate. When James Dark died, Frank Dark bought his interest in Lord's in addition to the bat business from Mrs Matilda Dark. The continuing Dark influence at Lord's came with James Dark's nephew, Sydney, who was installed as assistant secretary and clerk to the MCC from 1862 to 1871. Sydney Dark was among the MCC welcoming party when Charles Lawrence's 1868 Aboriginal Australian team came to Lord's.[20]

The day he visited Lord's, Charles noticed a pond in the south-east corner. It was in this pond that Steevie Slatter taught himself to swim. Slatter later became Lord's groundsman. The Lord's pitch was loved by bowlers throughout the land. The pitch was bumpy and often dangerous: one at the throat, then next rapping the ankles (little wonder Fuller Pilch used to bring a scythe with him to every Lord's match). Under-arm bowling was being phased out and replaced by the new-fangled round-arm, which was legalised in 1835 and for which Alfred Mynn became famous. To celebrate the MCC Jubilee year, Lord's turned on a 'grand match', The North with Box and Cobbett versus The South. Each MCC member was asked to donate one pound towards the promotion of cricket, for this match was, in effect, a double celebration: MCC's first fifty years and Queen Victoria's accession to the throne. William Lillywhite took 14 wickets to help The South win by five wickets. The father of Frederick, the historian, Lillywhite took 1355 wickets at 10.89 in 245 big matches. His season's best tally of 115 wickets came in 1844, when aged 52. Lillywhite opened the batting the day Charles first went to Lord's and stayed at the crease only slightly longer than Pilch.

Lillywhite always considered himself able to dismiss Pilch and was often teased by those who knew him all too well. Lillywhite bowled slow medium and, like all the early round-armers, he operated around the wicket, which was definitely safer for umpires. He was accurate and combative. 'I suppose,' he once said in earnest, 'that if I was to think *every* ball, they would never get a run!'

One day at Lord's, when he was awaiting the arrival of Fuller Pilch to the batting crease, someone yelled: 'Hallo, Lilly, here comes your master!' To which Lillywhite replied, 'I wish I had as many pounds as I have got out Pilch.'[21]

James Dark did not always have a lot of big games played at Lord's, but he did have entrepreneurial flair. In 1837, apart from the Jubilee match, Dark had the balloonist Monsieur Garnisin ascend over Lord's, watched by a large, appreciative crowd. Dark also instigated hopping races, canary shows — which continued to be staged in the MCC Members' Dining Room as late as 1898 — pigeon flying, a cycle (velocipede in those days) record attempt, running on a travel track and, in 1844, a spectacular show by 'Red Indians of the Iowa Tribe'.[22]

The visit to Lord's by the Native Americans created enormous interest in Britain. They camped at Lord's for one week and gave displays of their athletic prowess and archery skills. The visit may also have sown the seed in someone's mind about a visit to England by Australian Aboriginal cricketers.

Charles heard the men talking of Pilch's extraordinary dismissal in another famous match, known as the 'Barn Door Match', in the July 1837 Gentlemen versus Players contest, in which the Gentlemen 'defended three wickets the size now in use, namely, 27 in by 8 in and the Players, defending four wickets, 36 in by 12 in'.[23] Fuller Pilch had scored 9 when his top hat fell from his head and on to the top of the off stump. The scorers wrote, 'Pilch hat knocked on the wicket, bowled Bathurst, 9.' Despite Pilch's modest tally, the Players won the match by an innings and 10 runs. 'No other match with these odds has ever been played. One of the four "monster" wickets was still in existence at Lord's about 1858.'[24] Charles then caught the eye of the stern man with the yapping dog. He did not recognise the man, but it was indeed Lord Frederick Beauclerk, both a tyrant and a man of the cloth. Charles heard someone speak in hushed tone about his Lordship's dog at his heel, for there were no dogs allowed at Lord's — none, that is, except for one belonging to Lord Frederick Beauclerk, who was a law unto himself. His Lordship was the Vicar of Hertfordshire and a Doctor of Divinity. For 35 years Beauclerk played in big matches and for some sixty years he made his presence felt at Lord's as an MCC member. He was president of the MCC in 1826, the year after fire destroyed the old wooden pavilion and, alas, most of the early records. Beauclerk was at his autocratic zenith at this time. He would walk from the old pavilion with his superior air, stop and look about him, then proceed to his left where invariably sat Mr Gully and his two 'legs'. Mr Gully usually sat to the left of the Lord's pavilion, and his two 'legs', who were ever calling the 'odds' when Beauclerk was out of range, invariably ducked for cover when the great man came into view.

His Lordship was the perfect hypocrite. He expressed public dismay at all forms of gambling yet privately boasted that his gambling on cricket was worth to him an average of 600 guineas a season. Lord Beauclerk was considered a capital bat, hitting a total of eight centuries at Lord's, although most were in 'lesser matches'. He began playing for Hampshire in 1805, the same year the poet Byron played for Harrow in a match against Eton at Lord's and 'were most confoundly beat'. In 1806 Beauclerk played in the first Gentlemen versus Players match at Lord's. He was a canny customer on the field and never reluctant to bend the rules, or if need be break them for his own purpose. He was, apparently, completely devoid of any feeling for his fellow man. In addition, he had an uncontrollable temper. He must have been among the most mean-spirited churchmen to draw breath. It was said that he delivered his Sunday sermon while astride a saddle, specially mounted in the enclosure behind the pulpit. His Lordship liked to ride roughshod over all and sundry.

The day Charles Lawrence first set eyes on his Lordship, Beauclerk was rising 67 years of age. But he had not mellowed. Indeed, those oldies about Charles reckoned Beauclerk was meaner than ever. Charles was left in no doubt about the extraordinary Lord Frederick Beauclerk.

Charles didn't get the opportunity to use his bat. Officials did not allow the youngsters to take to the field while the players practised before the match began. There were impromptu games being played on the grassy outer, but Charles was so keen to catch a close look at the players and then watch Fuller Pilch bat that he did not take part in any of the games. He felt even less inclined to do so after Pilch fell for a first-ball duck.

Charles began his walk from Lord's back to Merton long before the wily old William Lillywhite dismissed Alfred Mynn for 2, but not before Felix completed a neat and compact 35 for Slow Bowlers. He put his priceless Dark bat under his arm and walked from the ground.

Dr Samuel Johnson tells us that the name cricket was derived from the old English word 'cryce', a stick. It is written that a primitive form of cricket existed in the Middle Ages, popular with monks, which Edward III attempted to suppress on the grounds that it interfered with archery. Oliver Cromwell was said to have been addicted to cricket, yet in 1656 'krickett' was proscribed by Cromwell's Commissioners throughout Ireland, and all sticks and balls were to be burnt by the common hangman. Cricket's evolution was slow, even in England. It was not until 1744 that the full scorecard of a big match (Kent versus All England at the Artillery Ground, Finsbury) was recorded. Some say the matches of Hambledon at Broadhalfpenny Down marked the start of cricket in the modern era. However, the games seem to have had more 'drinkin' than playin' ', with John Nyren's immortal words giving us an insight into what days these must have been:

> There was high feasting held on Broad-Halfpenny during the solemnity of one of our grand matches. Oh! It was a heart-stirring sight to witness the multitude forming a complete and dense circle round that noble green. Half the county would be present, and all their hearts with us. Little Hambledon pitted against All England was a proud thought for the Hampshire men. Defeat was glory in such a struggle — Victory indeed made us only a 'little lower than angels'. And then what stuff they had to drink! — Punch! — not your *Ponche a la Romaine*, or *Ponche a la Groseille*, or your modern cat-lap milk-punch — punch be-devilled; but good, unsophisticated John Bull stuff — stark — that would stand on end — punch that would make a cat speak! Sixpence a bottle! We had not millions of interest to pay in those days ... Then the quantity those fellows would eat! Two or three of them would strike dismay into a round of beef ... There would be this company, consisting most likely of some thousands, patiently and anxiously watching every turn of fate in the game, as if the event had been the meeting of two armies to decide their liberty. And whenever a Hambledon man made a good hit, worth four or five runs, you would hear the deep mouths of the whole multitude, baying away in pure Hampshire — 'Go hard! — go hard! — Tich and turn! — tich and turn!" ...' Like true Englishmen they would give an enemy fair play. How strongly are those scenes, of fifty years bygone, painted in my memory! — and the smell of that ale comes upon me as freshly as the new May flowers.[25]

Because Pilch fell first ball, Charles' lasting memory of the day was the pre-match warm-up. Felix revealed his artistry with the bat and William Lillywhite flexed his muscles by raising and lowering his arms in a lazy half circle. Charles was enthralled, but Fuller Pilch held, for him, the greatest fascination. He watched Pilch's every move. He studied him, his mannerisms and, above all, his style.

Pilch played 229 matches, hitting 7147 runs at 18.61. He scored three centuries with a career-best of 153 not out. In Pilch's time the wickets were dreadful in comparison with today's manicured turf rolled as hard as a half-crown piece. Batting in the early to mid-1800s was a hazardous business. Even wicket-keepers of the brilliance of Box struggled to stop the shooters and flyers scuttling through to the ever-reliable long-stop. Few batsmen wore pads and none wore helmets. The ball tended to bite and turn, jump and skid. Anyone who averaged above 15, as did Felix and Pilch, were exceptional.

It was late afternoon by the time Charles reached London Bridge — no ride in a dogcart on the return journey. The sunshine spread late into the evening. Charles reached his home at nine o'clock. He was scolded and put to bed without any supper. However, Charles had left the bulk of his rations for the return trek, so he was not hungry. His appetite was unlikely to improve that night, for he knew that a belting from the headmaster was as certain as Fuller Pilch getting bowled first ball by Samuel Redgate. Charles' parents were angry with him over the Lord's excursion, but they did not inhibit his natural aggression or sense of adventure.

Charles' early days were filled with schoolwork and adventures. He was always on the go. He once nearly drowned in the River Maudel, having decided to swim as far as he could. However, he tired and began to sink. Someone came to his rescue. 'I could not rise and all I could think of was what would mother say when she heard of it.'[28] There were personal confrontations. One particular boy, a chimney sweep, targeted Charles one day. He was on his way to school when the boy leapt at him and wiped his sooty hands all over Charles' face and clothes. Such was the state of his clothes after the attack, Charles had to return home to put on a clean pinafore. However, Charles took the attack as a personal affront. He declared war on the chimney sweep. Next time he would hit back. Sure enough the chimney sweep came at him again next morning. The sweep grabbed Charles by the hair and someone yelled out to the boy to leave Charles alone. But the sweep held on and Charles, in desperation, hit his attacker in the face with his closed fist. The sweep closed again on Charles and fought like mad. The pair were rolling in the mud and scraping along the main road. A woman broke up the fight and took Charles in to her house, washed him, put him to bed and dried his clothes, sending word to his mother that the fight was not Charles' fault and that she hoped he would not be punished. Charles' father visited the sweep's father and asked that his son refrain from using the particular road Charles used to walk to school. He never again set eyes on that little street-fighter.

Charles learnt his cricket on Nelson's Field in Merton. His first bat and ball were bought for him by his father at a stall at the Mitcham Fair. Charles was then just three years old. He was so delighted with his bat and ball that he usually took them to bed with him.

Charles got to know and like a young fast bowler, round his own age, named Tom Sherman. Charles and all his mates considered Sherman to have the perfect bowling action.

> When I think of him now, I can safely say his delivery was the most perfect I have ever seen. I tried for years to imitate him but could not get the same action. Had Tom been as good a batsman he would have been a champion. When us boys were on the Mitcham green and saw Tom we were delighted as he was so natural he would stay for a little while bowling to us. As time went on Tom and I became close friends and played in several matches together. Our first match that we were asked to play with men gave us great delight as we were only just about fourteen. We played for Merton against Crayford in Kent on Crayford heath. We started from Merton at 6 o'clock in the morning in a bus (four horses) [and] had breakfast half-way (Black Heath, I think). I recollect the quantity of eggs there were on the breakfast table and the throwing them at each other which afforded us great amusement for this was our first match with men ...[29]

The cricketing chums, Charles and Tom, combined to bowl out Crayford for a paltry 70 in the hot conditions. The pair were greatly pleased with their efforts. Soon after they had settled down during the break between innings, a big, jolly fellow approached them and urged them to have a drink of a brewed concoction of sherry and water that was held in a large pewter mug. As it turned out, the man had put rather more alcohol than water in the mug. A few mugs of the brew and the boys began to feel wonderful.

> Being so thirsty we soon finished the lot, which made us feel that we could soon get the runs required. The captain said, 'you boys go in first and get these runs' which we thought would be an easy job. We started with too much confidence. Tom was to receive the first ball and I was so anxious to start that when the bowler was about to deliver I left the crease. He stopped, turned around and knocked the wicket down. Tom played forward, fell down out of his crease and was stumped. We got into the bus out of the way as we were too giddy to stand up. So we went to sleep, but awoke to a great noise and slapping for us to get up for we had won the match by one wicket. The last man went in with four runs required to win. He was our worst player and not worth a run, however, the ball hit the bat and glanced into a furz bush, not far from the wicket, and could not be found in time. They were afraid to call 'lost ball', so Merton got the required runs.[30]

Merton officials held an impromptu enquiry over the boys' behaviour. Charles and Tom said they had felt giddy after drinking the brew offered by the big man and that they did not know what they were doing. The alleged 'offender' was not to be seen. However, at the dinner that night someone pointed him out, and one of Merton's most passionate players reacted immediately, aiming an apple dumpling in the man's direction.

However, the dumpling missed its target and hit an innocent sitting next to him. The 'innocent' was not quite so innocent for he returned the compliment (and more), hurling a glass bottle at the Merton player. An all-in brawl ensued. All the lights were knocked out in the dining room and some fighters found refuge under the table. Later Charles learned that the big, jolly man had bet heavily on Crayford. He had obviously seen Crayford's biggest threat in the all-round pair of Lawrence and Sherman, so he aimed to nobble the boys. Instead of sherry and water, it was brandy and not much water at all. The boys were drunk.

There was a stage in his young life that Charles became frustrated at not getting enough quality cricket. A man in his father's employ used to travel from Merton to Bow in Essex and one day Charles asked him for a lift to Kensington Common, a known venue for cricket.

> We arrived there at 5 o'clock and I watched the boys playing, but they did not invite me to join them. In any case they could not play very well, so I left and fielded for some men, who were not much better but they were more generous and asked me if I could bowl and gave me the ball to try. This pleased me beyond anything and delighted them for I had no difficulty in knocking their wickets down. They kept me at it until it was too dark to see the ball and I forgot the distance I was from home. When I told them they said, 'mind you don't lose yourself in London'. Advice which did not help at all, because that is exactly what happened. After getting to London Bridge I became lost, for I turned up Cheapside, got into the Strand and Charing Cross and was a long time finding the road to Bow Church. I felt safe when I got to White Chapple. It was midnight when I arrived home. My parents were very angry.[31]

At the age of fifteen Charles was apprenticed as a block cutter and designer to Littler's Print Factory in Merton. He stayed for two years. In the meantime his father was engaged as manager for a printing works in Perth, Scotland. Charles had become disenchanted with his lot. He wanted to play cricket, not become ensconced in the printing trade. So he ran away from Merton and travelled to Perth to join his father. He had a desire to join the navy, but one short, rough trip to Dundee by tramp steamer saw him forget his dreams of a life on the high seas. He was violently sick all the way. Charles promised his mother that he would return to Merton to complete his printer's apprenticeship after a few months in Perth, where he enjoyed three months' cricket with the Perth club. The regular cricket helped him improve all aspects of his game. Cricket was played on a stretch of land known as the Domain. There he came across some red-coated figures, whom he took for golfers on their way home. They seemed to be calling out to him and their yells became more urgent, when his eagle eye caught sight of a golf ball in flight. He bounded towards it and judged the catch perfectly. He then threw it back towards the approaching figures. The red-coats roared.

Cattle roamed the Domain and the wickets were not free of tufts of grass. Charles joined other players to help prepare wickets for practice and matches. The scythe was banned, as it was in other parts. The players cut clumps of grass with their knives and used any flat instrument to try and achieve a reasonable playing surface. The home ground advantage worked. Perth won in Perth but invariably lost in Edinburgh. Edinburgh won in Edinburgh but lost away.

Charles quickly met new friends. He was both skilled at cricket and popular with his fellows. He regarded his rapid improvement as being due to his being able to imitate the players he revered: Thomas Box for wicket-keeping, Alfred Mynn for bowling and, of course, Fuller Pilch for batting. 'With these models in my mind's eye, I was bound to improve.'[32]

Those three months flew. When Charles told the club that he must leave and return home to Merton to complete his apprenticeship, the club would not hear of it. They offered Charles a substantial sum of money to stay on in Perth as a professional. Charles reckoned that the amount was far in excess of what he could earn as an apprentice printer, but his father would not allow him to accept the offer. Running away was an option, but Charles hoped that things could be worked out. His mother saw the passion for cricket in his eye and she influenced his father to have a change of heart. Charles played out the season on the proviso that he return to Merton to finish his printer's apprenticeship in the winter of 1843–44. His father wrote to Charles' employer and his return to work was duly sanctioned. Before he left Perth, the Scottish club feted Charles in the hope that the youngster would return to play in the summer of 1844. That second summer in Perth gave Charles the inspiration and the grounding to make cricket his profession, for 'either sleeping or waking, cricket was uppermost in my mind'.[33]

Charles became established in Perth. He was appointed clerk on the Scottish Central Railway and he was the Perth club's key all-rounder. He lived with the stationmaster at Greenhill Junction, Mr Thomas Ash and his wife. They had no children and took Charles under their wing and looked after him as if he were their son. Mr and Mrs Ash were friendly with Mr Douglas McLeod, a stationmaster down the line. McLeod, who was then aged about 50, got to know Charles and during their frequent chats he told Charles of his early prowess as a cricketer. Charles was completely taken in by McLeod and he recommended McLeod to play for Scotland against William Clarke's celebrated All England Eleven in Edinburgh.

Charles decided to see first hand just how talented was the man he had so warmly recommended to the Scotland cricket selectors. He and McLeod turned up at the Edinburgh cricket ground, late on the afternoon of 6 May 1849 — the eve of the big match.

> He was rigged up in a new suit of flannels and white shoes. He put on the leg guards and gloves and I bowled to find my friend could scarcely bat. I did all I could in the short time before other players came on to the ground, got him to stand in position which straightened him up a bit, so he had a little look of a hitter.[34]

McLeod's batting practice did not help. He was bowled first ball in each innings. His fielding was probably worse than his batting. Twice he fell in trying to pick up the ball which sat in a stationary position on the turf. Charles was chafed to bits by his fellows who could not resist the urge to remind him that he recommended McLeod. In later years Charles also picked the likes of Sundown for the 1868 tour. Sundown's solitary run of that tour was apparently the only run he scored in his life.

England won the match, but the outcome and every other individual feat paled into insignificance in the light of Charles Lawrence taking all ten All England XI wickets in their second innings. He took 3/59 in the first innings, then bowled unchanged in the second dig to take 10/53. It was possibly the first international ten-wicket haul. Jim Laker took 9/37, then 10/53 against Australia at Old Trafford in 1956 to emulate Lawrence's feat. For the first time since he walked to Lord's as an eleven-year-old Charles was again in the company of all his heroes. All, that is, except Fuller Pilch, who by then was the proprietor of the Saracen's Head, a popular pub in Kent.

At this time some of the most famous names in cricket history were playing for All England: William Clarke, the great and canny all-rounder, led the likes of Johnny Wisden, George Parr, Thomas Box, Nicholas Felix and Alfred Mynn. Sir Thomas Moncreif was the Scotland captain. Moncreif was an honest, tough cricketer, if not a brilliant one. His great gift as a leader was his ability to judge when a man was about to perform or that he was nearly spent. He noted that Charles had bowled fast and straight in the England first innings. He picked up Clarke for a duck, courtesy of a great catch by Fairlie and clean-bowled top-notchers Wisden (14) and Gunn (2). England was dismissed for 165 and the Twenty-Two of Scotland replied with just 84. Lawrence contributed 3. Clarke's men batted again and were dismissed for 132. Sir Thomas Moncreif had watched Lawrence keenly and he suggested that Charles go off his long run. He had two approaches for his fast medium bowling: a shortish run and a long, bounding run. George Parr and Johnny Wisden were well set, although it was Parr who did the bulk of the scoring. In fact, Wisden fell almost immediately for 1, then Box (13), then Parr (43), again clean-bowled by Lawrence. His bowling was fast and accurate.

Testimony to his accuracy was his hitting the stumps of five of his England victims — Parr, Felix, Guy, Mynn and Chatterton. He bowled Nicholas Felix with a magnificent delivery which fairly shot along the turf like a scurrying rat, taking all three stumps clean out of the ground. The crowd roared and Felix stood gaping. He had reached 18 and was hitting the ball with growing confidence before that Lawrence beauty.

'The ball would have bowled me out in my wicket, anywhere,' said Felix walking down the wicket. He stopped to speak to Charles, reached into his fob pocket and produced a half-crown. 'Take this in remembrance of me ...'[35]

Charles bowled 216 balls, with 24 maidens, in taking the 10/53. This performance brought the sort of instant fame all performers crave, for now both his Scottish peers and such celebrated opponents as William Clarke's All England XI hailed his skill. His performance that day of 7 May 1849 would soon pay handsome dividends.

Charles dismissed Wisden in both innings. John Wisden was to take all ten wickets in an innings twice, the first time for North versus South at Lord's in 1850 when he clean-bowled the entire ten. Wisden toured North America with George Parr's England team in 1859 and in 1864 he published *Wisden Cricketers' Almanack* for the first time.

The All England XI was a wandering band of professional cricketers. Richard Daft, the Nottinghamshire batsman and cricket scribe, loved to write of the 'Eleven'.

What fun we have had in these matches to be sure! We would arrive early, breakfast on bread, cheese and bottled ale. Tom Foster would leave his umpire's post and come into the pavilion for more at the fall of each wicket ...[36]

Led by that sardonic old warrior William Clarke, who was the side's first captain, secretary and manager, the All England XI travelled the length and breadth of England. They spread their fame and the cricket message. They inspired the young cricketers and tickled the fancies of the old, whose memories went back long before the Victorian Age. W. G. Grace was only six years old when his elder brother, E. M. Grace, played against this wandering Eleven. It was W. G.'s first glimpse of famous cricketers. Perhaps the stern and commanding presence of 'Old' Clarke, who was then aged 56, yet at the peak of his bowling prowess, inspired young W. G.

William Clarke was the driving force for professional cricket. He did not play his first match at Lord's until 1837 at the age of 39, but he made up for it. At 48 the MCC offered Clarke a job as practice bowler at Lord's. During the next seven years, Clarke took 2385 wickets, his lowest season's haul in that seven-year 'pitch' being 222. In his last year, 1855, he took an incredible 476 wickets. The All England XI played mainly against local eighteens and twenty-twos, which probably had a high percentage of batsmen of the ability of Scotland's Douglas McLeod, although the opposition were not all 'rabbits'. His extraordinary wicket hauls were perhaps more likely to be because he hated taking himself out of the attack.

Clarke apparently just ambled to the crease, then he would

... swing his arm back in a peculiar way, till it was almost level with his armpit, thus shooting the ball out from the highest point at which it could decently retain the name of underhand. When it landed from this horrid height, it was apt to sit up like a dog begging. Delivered with bewildering changes in flight and a deadly spin, it is perhaps no wonder that this ball, with its myriad of variations, took 2385 wickets.[37]

The team collected appearance money and a lion's share of the gate, but Clarke kept most of the loot for himself. He paid his professionals anything from four pounds to six pounds a week. On the surface it seemed fair pay, but Clarke himself made a packet. (In

1873 W. G. Grace was paid 1500 pounds to tour Australia, while the professionals in W. G.'s side got about 250 pounds for their efforts.)

Clarke had a wicked sense of humor. 'I'll bowl from this end', he would tell his fast bowler Joseph Guy. 'You can have any end you like.' Once a young player's mother approached Clarke at the Trent Bridge ground, extolling the virtues of her son's bowling and how he was physically a good specimen. 'Why, Tom's six feet in his stockings,' she said. Clarke gave the woman a long stare with his one good eye (he lost the sight in the other, his right eye, when it was struck during a game of Fives in 1828) and said, 'What a lot of toenails to cut!'[38]

Born on 24 December 1798, William Clarke was the son of a bricklayer living on Bunker's Hill. William followed his father into the trade and became a bricklayer, but by 1816 his bowling had developed to the point where he had become a regular in the Nottingham team. By 1831 Clarke was landlord of the 'Bell Inn' in the Market Place. But Clarke had his eye on the Trent Bridge Inn, for the grounds about the Inn were perfect for a cricket field. A woman named Chapman was landlady of the Inn. Clarke's first marriage was dissolved and he married the Trent Bridge Inn landlady. Cricket historians do not record whether the union was a marriage of true love or was one of crass opportunism. Clarke immediately set about laying out the Trent Bridge ground. He opened the ground in 1838, upsetting the locals by charging admittance. The Nottingham people were used to watching cricket at Forrest for nothing. Clarke's popularity was not enhanced in those early cricket days at Trent Bridge. He led Nottingham from 1835 until 1855. George Parr used to say of Clarke that he played 'not by sight, but by sound'.

'Old' Clarke was a craggy, mean bastard, who played the game both fair and foul, but he did cricket its biggest favour by driving the All England XI. His wandering cricket team was the forerunner to county cricket. An unofficial championship between the counties began around 1860, but the English County Championship was not established until 1873.

William Clarke died at Priory Lodge, Wandsworth Road, London, on 25 August 1856, aged 57. At 52 he had fallen and broken his right arm, but he bounced back and played right up to shortly before his death. He took a wicket with the last ball he ever bowled, for the All England XI versus Twenty-Two of Whitehaven in June 1856.

'Old' Clarke had a huge impact on cricket generally and on the future of Charles Lawrence, for it was Clarke, so taken with Charles' ten-wicket innings haul against his All England XI at Edinburgh, who went in to bat for Lawrence.

Charles Lawrence married in Scotland, but we are not certain of the year, probably around 1849. He continued to work with the Scottish railways but reckoned that with the combination of his own savings and his wife's money he might venture into the world of business. The Lawrences opened a cricket depot and tobacconist shop in Edinburgh, but the business was not a success.

Lawrence even toyed with the idea of gaining a place in the famous wandering eleven. However, he instinctively knew he needed to play in a tougher competition. The Lawrences decided to move back to England. Charles was nearly 22. The year was 1850. Cricket was in transition. It was already four years since the last great single-wicket match between the 'odd couple', Alfred Mynn and Nicholas Felix.

In 1852 Johnny Wisden became secretary of a breakaway wandering eleven, the United All-England XI, rivalling William Clarke's band. While there was fierce rivalry between the two elevens, neither was about to fold, for there was more than enough interest to cater for two professional bands of cricketers. However, good relations were impossible to maintain while Clarke was about. After his death old animosities softened and the enormous gulf between the two bands was bridged. They met at Lord's for the first time on 1 June 1857 before a crowd of 10,000: the biggest attendance ever recorded up to that time. Their clashes became the big match of the summer and remained so until W. G. Grace began his dominance in the Gentlemen versus Players fixture.

A chance meeting between Charles and 'Old' Clarke at a London theatre in early 1851 probably changed Charles' life forever. The old warrior instantly recognised Charles as that slip of a boy who had bowled his team out in Scotland. Opportunity knocked.

Clarke said he had been asked to recommend a tutor for the Phoenix club, Dublin or the Earl of Leicester's club, Norfolk. He said, 'think of it and let me know in a day or two.' At that stage we had no children. We thought it over and decided upon the Phoenix Club in Dublin.[39]

Charles Lawrence began his professional engagement at Phoenix in May 1851. For the first couple of years there were few matches of importance. The Military played a game against the Civilians of Ireland, and Charles arranged a few games against the Gentlemen of England, but he believed the big turning point for Irish cricket came in the wake of the Earl of Carlisle's appointment as Lord Lieutenant of Ireland. Carlisle called on Lawrence to build a cricket ground at Carlisle's vice-regal lodge. With the backing of nobility, Lawrence soon established his own Irish equivalent of the English wandering elevens. He formed the United All Ireland XI. They played their first match against Twenty-Two of Ireland. Lawrence was afforded a benefit match. His first task was to ensure that the ground was 'enclosed' to enable him to charge admittance to the ground.

Lawrence surrounded the ground with canvas sheeting. He wrote to his contacts in Scotland and England, and found that with money and the support of the landed gentry virtually any entrepreneurial endeavour could be achieved in Britain. However, the weather turned foul. The military band couldn't play, the canvas was blown away and the match was a financial disaster. Lawrence was again lucky, for Carlisle took pity on him and allowed him another match to make good the finance. In 1854 Lawrence arranged for a side from Liverpool to play a combined team of the Military and Civilians of Ireland.

Tom Wills played for Liverpool. In fact he took ten wickets. Wills and Lawrence would not have dreamed of the extraordinary part they would both play in the historic 1868 Australian tour of England

In 1858 Lawrence took his All Ireland XI to Lord's. There he again showed his amazing ability with the ball, taking eight wickets against a team of English gentlemen (no professionals were allowed to play in the MCC team). The match was played in 'thick mud'.

Lawrence's spirit of adventure had been fired when George Parr took an England team to North America in 1859. Parr's men were each paid 50 pounds for the tour. The team left Liverpool on 7 September. Parr led a team of twelve, including John Wisden, and they were to play a total of eight matches. The players experienced great anxiety during rough weather on the voyage across the Atlantic. Parr was among the worst of the travellers. Another of the players was the dapper little Julius Caesar, who would umpire in England in 1868. He hailed not from Rome but Godalming in Surrey. Caesar was a mild mannered little man, but he could become argumentative if a scorer failed to write out his first name, 'Julius', in full. Caesar was a good boxer, and was generally able to maintain admirable self-control. After taking some good-natured taunts about England and Englishmen from the Americans, Julius found himself drinking port with a local in a New York saloon. Their conversation began well enough, but the port gradually began to take its toll and eventually Caesar announced to all and sundry that he intended to punch the man's nose, whereupon the American produced a six-shooter and pressed it to Caesar's nose. Caesar retreated.

Historians are at odds as to just how the 1861–62 England tour of Australia came about. Felix Spiers, who kept the Royal Hotel and Café de Paris in Bourke Street, Melbourne, and Christopher Pond, the host of the Piazza Hotel on the corner of Bourke and Kings Streets, decided to form an entrepreneurial duo. They offered the novelist Charles Dickens 10,000 pounds to undertake a reading tour of Australia. However, it is not certain whether the offer was made before or after the highly successful 1861–62 England tour of Australia.

Dickens found his reading tours of North America financially rewarding but exhausting. An Australian tour was a real possibility given that his American source of income had been severed due to the American Civil War. Dickens pondered the offer for some time. He envisaged a new book with the working title *An Uncommercial Traveller Upside Down*. He had just finished polishing *Great Expectations*, and he was turning *Our Mutual Friend* over in his mind at the time he decided to reject the lucrative Spiers and Pond offer. On 5 October 1862 Dickens wrote an explanation:

If it was for the hope of a gain that would make me more independent of the worst, I could not look the travel and absence and exertion in the face. I know perfectly well before-hand how unspeakably wretched I should be. I can force myself to go aboard a ship, and I can force myself to do that trading desk what I have done a hundred times; but whether, with all this unsettled fluctuating distress on my mind, I could force an original book out of it, is another question.[40]

I am inclined to believe that the Spiers and Pond offer came after the England tour, not before, so the offer was made to Dickens in London in June 1862, not a year earlier. Spiers and Pond could have made such an offer to Dickens in the wake of a large financial gain. As Lawrence later confirms, Spiers and Pond made a far greater amount of money from the 1861–62 tour than they let on at the time.

Charles Dickens and the start of international cricket between England and Australia are inextricably entwined, for cricket has been the common denominator. Whether Dickens was offered the chance to come to Australia before or after the English cricketers toured in 1861–62 is a relevant historical point. Big cricket Down Under either got its start because Dickens refused a 10,000 pound reading tour of Australia or Dickens' huge offer came in the wake of Spiers and Pond making so much money they could take an entrepreneurial punt on the great novelist. The game of cricket was the catalyst.

To entice the cream of English cricket, Spiers and Pond needed a messenger, someone who could be trusted to sail to England as their international agent to sign up prospective England players. William Mallam was the chosen agent. Spiers and Pond put up an advance of 7000 pounds. They wanted to ensure that the tour was successful, so it was vital for them to secure the best cricketers in England.

In Ireland Lord Carlisle was replaced for a time by Lord Eglington as Lord Lieutenant of Ireland and he assured Charles that he would encourage cricket in the land with a like passion to his predecessor. In 1861 he asked Charles to bowl a few down to him as he wanted to rediscover the batting form of his youth. Charles knew that the state of the wicket could prove dangerous and he asked the Earl to put on pads and gloves. However, the nobleman would have none of it, saying he did not have time. Within an over, Lord Eglington was nursing a broken left index finger and Charles was lamenting not having insisted he wore batting gloves. Two days later, Charles was called to Lord's to play in a match. Lord Carlisle saw him and set about questioning him as to how Lord Eglington's finger came to be broken.

Events moved rapidly from that match. Lord Carlisle was again appointed Lord Lieutenant of Ireland and within days Charles played in a match with the Prince of Wales and received an offer from an important visitor from Australia. It was William Mallam, offering Charles a spot on the England team to tour Down Under. His old Surrey captain, H. H. (Heathfied Harman) Stephenson was to lead the England team. Charles was offered 150 pounds for the tour, plus all expenses and first-class travel.

Stephenson's team left Liverpool on 20 October 1861 on the *Great Britain*. Lawrence wrote in his journal: 'The passage out was very pleasant any amount of games and a good feeling which made the time pass quickly, although Tom Sewell and Thomas Hearne were sea sick for most of the voyage.'[41]

The team arrived in Australia to an extraordinary welcome. There was a myriad ships in the harbour of all shapes and sizes, decorated in the England colors. Stephenson's men were given a right royal greeting. Messrs Spiers and Pond must have been rubbing their hands with glee. The Melbourne streets were crowded with well-wishers as Stephenson's coach, led by eight handsome horses, rolled into the central business district. Some ten thousand people gathered in and around the Café de Paris in Bourke Street, where the England team got off the coach.

Stephenson's men were feted everywhere they went in Victoria. They banqueted for a month and then came the first match, against Twenty-Two of Victoria at the MCG. It was New Year's Day, 1862 and some 15,000 people turned up to watch the game. The Yorkshire batsman Roger Iddison was not complimentary about the Victorian players, but he was mightily impressed with the Australians' ability to consume alcohol. Lawrence did not get a lot of runs, but he bowled well, taking 0/32 against Eighteen of Victoria, 11/38 against Twenty-Two of Owens, 9/36 against Twenty-Two of New South Wales and Victoria, 2/12 against Twenty-Two of Ballarat, 4/12 against Twenty-Two of Bendigo, 7/22 against Twenty-Two of Castlemaine and 0/11 and 1/13 against Twenty-Two of Victoria.

The tour was a great success, not so much for the brilliance of the cricket but for the interest of the people. Spiers and Pond cleared £11,000, a veritable fortune, which enabled them to return to England and buy a restaurant in London's West End. (The entrepreneurs may have taken an even greater slice of the cake. According to Lawrence, when he was in London in 1868 the pair confessed that the profit from the tour was actually £19,000.)[42] And, contrary to the initial offer, each of Stephenson's men returned to England with £250 in their pocket.

On top of his tour allowance, Lawrence was offered a further £300 a year to stay in Australia and coach cricketers at the Albert Club in Sydney. He accepted and became the first professional cricket coach in Australia.

Lawrence had urged H. H. Stephenson and all of his players to stay in Australia, for he believed that there was a great deal of money to be made in the colonies. But neither Stephenson nor any of his men agreed with Lawrence. They sailed home to Blighty and left Lawrence in Australia dreaming of riches.

> I thought I should soon make a fortune for I had an idea on a presentment after I had seen the Blacks throw the boomerang and spears. If I could teach them to play cricket and take them to England with success … this impression never left my mind until I had succeeded in forming an Aboriginal team …[43]

Lawrence's diary entry is not dated, so we do not know exactly when he got the idea of taking a team of Aboriginal cricketers to England. But we do know that he wanted to shove Wills aside from the time a tour of England was mooted. The George Parr-led England XI touring Australia in 1863–64 was a further boost to international cricket and helped inspire Lawrence to make a tour 'home'.

Parr was a great character. He took over from William Clarke as the driving force in Nottingham cricket. An old elm tree at Trent Bridge came to be known as 'Parr's tree' for he had the up-and-under stroke which he used to dispatch many a ball into its branches. Parr also had a rather strange habit of carrying a hatbox (contents unknown) with him wherever he travelled. His peers heard rattles from within, so they concluded that the hatbox did not contain a hat, but what it did contain they could not tell. A nervous traveller, Parr was holding his precious hatbox on 7 April 1864, when the steamer *Wonga Wonga* in which the England team was sailing collided with a sailing ship, the *Viceroy*, when just clear of the Sydney heads en-route to Melbourne. The undamaged *Wonga Wonga* lowered a life-boat and all the sailors from the *Viceroy* were rescued. William Caffyn, who toured with Lawrence in the first England Eleven to tour Australia, was another who was not enamoured of the high seas. He vowed after the voyage to North America, in which the players were knocked about in huge seas, that he would never venture overseas again. Yet Caffyn did tour Australia a second time and, as did Lawrence in 1862, he stayed Down Under to take up a coaching appointment in Melbourne.

A neat, dapper little man with billowing side-whiskers, Caffyn was known variously as 'Terrible Billy' or 'The Surrey Pet'. The Melbourne Cricket Club engaged Caffyn as 'a coach and general instructor of members'.[44] He was paid 300 pounds a year. He spent a year in Melbourne, then moved to Sydney, where, with his wife, he began what was to become a successful hairdressing business. In 1864 the MCC at Lord's made over-arm bowling legal. Caffyn deplored the new style of bowling. He reckoned that over-arm bowlers would not achieve the brilliant length or change of flight of the old round-arm style. He claimed that the 'shooter' might disappear from the game. However, the shooters so often seen on the furrow and ridge pitches at Lord's might well have occurred through the state of the pitch rather than the height of the arm of the bowler. Impressed with the progress Australian cricket had made between 1861 and 1863, Caffyn later wrote:

> They were delightful pupils to teach, even as far back as the 'sixties' — always willing to be shown a new stroke and quick to do their best to retrieve an error, never taking an offence at having their faults pointed out and never jealous of one another. When I remember all this it is not so much a matter of surprise to me to see what Australian cricket has become today as perhaps may be the case with other people.[45]

The England tours of 1861–62 and 1863–64 inspired Australians to play cricket. The game captured the imagination of the public and no doubt helped many people identify with the Mother Country so far beyond the seas. Teams started to bob up throughout the land. Pastoralists, particularly those in Victoria, were beginning to take great interest in cricket. Many farm workers were lost to the big land-holders through the gold rush of the 1850s. Labour was in short supply, which might explain why Aboriginal workers were so well treated on land holdings in Victoria at that time.

Many Aboriginal workers of the Western Districts of Victoria were playing cricket on pastoral holdings from that pivotal year, 1864. Men such as Lawrence, Wills and Parr had made their mark. Some of the pastoralists saw cricket as a genuine unifying force, something tangible in what was really an early attempt at reconciliation. A revealing article appeared in the *Hamilton Spectator* of August, 1866. It is reproduced here in part:

> Those of our cricketing friends who are interested in the development of 'muscular Christianity' will be glad to find that the long-contemplated match between the Aboriginal Eleven and one of the Melbourne clubs, is likely to eventuate in a real contest. A professional from Melbourne will shortly proceed to coach the Lake Wallace, and other Blacks in the higher mysteries of cricket ...[46]

The cricketing prowess of the Aboriginal team had captured the imagination of the Victorian public. The side was due to play more matches in Victoria, but arrangements had to be changed swiftly when Lawrence read a notice in the newspapers indicating that the Central Board for the Protection of Aborigines was lobbying the Victorian Government to stop the tour. Lawrence feared their venture would have to be abandoned. In consultation with Smith, Graham and Hayman, Lawrence planned for his men to leave Victoria without anyone knowing.

Lawrence did not wish to alarm his men, so he told them they were taking a few days off to go fishing at Queenscliff. The players were taken from Geelong by four-in-hand driven by George Whar-low. Indeed they did fish for a day or two, then they boarded the good ship *Rangatira*, a regular passenger vessel between Melbourne and Sydney. The *Rangatira* lingered long enough off Port Phillip heads to pick up Lawrence and his precious cargo, the long boats shuttling them from Queenscliff. The speculative foursome — Lawrence, Hayman, Smith and Graham — had effectively outsmarted the Board.

Team morale was high upon reaching Sydney. The Aboriginal team won the return match against Illawarra at Wollongong and won at Singleton and Newcastle before a loss at Bathurst. Then came the last work-out before they sailed for England, against the Army and Navy at Redfern. On 4–5 February 1868 the Duke of Edinburgh, denied seeing the Aboriginal players in Melbourne, twice drove his four greys to the Albert Ground in Sydney to watch Lawrence's men. He was intrigued by their cricket and by their tribal skills. The Aboriginal team scored 237, with Cuzens blasting 86, and Mullagh and Bullocky 39. The match ended in a draw, but the players showed clear signs that they would match it with many an English eleven. Mullagh cleared five feet seven inches in the high jump, his effort a highlight of the sports that delighted the crowd of some 4000 fans. Team-mates Charley Dumas and Jimmy Mosquito would better that mark in England later that year, jumping to within one inch of the world high-jump record, set co-jointly on 23 March 1866 at Beaufort House, London, by T. G. Little and J. H. T. Roupell, both of Cambridge University, with a clearance of 5 feet 9 inches.[47]

Soon after the Aboriginal team sailed for England, the Duke of Edinburgh was lucky to survive an assassin's bullet in Sydney, but survive he did, and he caught up with Lawrence's men on the green cricket fields of England.

There was some confusion as to just who among the Aboriginal players actually sailed on the *Parramatta* on 8 February 1868. Tarpot didn't sail. He became ill and left the ship just before it departed. This was a great pity, for Tarpot was a terrific draw-card. He had already demonstrated his great athleticism, being able to run 100 yards backwards in 14 seconds, a feat that might even have been beyond the likes of Jesse Owens or Carl Lewis. Harry Rose had left the party at Geelong. Charley Dumas and Twopenny were not from the Wimmera. They were believed to be Lawrence recruits from New South Wales. William Hayman was not with the party. He had sailed for England six weeks previously to confirm fixtures. Lawrence's players comprised Dick-a-Dick, Peter, Mullagh, Cuzens, Sundown,

King Cole, Tiger, Red Cap, Bullocky, Mosquito, Jim Crow, Twopenny and Charley Dumas.

Most of the Aborigines had been born on stations and had links to pastoral holdings. They were full-blood Aborigines, brought up in the tribal ways. They could hunt with boomerang and spear and survive in the bush. They were proud tribal men who had plunged headlong into the dangerous waters of the white man's world. This was no dugout canoe on Lake Wallace. The *Parramatta* was a fully-rigged sailing ship of 1521 tons. It was a sturdy craft with an able skipper of vast experience at the helm, Captain John Williams.

The Australian Cricket Team was on its way.

CHAPTER FOUR

THE afternoon of Friday, 7 February 1868, was wet and windy and Lawrence and his men were glad to be on board, under cover, settling their baggage and meeting with friends and relatives. Tarpot had been coughing non-stop and Lawrence envisaged disaster a few days out to sea if Tarpot had been allowed to sail. There had been no chance to get a replacement player. There were none available in the Sydney area and there was no time to call one up from Victoria. They would have had to make do with thirteen players.

The players packed all their cricket gear in their quarters, which was a large, separate cabin between the first and second class areas. Dick-a-Dick carefully placed his parrying shield and leangle under his bunk and Charley Dumas's collection of 15 boomerangs, which varied greatly in size and weight, were neatly wrapped in calico pillow slips and stored under a bunk. Dumas was the expert boomerang thrower and his displays were to enthrall the English spectators. Costume and spears and shields were all safely put away for the long voyage.

Lawrence kept the players busy and in any idle moments he gathered them around and spoke passionately about the the joys of sailing the high seas and how Jesus Christ, through the gifted hands of Captain Williams, would ensure that they all arrived safely in England. Lawrence expected the men to be apprehensive, and they were afraid. But he also sensed within their ranks a refreshing air of expectancy, something he noted with these men when they were loading their guns before a foray into the bush to shoot game.

Among the passengers was the much-travelled Reverend Henry Nisbett (1818–1876) who had a penchant for writing about his travels. Born in Glasgow, he served as a missionary for the London Missionary Society in Samoa in 1841. His journal of the 1868 Sydney to London trip contains daily entries from 8 February 1868 until the *Parramatta* berthed at Gravesend on 13 May. It features mainly weather reports and compass readings, plus his particular sermon for that day, and the 'inevitable' headache, which seemed to visit him almost as frequently as he put pen to paper.

> Saty, 8th Feby. — After daylight preparations made for leaving — Towed out of harbour by two steam tugs — and certainly our good ship *Parramatta* looks and is a magnificent vessel — By breakfast time we were out at sea — Had a fine run for some hours — but towards evening a 'Southerly Buster' came on … as the wind continued high with a heavy sea, we lay to all night under close reefed top sails …[1]

The *Parramatta* heaved under the heavy swell and fear spread throughout the players' ranks. Lawrence arranged for Captain John Williams to talk to the men. Captain Williams invited the Aboriginal players into his cabin that first stormy night at sea. When they heard the captain pray, Cuzens quizzed Lawrence.

> 'Does he know Jesus Christ and the little piccaninny you used to tell us about … the one we saw in the picture and Dick-a-Dick said, "they kill him".'
> I told them that Jesus was in heaven now and that the captain prayed to him … that we should all arrive safely in England. Nothing seemed to bother them for they thought the captain was so good that the ship would never sink …[2]

On the second night the wind howled, the seas rolled and the thunder roared. All but Reverend Nisbett fairly shook with fear. The Reverend slept through the entire storm, but he learnt next day of the vivid brilliance of the lightning and the continual crack of thunder. Before the storm that Sunday, Captain Williams read the litany in the first of Reverend Nisbett's Sabbath services. Nisbett held daily readings and never failed to hold his Sunday specials. In three months, however, Reverend Nisbett made no mention of the Aboriginal cricketers on board, although he saw fit to record that some of the passengers or crew dressed up as negro singers to entertain the ship's company.

On Monday had a racket in the saloon by part of the company

performing dusky minstrels — with blackened faces and hands — The place filled with passengers and crew too I suppose, as spectators, who increased the noise very considerably ...[3]

According to Lawrence the Aboriginal players were extraordinarily popular on board. Initially he gave the players notebooks, with ruled lines, for he had hoped to teach them to read and write during the voyage, but they soon tired of such lessons and began to draw trees and birds, lizards and snakes. They drew the animals of the time and also animals from the Dreamtime. The players' bodies were at sea, but their hearts were back in their tribal homelands.

Lawrence gave them drafts and playing cards, which they enjoyed. He also arranged for the ship's carpenter to provide the players with bits of wood, from which they created a variety of wooden implements for the women passengers and toys for the children. One of the women gave Dick-a-Dick a tatting shuttle and asked him if he could make her a replica. Dick-a-Dick succeeded and soon the women had the Aboriginal players busier than ever. Their popularity soared. It is astounding that with the sometimes feverish activity involving the women and children and the Aboriginal men on deck the Reverend Nisbett did not acknowledge the players' presence in his journal. Perhaps it was a sign of the times that it would not have been acceptable to acknowledge the 'dusky heathens' in the written form. The Reverend demonstrated his ability to sleep through a violent electrical storm and it seems he was also quite adept at turning a blind eye to reality, if it meant keeping the numbers in his congregation.

Charles Lawrence had more pressing considerations and ones of an earthly nature. He was the father-figure and mentor to thirteen Aboriginal people, embarking on an adventure as bizarre and as potentially frightening as a bunch of amateur geologists today would experience winging their way towards a working tour of the moon.

The men had been given sobriquets, because their pastoral landlords apparently could not pronounce their tribal names. That was the popular theory, although there is a condescending tone in some of the nicknames. The Aboriginal players on the *Parramatta* were:

Dick-a-Dick	(Jungunjinanuke)
Peter	(Arrahmunijarrimun)
Johnny Mullagh	(Unaarrimin)
Johnny Cuzens	(Zellanach)
Sundown	(Ballrinjarrimin)
King Cole	(Brippokei)
Tiger	(Bonmbarngeet)
Redcap	(Brimbunyah)
Bullocky	(Bullchanach)
Jimmy Mosquito	(Grougarrong)
Jim Crow	(Jallachmurrimin)
Twopenny	(Murrumgunarriman)
Charley Dumas	(Pripumuarraman)

Dick-a-Dick (Jungunjinanuke) was one of the great characters among the Aboriginal cricketers. He was the great dodger, whose hand–eye coordination was exceptional and perhaps better even than the greatest batting marvel of them all, Don Bradman. He would challenge a person to stand about 10 paces away and hurl a cricket ball at him. He defended himself with a parrying shield, which he held in his left hand, and a leangle or killer boomerang, held in the right hand. Deliveries thrown at a height above waist level were fended off with the parrying shield. Low-flying missiles were deflected with the L-shaped boomerang. His cricket paled into insignificance in comparison with his dodging and tracking skills. He batted in the middle to lower order and he bowled a bit of medium pace, but his dodging of cricket balls was the thing he is remembered for on the 1868 tour. Few people knew of Dick-a-Dick's efforts in saving the Duff children four years earlier, and he may never have never been given any recognition for that effort had he not won fame through the 1868 tour.

Peter (Arrahmunijarrimun) was a specialist batsman but he didn't excel with either bat or ball. He hailed from the William Hayman property and was one of the foundation members of the Edenhope Cricket Club. Peter was said to have been an expert with the stockwhip.

Johnny Mullagh (Unaarrimin) was the star all-rounder of the squad. He could bowl straight and fast and was a brilliant fieldsman, but it was his batting which so impressed good judges. Lawrence believed that Mullagh could have played years of county cricket and was a potential regular State player for Victoria. Only injury prevented him from playing for Victoria before the 1868 tour. He was to make a big impact in England. Mullagh had come under the early tutorship of Tom Hamilton, who taught the Aborigines cricket at Bringalbert Station. Through cricket, Mullagh had come under European influence to such an extent that, although he was proud of his heritage and he did not see himself as a 'white' man trapped in a black man's skin, he yearned for acceptance within the dominant white community. Long after the 1868 tour, Mullagh confided in Hamilton, a man he trusted implicitly: 'a white woman won't have me, Mr Tom, and I will never have a black one.'[4]

Johnny Cuzens (Zellanach) was a brilliant all-rounder. He bowled with a high arm and was the quickest of the Australian bowlers. He was the Jeff Thomson of his time, for he bowled with explosive and unpredictable pace and he could hit like a thrashing machine. He could also run like the wind, running bare-footed. He was your classic sprinter, the sort we see today in the Olympic Games. He proved one of the finds of the tour.

Sundown (Ballrinjarrimin) was a specialist batsman, but he was always a bit out of luck with the bat. He is said to have scored only one run in his batting life and that was on the 1868 tour. He is thought to be the inspiration for the legendary character who 'scored only one run in the first innings, but was not quite so successful in the second'.

King Cole (Brippokei) bowled some lively medium pace and batted in the lower order. He fielded at point and had a good throwing arm. King Cole may well have been the 'C. Rose' named in scorecards in the mid-1860s. King Cole played only a few games on the tour before tragedy struck. He contracted the dreaded pneumonia and he died in London on 24 June 1868.

Tiger (Bonmbarngeet) was an all-rounder and good fieldsman. He had amazing stamina and didn't mind a drop of ale.

Redcap (Brimbunyah) was a middle order batsman and medium pace bowler. He held the bat low, the 'choke' grip, and was more adept at the horizontal bat shots such as the cut and the pull than the drive.

There was none of what the moderns might call 'soft hands' with Redcap. When he snicked one it flew hard and fast straight to first slip. Redcap was one of the trackers who saved the Duff children.

Bullocky (Bullchanach) was a hard-hitting opening batsman and the side's number one wicket-keeper. A big man, Bullocky played for Victoria against a Tasmanian sixteen in 1867. He batted number four, but failed, scoring just four runs. He proved a solid and consistent performer on the 1868 tour.

Jimmy Mosquito (Grougarrong) was another of the side's specialist batsmen, but his talents appeared much better suited to wielding the stockwhip. Mosquito carried an 18-foot rawhide stockwhip, with which he could perform the most amazing feats. Mosquito and his stockwhip became one of the many talking points about the Aboriginal cricketers in England. He was said to have been a brother of Johnny Cuzens.

Jim Crow (Jallachmurrimin), like Sundown, was a disappointment in purely cricketing terms. And like Sundown he probably just made up the numbers on tour. Both men were destined to return to Australia early due to illness.

Twopenny (Murrumgunarriman) is generally regarded as the first Aboriginal first-class cricketer. His bowling action was regarded as 'doubtful'. By the time he first came under the eye of Charles Lawrence in Sydney cricket in 1867, over-arm bowing had been in vogue for only three years. Twopenny was one of the few players on the 1868 tour not to come from the Wimmera in Victoria. He was said to have been born in Bathurst in 1845. Because of his apparent doubtful action Twopenny didn't bowl a great deal on the 1868 tour, but when he did he made a big impact.

Charley Dumas (Pripumuarraman) was another of the side possessing dubious ability with both bat and ball, but he was an absolute magician when it came to throwing the boomerang. Charley had such control over this aeronautical marvel that he could hurl the instrument some 150 yards, have it smack the ground hard then soar upwards towards the heavens, do a wide sweep of the ground, swooping to create a thousand ducking heads and then return to within an arm's reach of its owner, where it would hover, then fall between his bare feet. As with Twopenny, Charley Dumas came from New South Wales.

There were those who believed that Twopenny was a chucker. Some thought similarly of Tom Wills' bowling and there were some who reckoned that Twopenny was recruited by Lawrence with the idea that Lawrence would 'use' Twopenny's chuckers against Wills' chuckers in the inter-colonial New South Wales versus Victoria matches. Twopenny and Charles Dumas suddenly appeared for Lawrence's team at a time when Wills was being shoved aside. In A. G. Johnny Moyes' *Australian Cricket, A History* Moyes states that many of the players who took part in the celebrated Boxing Day match of 1866 under Tom Wills against the Melbourne Cricket Club failed to make the team for England.[5] Moyes apparently was unaware that Jellico and Paddy had died soon after the first abortive tour of Sydney in 1867, Tarpot fell ill and left the *Parramatta* the day before she sailed, and Officer was virtually a non-starter for the tour because of a sly-grog charge hanging over his head in Edenhope in the early part of 1868.

The Aboriginal cricketers from the western district of Victoria were proud full-blood warriors. They knew the old ways and they were highly skilled in the use of a variety of weaponry. The spear was the most important and deadliest weapon in the Aboriginal warrior's armory. Stone spearheads of varied sizes and types, flaked, chipped and edge-ground have been found throughout Australia. The Aboriginal people have proved to be magnificent improvisers, for, over the past 200 years since European occupation, they have fashioned superb spearheads from bottle glass and even porcelain from the insulation 'cups' obtained from atop poles on the Overland Telegraph line. Stone axe-heads as old as 20,000 years were found in three rock shelters near Oenpelli in Arnhem Land. In 1967 Carmel White dug up an axe-head which might be the oldest axe-head made. The axe-head had been sharpened and polished by grinding and the head was clearly grooved to facilitate fitting to an axe-handle.

Bark was stripped and cut from trees to make canoes, shields, shovels, and water and general purpose carriers. The craftsmen handed down stone-age skills learned during and after the last great Ice Age. Bark was stripped from a growing tree, using the stone hatchet.

Wooden 'plugs' were used to help maintain the envisaged shape and to prise the wood from the tree. Great care was taken to ensure that the tree was only scarred, not fatally injured. Scar trees hundreds of years old can still be seen today along waterways and in bushland throughout the nation. Aboriginal women had a myriad of uses for the coolamon, a clever bark vessel shaped like a saucer. It was usually half a metre in length and about 25 centimetres wide. It was used to carry seeds, water, small game and even babies. All tribes used spears, throwing-sticks, digging-sticks, stone-core and flake tools, hafted axes and coolamons. However, the implements varied slightly from region to region, depending on the raw materials available. Wooden-tipped spears, believed used almost exclusively in Tasmania, were beautifully crafted in the age-old way. The men of the tribe went to great pains to find the right wood for the intended spear. They could 'see' a spear within the uprights and the branches of a tree, just as others envisaged a boomerang from a curved branch of a white gum or mallee. While the Aborigine 'saw' a potential battle weapon in the tree, a settler might 'see' fence posts in the same tree.

A tea-tree was perfect for the all-wooden spear. Great pains were taken to select the best of the branches. It might be a shaft some four metres long. The bark was shaved off, then the shaft straightened by passing it through the flames of the camp fire. When the owner was satisfied with the straightness of the shaft, he sharpened the point and hardened it by further scraping the heavy pointed end and pushing it round in the coals of the fire. In 1974 an amazing collection of remarkably preserved wooden objects, believed to be at least 10,000 years old, were found at Wyrie Swamp, near Millicent in the south of South Australia. One boomerang, believed to be among the oldest discovered anywhere in the world, was completely intact. It now takes pride of place with hundreds of other boomerangs of varying ages, colours and shapes at the Adelaide Aboriginal Museum. The modern town of Millicent, built on land reclaimed from hundreds of swamps, is situated just north of Mount Gambier, near Casterton (Jardwadjali territory) and within the Buandig language group, almost certainly people who both traded with and fought against the Djab wurring and Jardwadjali people.

The prize archaeological 'find' at Millicent provided ample evidence that the Aborigines were advanced in the crafting of a variety of weapons and implements as far back as the last great Ice Age. The natural processes which eventually break down all vegetable matter have caused most artifacts made from perishable material to vanish. Unless preserved in a freakish manner such as happened in Millicent, such artifacts disappear after a few hundred years, whereas stone tools retain their original shape for thousands, sometimes millions of years.

Many colonialists, clergymen and laymen such as Charles Lawrence felt it was their moral duty to help 'assimilate' the Aboriginal people and help them on the path to 'salvation'. This arrogant attitude among the settlers assumed that their Christian religion was the only religion and that the 'pagan' Aborigines must be shown the light.

Before the European invasion, what did Australia's Aborigines believe? Did they believe in God? There are many theories, although we have learned that each group or band looked up to their elders or 'clever-men', but there was no lineage of rule in their society, no specialist priest to teach religion as we might understand such matters in our society. If the Aborigines did not believe in one God, they certainly had a wonderful sense of belonging in the universe. They believed in the transmigration of souls, a belief more in keeping with the karma of Buddhism than anything in Christianity. The Aborigines did not believe in an after-life, but they believed in reincarnation or the spirit of the dead returning to earth in the body of another human being. Each tribe or band had its 'clever-man'. He was usually the man who could do things better than his peers: the best spear maker, the best boomerang thrower, the best dodger of spears. The clever-man was the tribe's executioner and medical practioner: he killed and he healed.

Clever-men also called upon the spirits to make rain in the dry periods, and generally were considered to have supernatural powers which would help the tribe.

The Aborigines' belief in the transmigration of souls might explain the bizarre story of William Buckley. Buckley was among a group of convicts in David Collins' Port Phillip landing party in 1803. Collins stayed long enough to look at the River Yarra and the general region where the city of Melbourne would later rise. He was less than impressed and any notion of settling there was aborted. Free from their chains for an instant, three convicts absconded. Two were quickly recaptured, but the third, William Buckley, got away. There was a token hunt for Buckley, but when the soldiers returned to their ship the general feeling was that the prisoner had no chance of surviving. But Buckley did survive. He was befriended by the local Aborigines and lived 'regally' among them for more than 30 years. When Buckley was 'found' in 1835, Australia learnt of his adventure and extraordinary survival through his scribe, John Morgan:

> … they called me Murrangurk. I afterwards learnt [that Murrangurk] was the name of a man formerly belonging to their tribe, who had been buried at the spot where I had found the piece of spear I still carried with me. They have a belief that when they die, they go to some place or other, and are made white men, and that they return to this world again for another existence.
>
> They think all the white people previous to death were belonging to their own tribes, thus returned to life in another colour. In cases where they have killed white men, it has generally been because they imagined them to have been originally enemies, or belonging to tribes with whom they were hostile … They fancied me to be one of their tribe who had been recently killed in a fight … [6]

Over time Australians found a new saying. To have no chance at all was to have 'Buckley's chance'. In 1803 David Collins had reported that the Port Phillip area was not a fit place to settle: he was just as wrong about Melbourne as they had all been about William Buckley.

In the western districts of Victoria, as in other parts of the continent, Aboriginal men hunted kangaroos, emus, possums, wombats, gliders and goannas. Men and women had a shared experience in spearing and trapping fish, tortoises and eels. However, the women concentrated mostly on digging for edible plants and catching small animals, such as lizards, bandicoots and echidnas. The hunters moved out of camp early in the morning, armed with boomerang and spear. The women fed the children, tucked the infants in a woven string basket slung in front of them and carried their long digging stick, which could be up to 3 metres long. The older children also walked with their mother, each carrying a digging stick. The women returned to camp first. They lit the fires and prepared a welcoming homecoming for the hunters. All food was shared. The hunters offered any caught game to the rest of the band before they selected a portion. Anyone who has braved a Victorian winter knows how bitterly cold it can get there, yet the Aboriginals wore little clothing save for a small apron front and back for the men and a bush 'mini-skirt', a short kilt of emu feathers, for the women.

At night the people slept with their feet pointing towards the coals of the fire. They had possum skin coats which doubled as blankets and they snuggled up close. A possum-skin coat was a prized possession. The cloaks were fixed around one shoulder with a pin made from the small bone of the hind leg of a kangaroo. Some 70 medium-sized possums were needed to provide enough skins to make a coat. The Djab wurrung and Jardwadjali had both a physical and a spiritual bond with the land. By the 1860s when the invader had distributed all the land and brought in white-man's laws to further segregate the Aboriginal tribes, the people became dispirited. Forcing the Aborigines from their sacred land was akin to tearing out their hearts and feeding it to their enemies.

Aboriginal people didn't kill any animal for the thrill of the hunt. They did so out of necessity. They carved a canoe or a shield out of a tall, strong gum tree, but they did not ring-bark it; they didn't kill the tree. Their spirit, culture and tradition leads to totemism. Totemism is a potent force in Aboriginal culture, for it means that humans and all living things are integral parts of the whole; there is no struggle for supremacy between human beings and the rest of nature. Totems link the individual with the Dreamtime. The anthropologist William Stanner once recalled a talk he had about totemism with an Aboriginal man in the western districts of Victoria. The Aboriginal man told Stanner:

> 'There is my Dreaming place. My father showed me this place when I was a little boy. His father showed him … He said, "my boy, look! Your Dreaming is there; it is a big thing: you never let it go; all Dreamings come from there; your spirit is there." '[7]

Captain John Williams and Lawrence read to the players from the Bible as the *Parramatta* lurched and rolled in big seas. She was heading towards the southern side of New Zealand, towards cold deep water.

Twenty-one days from Sydney she wove her perilous way through a field of icebergs. Their sheer size dwarfed the ship. We can imagine Charley Dumas hurling a boomerang from the quarter deck, watching this strange and ancient aerodynamic wonder soar over, around and between the field of ice skyscrapers, 200 yards out and 200 yards back, the instrument returning to the feet of Charley as if flown by some unseen aviator. The humorless Reverend Nisbett befriended a Mr Mell, after he discovered that the fellow was a Methodist Minister and that he was accompanied by 'an agreeable looking young wife'. The Reverend writes almost exclusively about his preparation of sermons, the weather, interminable headaches and any ships sighted and rarely speaks of the passengers, his congregation, other than to criticise. He was indignant, for example, when Captain Williams allowed a raffle to be held to raise funds for a newborn baby girl and her mother. Five pounds was raised. The Reverend thought gambling to be a dastardly thing, akin to devil worship. He was from the old, hard school of fanatical 'Bible-bashers'. Judging from his writings, his attitude towards his fellow human beings was decidedly intolerant.

The travellers were unaware that on 12 March 1868 at Clontarf in Sydney an attempt was made on the life of one of their greatest admirers, Prince Alfred, the Duke of Edinburgh, second son of Queen Victoria.

On 4–5 February 1868 Lawrence's men had played the Navy and Army team, mainly officers from the HMS *Galatea*, Prince Alfred's royal sloop, plus two famous cricketers, Ned Gregory and 'terrible' Billy Caffyn. The Duke watched much of the match, plus the sports at the end of each day's play. The Duke loved the sports best of all, and especially the Aboriginal sportsmen. Just five weeks later Prince Alfred faced the greatest danger of his life. When he and his entourage arrived at Clontarf for a gala picnic, Irish-born Henry James O'Farrell lurched out of the crowd of cheering people and fired two shots at him. The Prince was hit, but suffered little more than a flesh wound.

Although quite obviously mad and despite defence pleas of insanity, just five weeks after the shooting, on 21 April 1868, with the *Parramatta* nearly a month from England, O'Farrell was hanged. Prince Alfred had long since recovered and had left for England in the HMS *Galatea*. He was destined to once again see the Aboriginals play cricket and once again delight in their running, jumping, and spear and boomerang throwing. The company aboard *Parramatta* was oblivious to the shooting drama back home.

The *True Briton*, a 685 ton fully-rigged sailing ship, fell in with the *Parramatta* for seven days from the time they met mid-ocean on 24 March. On Friday, 27 March Captain John Williams boarded the *True Briton* and her chief officer came on board the *Parramatta*. Reverend Nisbett noted that the *True Briton* was carrying some 200 steerage passengers and 'some troops'. More than a week after the *True Briton* sailed over the horizon, the Reverend Nisbett complained of rodents:

> Thursday morning, April 9: The rats have become very troublesome in All the cabins — this morning found one lying dead on the top of one of our little boxes — Had a turn out of things under the bed and found some of their depredations — in the way of spoiling & etc.[8]

After successfully negotiating a 'field of seaweed', the ship cruised into the month of May. On Tuesday, 5 May the women on board held a 'bazaar', selling all manner of needlework and implements such as wooden needles and tatting shuttles made by the Aboriginal men. More than £40 was raised for the benefit of the Orphan Asylum for Merchant Seamen. Reverend Nisbett entered into the spirit of the occasion: 'I furnished a few things from which they realized two to three pounds.' Captain John Williams was delighted with the outcome of the bazaar.

The *Parramatta* reached the Thames estuary on about 11 May. Captain Williams was to leave the ship at Penshurst from where a pilot would take the *Parramatta* directly to Gravesend. The pilot arrived with the news of Prince Alfred's brush with death in Australia. According to Lawrence, the players 'got very frightened and thought we would not be allowed to land in England', but on hearing of his recovery said, 'when we get to England we will go and see him for he will like to see us play cricket and throw the boomerang and spear, won't he?'[9]

The players had become very fond of Captain Williams and he of them. So before he left he spoke to them in their cabin:

> 'Now boys I have to thank you for your good behavior during the passage and to give you a little advice as you will meet with as many thieves and

vagabonds as hairs on your head and they will tell you that you are very clever and then ask you to have some drink and then rob you, so don't have anything to do with them, but do just what Mr Lawrence wishes you to do for he knows what bad men there are in London.'

He also spoke kindly to them, shook hands and bid them goodbye. They cried a great deal when he left.[10]

The *Parramatta* berthed at Gravesend on a hot English summer's day. It was 13 May 1868, exactly 81 years from the day that the First Fleet of eleven ships under Arthur Phillip sailed from Gravesend to undertake the European occupation of Australia.

CHAPTER FIVE

A week from Britain, the Reverend Henry Nisbett noted in his journal that on Thursday morning, 7 May 1868, the *Parramatta* exchanged signals with the *Astracan of Calcutta*. Seven other ships were sighted during the day. On Monday, 11 May the pilot had taken over from Captain Williams: '… having been taken in tow by a big steamer during the night of Monday we made fine progress during Tuesday along the coast — very close in — had a fine view of it — a fine, warm summer day — up the Thames during the night under the care of two tugs.'[1]

The sun shone as the pilot successfully guided the *Parramatta* into safe anchorage at Gravesend. There was a flurry of activity on the harbour; ships of all manner: schooners, steamers, ships which complemented sail with steam and fully-rigged sailing vessels such as the *Parramatta* herself. One great adventure had ended, and an even more stimulating adventure was about to begin. *The Australians* had arrived.

Team manager William Hayman, who had sailed to England six weeks in advance of Lawrence and his men, was at the wharf to greet the players. His connection with Kent player and secretary, William Norton, was a winner. Hayman had married Norton's sister and that family connection led to the Australians making Malling in Kent, sometimes called West Malling, their base while in England. The Nortons lived at Cade House, in West Malling. The team, minus Lawrence who continued on with the *Parramatta* to London where he was reunited with his brother and friends, took a coach from Gravesend to travel to West Malling, taking the main road to Strood, passing none other than Charles Dickens' house at Gadshill, but presumably not stopping to greet Dickens or practise on his private cricket ground at the rear of his home. Malling was due south from Dickens' Gadshill abode. That Dickens changed the name of Malling to Muggleton in his fictional All Muggleton versus Dingley Dell cricket match should come as no surprise.

Could Dickens himself have been standing at the front of his house when Hayman and the Australians drove by? Or perhaps he was in his study, pouring over a new masterpiece, occasionally taking time to look across the green sward that was the Dickens' back garden, where a game of cricket may have been in progress. The coach proceeded directly to Cade House where the Norton family were expecting them. William Norton played 87 first-class matches for Kent as a steady, middle-order batsman and medium-paced round-arm bowler. He led Kent for a number of seasons prior to the advent of the county championship. Years later Norton recalled the arrival of the Aboriginal players at his West Malling home:

> I had no notice of the exact time I was to expect them, so when they all walked one morning into my house after breakfast, they caused a good deal of excitement and curiosity. They had a little refreshment, and my two young daughters were brought into the room to inspect the blackies. The little ones were not at all frightened.[2]

When Lawrence was unavailable for the match against Hastings on 22 June, Norton stood in to lead the team. The family tie with Hayman was complemented by a link with Lawrence: in 1859 Norton managed Tom Sherman's New England XI, a professional team competing with other professional teams on the English summer circuit. Sherman was a schoolboy chum of Lawrence's and they played a good deal of their early cricket together in Surrey.

Some matches had been arranged before the side left Australia, but Hayman did not have a full itinerary. Lawrence had great influence with Surrey and Middlesex clubs, and also with noblemen in Ireland, all of whom had strong ties with the Marylebone Cricket Club at Lord's. When the MCC agreed to schedule a match against the Australians at Lord's to be played over 12–13 June, a full itinerary was assured. Offers of matches came thick and fast to the promoters. Until the MCC acted, Lawrence and his fellow promoters were concerned that they would play too few matches and thus miss financial opportunities. Eventually the side played 47 matches, but few of the games and venues had been confirmed in the first few days the side was in England.

Lawrence's arrival in London on 13 May coincided with the Surrey County Cricket Club's annual dinner at the Bridgehouse Hotel, London Bridge, a hotel owned by the family of Julius Caesar, the cricketer and umpire. Surrey CCC secretary William Burrup was instrumental in arranging life insurance for the players in the 1861–62 England tour of Australia and was to prove a great ally to Lawrence and his team in 1868. In all likelihood it was Burrup who initiated the Australians first match, against Surrey at The Oval in Kennington.

Lawrence returned to Town Malling to oversee training. The Aborigines had gained considerable weight as a result of the relative inactivity on board the *Parramatta* during the three-month voyage. Lawrence had his men busily practising their cricket and their skills with spear and boomerang. They became regular visitors to William Norton's West Malling residence and drew a big local audience to their training sessions. The London *Daily Telegraph* heralded the Aborigines' arrival in England with the comment 'Nothing of interest comes from Australia except gold and black cricketers'. The Britain of 1868 did not contain many black people. In fact, they were something of a novelty. A certain W. B. Tegetmeier, who travelled from 'Snodland' to Town Malling at the invitation of team manager William Hayman and Birmingham-based printer E. F. Hingston, met the team in the days leading up to Derby week, when the Australians were due to play a strong Surrey side. The correspondent was not a cricket writer, for he wrote:

> … as to their prowess as cricketers, I shall leave that to be described by other pens than mine; but, speaking as a mere outsider, I should say they will distinguish themselves far more as batsmen than as bowlers. A man who can stand with a small shield some six inches in width in his hand, and protect himself from a shower of balls, is not likely to keep an indifferent guard over his wicket; moreover their wonderful quickness of eye and precision of muscular movement must be greatly to their advantage in the game.[3]

Tegetmeier wrote in detail about the Aboriginal players' physical characteristics, writing that he was taking a greater interest in them as a naturalist than as a cricketer ('I trust the editor will not put this in the cricketing department'), and after observing their practice and their table manners, he delivered a treatise that was more in keeping with a paper for the Royal Zoological Society. All of the men, he wrote, were of the true Australian type:

> … the dark skin of various shades of blackness, the straight, black wiry hair and beard, the black eyes and broadly expanded flattened nostrils, are all characteristic of the natives of the vast Australian continent. The men were dressed in ordinary European costume, and were of sinewy rather than of muscular build.

He joined the players for dinner and could not fault their manners, apart from the occasional use of a knife instead of a fork or 'beyond taking mustard with roast mutton'. He noted with great joy that the Aborigines were adept hands at cribbage, billiards and draughts. 'I am desirous of mentioning their skill at these games, inasmuch as we are so frequently in the habit of speaking of the Australians as savages of so low a type that they are incapable of civilization.' Tegetmeier's article would not have ruffled the feathers of the British society of 1868, for such condescending attitudes were almost universally held.

Bell's Life in London ran a curious article, in parts breathtaking in its crassness, on the arrival of the black cricketers:

> The Aboriginal black cricketers who make their appearance at The Oval next week are the first specimens of the Australian native we have seen in this country. They are veritable representatives of a race unknown to us until the days of Captain Cook and a race which is fast disappearing from the earth. If anything will save them it will perhaps be the cricket ball. Other measures have been tried and failed. The cricket ball has made men of them at last. Since their arrival in England the Australians have been resident in the quiet little town of Town Malling in Kent, where they have been engaged practising the game in which they are to make their fame in England. Every day they have been hard at work and the labour has been requisite for causes not anticipated when they arrived. It was to be expected that after a sea voyage of many thousand miles they should want some rehearsal, but it was not thought that the atmosphere in England would render it necessary that would modify their play to suit the sunlight of the land. The clear air and brilliant sky of Australia are very unlike the vapoury atmosphere and cloudy heavens of our own

clime. The Aborigines assert that when they commenced playing here the effect of the light was so peculiar that they saw two balls instead of one, yet they are almost teetotallers.[4]

There is no doubt that it takes time to adjust to the English light and the pace of the wickets. Even today our professional cricketers take time to adjust, so how must it have been for these men, some of whom had been playing the game for only a year or two. In England when there is thick cloud it forms a blanket and seems to close in on you like an enveloping mist. The Aborigines needed much comforting from Lawrence over the English weather.

The Australians had been in England for nearly two weeks before the first match of the tour, against Surrey at the Oval, got under way on 25 May 1868. The first day attracted a huge crowd, the newspaper reporter noting proudly, 'there could hardly have been less than 7000 spectators, among whom were several ladies many of them in carriages and on horseback'. The players stayed in a hotel in Kennington and on their way to the ground they stopped at the factory of a sports goods manufacturer, owned by Mr S. G. Page, who presented each player with a cane-handled cricket bat and a copy of the *Cricketer's Pocket Book*.

Among the throng of excited spectators was George Brockwell, a former slow left-arm spinner with such an unusual delivery that it had the crowd roaring with delight. Brockwell, who played 34 first-class matches for Surrey between 1844 and 1857, had the curious (and painful) habit of striking himself on the chest just before he released the ball. In wet weather this left a large round mark in the centre of his shirt. Brockwell was employed by The Oval from the opening of the ground in 1845 to 1862, when he was retired on half pay.

Johnny Cuzens could not take his place in the side as he was ill, suffering from a bout of enteritis, so both the batting and the attack was considerably weakened. Surrey batted first and amassed 222, of which Thomas Weeding Baggallay, right-hand bat, slow round-arm bowler and occasional wicket-keeper, top scored with 68. Within a couple of years Baggallay became keen on yachting and he took up sailing to the detriment of his cricket. Baggallay changed his name to Weeding in 1868, but he must have changed it after 17 October, the last day of the tour, for when the side played its final match, a return game against Surrey at The Oval, its was Thomas Baggallay, not Thomas Weeding, in the score-book — clean-bowled by Johnny Cuzens with a ripping yorker which dismissed his leg-stump.

The year 1868 was long remembered for the searing heat of the summer. There was rain in the two days leading up to the first game, but from then on England shone. Surrey fielded a top-notch team, not, as some historians have noted, a weak team due to the absence of such notables as William Caffyn and H. H. Stephenson. In fact, ten of the eleven Surrey men had played first-class cricket. George Jupp and Charles Noble opened up and as they took up their place at the wicket Lawrence raised his right hand and the Aborigines gave a full-throated war-cry to welcome the English pair to the crease. Both openers had played for Surrey, as had Baggallay. An interesting ring-in was I. D. (Isaac Donnilthorne) Walker, who played 294 first-class matches for Middlesex from 1862 to 1884. While he was a fervent follower of Middlesex, Walker, like so many on this tour, helped make up the numbers of quality opponents. Then came George Greenfield, St John Boultbee, Charles Calvert, Henry Tobias Frere (who not only played first-class cricket for Sussex and Hampshire and a stint with Wiltshire, but was considered a 'crack shot'), Frederick Miller and H. Hibberd. The only Surrey player not to have played a first-class match was R. Barton Esquire, who scored 16 not out and was not asked to bowl.

The first day was taken up by the Surrey innings, but there was much to admire about the Aboriginal players' bowling and fielding. King Cole was at point, Charles Dumas was at mid-on, Jim Crow was at short-leg and Redcap was at long slip. Bullocky stood behind the stumps, Twopenny was at long-stop and Lawrence was at mid-off. Mullagh opened the attack, but it was Lawrence who made the early inroads, getting rid of Noble and Jupp. Then Mullagh got the prize wicket of Walker, caught by King Cole at backward point as he square drove, lifting the ball just inches from the turf where King Cole dived to his right to bring off a remarkable catch. Mullagh bowled 52 overs in taking 3/100. Lawrence was the star with the ball, taking 7/91 off 49 overs of round-armers and lobs. For a time Mullagh kept wicket to allow Bullocky a brief bowling stint of 5 overs and King Cole bowled 9 overs, but neither troubled the Surrey batsmen.

The visitors each wore a different coloured sash, which ran from the left shoulder to the right waist. The colours were printed on the scorecard so that spectators could easily identify each player. Tiger wore pink, Bullocky maroon, Mullagh dark blue, Dick-a-Dick yellow, Redcap black, Charley Dumas light blue, Peter green, Twopenny drab, Jim Crow brown, King Cole magenta and Cuzens white. Lawrence did not require any distinguishing coloured sash. The most preferred reason for the Aboriginal players being known by their English names, described as the most picturesque that have ever adorned a scorebook, was that their real names were 'too polysyllabic and not very euphonious'.

Before an even bigger crowd of 8000 on day two, the Australians replied with a paltry 83, of which Johnny Mullagh scored 33 and King Cole hit five twos in an impressive knock of 14.

Perhaps some of that Kennington crowd had joined the early morning mob to witness what became the last public execution in England, outside Newgate prison on 26 May 1868. Michael Barrett was hanged for his part in the Fenian bomb outrage near Clerkenwell Prison, London. The public executioner, John Calcroft (1800–1879), again officiated as he did for nearly every execution that took place outside Newgate Prison during his 'reign' from 1828 to 1871.

Batting again, Australia scored 132, Mullagh again top-scoring with 73. Any suggestion that this was a 'weak' Surrey team is nonsense.

The Australians performed well, given that they had played cricket for only a few years. Mullagh stood out as an outstanding bat. His poise and canny shot selection were impressive. In the second innings he batted for 130 minutes and was given a standing ovation by the crowd. As he neared the players' gate, the crowd converged on him and hoisting him up on to their shoulders carried him to the dressing-room. He would probably have made more than 73 given the brilliance of the thrust and parry of his batsmanship, but many of the balls were intercepted by members of the crowd and hurled in to the centre of the ground. All in all Mullagh had a good first-up match: 52 overs for a return of 3/100 and a batting double of 33 and 73. Immediately play ended, Surrey secretary William Burrup presented

Mullagh with a gold sovereign and watch and chain at an informal ceremony in front of the main pavilion.

During the lunch break on the first day, the great England fast bowler George Tarrant had gleefully taken up the opportunity to bowl to Mullagh in the nets. Lawrence had been speaking in glowing terms of his ace batsman and Tarrant wanted to test him out. The England pace-man bowled with his customary pace and fire, but he failed to dismiss Mullagh during their 15-minute session. Mullagh had unleashed a range of attacking strokes which amazed Tarrant. (The Englishman had toured Australia with George Parr's celebrated 1862–63 England team and had inspired Fred Spofforth, who was destined to become the demon Aussie fast bowler, to bowl like the wind.) At the end of the session Tarrant walked over to Mullagh, extended his right hand and said, 'I have never bowled to a better batsman!'

According to George Graham's ledger, the match against Surrey realised £603–2–6 in receipts. Expenditure was £299–13–5. The Surrey club was paid £150 and the police were paid £20 cash. Prizes totalled £6–10–0.

Lawrence and his men happily accepted an invitation to attend the Derby at Epsom. The Australians were cheered at the track almost as loudly as the winner, two-year-old filly Blue Gown (Beadman out of Bas Bleu). On the next day, 28 May, Lawrence and his men turned on a day of sports at The Oval. More than 4000 people turned up to see the Aborigines display their extraordinary skills as athletes and with the spear and boomerang. Two days of cricket and one day of sports had attracted more than 20,000 spectators at The Oval.

Charley Dumas was brilliant with his control of the boomerang. Kennington Oval is a vast expanse of land, but it was far too small to contain the amazing first throw. The boomerang soared high over the spectators' heads and swept high above the giant gas holders which stood beyond The Oval perimeter and back into view, sweeping low over ducking heads until the craft spun obediently above Charley's head. It hovered for a full minute before its gyrations began to slow and it finally fell neatly between Charley's bare feet. The crowd roared. Not all of Charley's throws were so well controlled. One wayward boomerang dived alarmingly into the crowd and almost sliced a man's top hat in half. Another swept across the vista of the gas holders, seemingly well beyond the precinct of the ground, and disappeared.

The Aboriginal players opened the 'games' with a mock hunt. Usually an even number of 12 men took part. They donned their traditional costume: black, fitting tights, a possum skin trunk and a cabbage tree hat that was lavishly bedecked with lyrebird feathers. The crowd sat in hushed silence. There was great expectation as the Aborigines walked on to the ground one by one. Each man held a spear: a hard wood shaft and a reed tip about 30 centimetres long. The entire length of the spear measured more than 2 metres. The spears and their wooden spear-throwers were the traditional ones of the Western District of Victoria. The men stood, spears at the ready, in line. Then Lawrence raised his arm and when he dropped it all the spears were thrown in unison. This was the start of the attack. Each man threw a total of six spears before the group gave a collective yell then divided into two equal parties. They stood about 70 metres apart and began a mock battle, one group throwing spears at the other group. Spectators were astonished at the speed and accuracy of the thrown spear. With the help of a spear-thrower, or woomera, the spear can be thrown fast and accurately over a distance of more than 100 metres. The defenders easily warded off the spears with expert use of their shields. The Aborigines also displayed their method of hunting and trapping animals, be they kangaroos or emus. The spears were thrown in such a manner as to encircle the animal with a wall of spears embedded in the ground. Crimean War veteran Lieutenant-General Pitt-Rivers was a student of the history of warfare and he visited The Oval for the express purpose of watching the Aborigines at 'war' with the spear. Pitt-Rivers was in the midst of preparing his essays on the evolution of technology. He 'commended the masterly skill of throwers and used his observations to support a detailed study of the evolution of throwing-sticks among primitive societies'.[5]

The English people were intrigued by the Aboriginal players' proud bearing and their extraordinary skill with their traditional weapons of war. Johnny Mullagh, Dick-a-Dick and Mosquito were excellent exponents of the boomerang, but no one could match the skill and control of Charley Dumas. Dumas hailed from New South Wales, although precisely which region he came from remains unclear. Pitt-Rivers noted that the size and shape of the boomerangs used by Charley Dumas differed from those used by Mullagh and the others. Certainly we know that the boomerangs of the Wimmera were different from those used in other parts of Australia. However, the method of throwing any boomerang is the same. The curved blade is held at the extremity of one end and so held with the concave side forward towards the direction the thrower wants the boomerang to start off. The returning boomerang held a great fascination for the English. Our writer W. B. Tegetmeier told his readers in *The Cricket Field* that an Aborigine could stand some 40 yards from a clump of trees and throw a boomerang towards them, and it would curve in flight, sweep around the trees and return to a spot behind the thrower. With the Fenian bomb outrage and Irish rebellion in the air, Tegetmeier was tempting fate with this statement: 'It [the returning boomerang] is the nearest realization that I have ever seen of the Irishman's wish for a gun that would shoot round a corner.'[6]

Tegetmeier takes captive the imagination with his description of Charley Dumas sending forth his aeronautical wonder at the crowded Kennington Oval:

> Thrown violently forward so as to tip the ground some twenty yards in advance, the boomerang has its motion altered by contact with the earth, and glides rapidly into the air. But the most graceful performance with this instrument is when thrown so as to rise to a great height, in which case it is impossible to conceive anything more beautiful than its movements; it skims upwards like a swift, now presenting its flat blade to the eye, and then, turning its sharp edge to the spectator it becomes invisible in the clear bright sky, appearing again as its plane of rotation changes and as it glides rapidly about, now this direction, now in another, as though guided by its own volition.[7]

William Hayman arranged for Tegetmeier to take possession of an example of every one of the Aboriginal weapons: spear, woomera, boomerang and waddy. The implements were on public display at *The Cricket Field* office for years. It is unclear whether Tegetmeier got hold of examples of Dick-a-Dick's shield and leangle; however, in 1946 Dick-a-Dick's leangle (sometimes called a 'leowell' or 'killer boomerang') turned up at the Lord's Museum and has remained there ever since. It is also not known whether Hayman sold the weapons or gave them away. No mention of any weapons' sale is made in the tour ledger. Pitt-Rivers would have been a potential buyer. He established a fabulous collection of artifacts from around the world, including shields and spears used by Aboriginal people, but it is not known whether any of those implements were acquired from the 1868 Australians. The old warhorse was fascinated by the Aboriginal method of warfare. He watched in awe at the Aborigines' display of tactical skill at The Oval in May 1868. He stood transfixed as a dozen Aborigines threw spears an enormous distance by using their wooden woomeras to help propel the weapon. A volley of spears headed towards a small group of men at the far end of the ground, standing near the huge shadows cast by the gas-holders. Their aim was so deadly that every man in the small group had to dodge or die. At Bootle Dick-a-Dick threw a spear more than 120 metres using the traditional method.

It is too easy to dismiss this tour as something akin to a circus. That cricket had always been associated with running and jumping and the long throw, years before the conception of the Aboriginal tour, gives the after-stumps sports much credence. Before that first sports day leading London newspapers carried advertisements of the coming event at The Oval. There would be a 100 yards flat race, a running high jump, a 150 yards hurdle race, a standing high jump, spear throwing, 2 mile handicap walk, throwing a cricket ball, pole vaulting, picking up stones one yard apart, throwing boomerangs, a 440 yards flat race handicap, a water bucket race, dodging cricket balls by Dick-a-Dick (with leowall and shield), a 100 yards backwards race, and Lawrence's feat with bat and ball.

The official umpires, Messrs Tanner and Street, were the games officials. The starter was W. Croucher. *Bell's Life* carried brief results in its edition of Saturday, 30 May. F. Ford of Lambeth beat Mosquito by 4 yards to win the 100 yards flat race, but the Aborigines proved superior to the Europeans in all other events except the walking race and the 440 yards. Mosquito won the standing high jump (4 ft 1 in) from Dick-a-Dick and F. Ford; Dick-a-Dick won the 150 yards hurdle (4 flights) from Johnny Mullagh and Charley Dumas, with Ford just missing a spot in the first three; Mosquito (8ft) defeated Jim Crow

(7 ft 8 in) in the pole vaulting (no other starters). The 2 miles walking race was won by Wren in 18 minutes 15 secs, then came Julius Caesar and Nicholls (disqualified), with Dick-a-Dick and King Cole bringing up the rear of the field. The 440 yards race was won easily, by 15 yards, by the determined F. Ford (scratch). He beat Julius Caesar (10 yards start) and Janus (10 yards start). The water bucket race was won by none other than Sundown, who did little on the cricket side of things — so little that one wonders how he got into the team in the first place.

Sundown played only two matches on tour before he and Jim Crow were sent home ill in September. He did not bowl a ball on tour and batted three times, scoring a grand total of 1 run. (History provides Sundown with a few historical rivals as poor batsmen. In 1975 Jim Higgs failed to score a single run on the entire England tour.)

By far the most astonishing feat in an extraordinary day of sports was Dick-a-Dick's amazing 'dodge'. A great athlete, Dick-a-Dick had tremendous hand–eye coordination. He offered the Surrey players and officials a challenge. Armed with a parrying shield and leangle, Dick-a-Dick played 'dodge the ball'. For the price of one shilling, anyone could have a shy at Dick-a-Dick with a cricket ball. Dick-a-Dick would stand no more than 10 paces from the thrower. At one stage Messrs Burrup, Garland, South, Norton, Shepherd, Croucher and Westhall Jnr threw in unison, but not one ball found its mark. The balls aimed at his head and chest he easily parried with the shield, and those thrown below the waist were deflected by skilful use of the leangle, giving the ball a new direction as would a hockey player using a stick with less length on the turn at the end of the stick. It was Dick-a-Dick's performance that day which won him much fame and a modest fortune, for every session from that day onwards earned him a pocketful of silver at every one of the 47 venues.

His performance that day was so good that it might have been perceived by some spectators as showing up the white man, for a number of ruffians began to hurl abuse and the odd bottle at Dick-a-Dick. Drink fuelled the fire and fights broke out in the crowd, some of whom spilled on to the arena to avoid a confrontation with ruffians. Police intervened and the 'roughs' ran out on to the field, thus bringing the games to a halt. *Bell's Life* noted: 'The least said, the soonest mended, but one or two of the ringleaders are known and at least some time or other will receive their deserts.'[8]

The publication criticised the police, saying that had they acted sooner the situation could easily have been contained, without the subsequent cancellation of the final events. But the Australian tour management must have been impressed for they handed over £20 to the police.

Earlier, in the cricket ball long-throw, Bullocky won with a mighty toss of 105 yards 6 in. Charley Dumas threw 100 yards 9 in to run second ahead of Dick-a-Dick and Surrey men Buckle and Harmes. Curiously *Bell's Life* does not mention that W. G. Grace took part in the long throw. Then aged 19, immensely strong and athletic, and in the very year he became the first batsman in the world to score a century in each innings of a first-class match, Grace is said to have thrown down a challenge to the Australians. In three goes he threw 116, 117 and 118 yards and, at his fourth attempt, he threw the ball 109 yards one way and 104 the other. Eminent cricket writer A. A. Thompson records the Grace effort, as does Alverstone and Alcock's *Surrey Cricket: Its History and Associations*, adding flavor to the Grace legend with, 'further to disprove the theory that no-one could throw both ways, he [Grace] exceeded the distance in a return heave'.[9] *Bell's Life* probably omitted the Grace throws because his challenge may have come after the official event.

Mullagh won the running high jump (5ft), with Dick-a-Dick (4ft 9 in) second. A few days later Charley Dumas and Jimmy Mosquito amazed the athletics world with wonderful high-jumping at Gravesend. Dick-a-Dick also excelled at Gravesend, beating his personal best jump by 9 inches. There is no official record of just who won the 100 yards running backwards race, although we do know that Dick-a-Dick was good at that event. Lawrence also showed his mettle with bat and ball. Bullocky stood some 70 metres from Lawrence, who held his cricket bat at the ready. Bullocky hurled the ball to Lawrence on the full toss and Lawrence with extraordinary timing allowed the bat to 'give' with the force of the ball and create the illusion that he had in fact 'caught' the ball on the bat. With a blink of the eye Lawrence extracted the ball from the bat's centre and held the ball aloft, much to the delight of the crowd. Such a feat demands fantastic timing, for it requires the man holding the bat to 'give' with the ball at precisely the right moment. A fieldsman can absorb a catch in similar fashion by 'giving' just as the ball enters his cupped hands.

Lawrence displayed his all-round skills in the second match of the tour, against Mote Park at the Earl of Romney's lovely oak-tree-lined ground at Maidstone in Kent. The organising committee of the Mote Park Club, which included secretary G. R. Streatfield, W. A. Crispe and H. Stacey, helped make the match a great event. In 1868 there was no permanent grandstand as there is today, so marquees were erected at strategic points around the ground for distinguished guests and the players. The match itself was drawn, due to rain, but Lawrence hit an unconquered 57 and took 4/68 in Mote Park's innings of 151. Tiger and Cuzens scored 20-odd apiece in the Aboriginal score of 4/119 before the heavens opened up. However, the inclement weather did not spoil the native sports, nor the splendid renditions of the bands of the Royal Horse Artillery and the 1st Kent Rifle Volunteers, whose music was a stirring accompaniment to the Aboriginal athletic show. Again Dick-a-Dick frustrated throwers and delighted the crowd as he ducked, dodged and weaved, and parried and deflected cricket balls thrown at him from close range. Jimmy Mosquito was gaining a like reputation for his expertise with a stockwhip. With his 18-foot leather whip he could 'disarm' someone holding a shilling between forefinger and thumb with outstretched arm. And Charley Dumas was at his mischevious best hurling the boomerang high over the heads of the crowd and chuckling as the crowd crooked their necks in a sort of collective trance straining to see where the boomerang was taking them. It 'took' them far over a large oak, where Redcap had inadvertently killed a squirrel with a throwing stick only hours earlier, and halfway round the ground before it obediently returned and hovered prior to a perfect three-point landing.

By coincidence I found myself at the Mote Park ground on 1 June 2000, 132 years almost to the day since the 1868 Aboriginal team played there. I was there to coach a number of emerging Kent County Cricket Club spin bowlers and it was only after having seen a photograph of John McGuire's 1988 re-enactment of the Aboriginal

Australian team in the pavilion that I realised that I was on historical turf directly linked to the story I was then researching. The ground itself looked pretty much as it would have in 1868, apart from the old pavilion which was built round the turn of the century and a little brick scorers' building which was built earlier than the pavilion but after 1868. Most of the tall oaks which surround the ground would have been small trees when Lawrence and his men played there. Perhaps Redcap's oak is still standing among the older brigade of trees on the southern side of Mote Park, but there is no way we will ever know.

Back in 1868 a big crowd attended, more people than had turned up to a match at Mote Park in living memory. They cheered when the Aboriginal players gave their customary war whoop at the arrival to the crease of the Mote Park opening batsmen, Marsham and White. Apart from Lawrence, Cuzens and Mullagh bowled superbly. Cuzens also excelled in the foot races. No one could match his speed and he scooped the prize pool. By the end of the second match at Mote Park, the general opinion in cricket circles was that only three of the team were of genuine county standard — Lawrence, who had proved himself in first-class cricket, Johnny Mullagh and Johnny Cuzens.

Officially the team was not confronted in an overtly racist manner. Certainly the newspapers referred to the players as 'darkies' and made reference to their physical and mental potentials and capabilities in a way that would not be tolerated in a non-racist society. However, these reports must be seen in the context of the prevailing attitudes of 1868. The British people were generally ignorant about the culture of the Aboriginal people, and the racist overtones evident during the tour were usually born out of ignorance, without malice or an intent to create tension. However, the sort of bias that was evident was exemplified by the behaviour of one hotel landlord. Through a fear that the Aboriginal team might wish to stay at his establishment for the third scheduled tour game, Thomas Elt, propietor of the Bat and Ball Inn at Gravesend, wrote to the Gravesend Board of Guardians in an effort to have that body 'lend him a quantity of beds and bedding for the accommodation of the black cricketers'.[10]

The inference here is that Mr Elt believed that the Board would reject his claim for extra bedding and so Lawrence and his party would have to seek alternative accommodation. If they insisted on staying at the Bat and Ball, Elt would then charge the earth. Either way Elt would win. The team did stay at the Bat and Ball and Elt insisted that they pay the sum of £40 — an extraordinarily high fee.

George Graham, the solicitor who provided the tour with substantial funds, was the man who kept the books. The Graham ledger became an invaluable research source. It mysteriously came into the hands of Bill O'Reilly, the greatest leg-spinner Australian cricket has produced. 'Tiger' O'Reilly was having a beer in his favourite Strathfield pub (in Sydney) in 1962 when a bloke unknown to him sidled up to him at the bar, plonked a hefty book down next to Bill's pint and announced: 'You'll know what to do with this lot, Tiger!' O'Reilly immediately understood the significance of the contents of the book.

(It is an extraordinary coincidence that 32 years earlier O'Reilly's great spinning mate, Clarrie Grimmett, was also presented with a link to the 1868 tour. Grimmett, the bowling star of the 1930 Australian tour of England, was bowling in the nets at Lord's when a stranger came up to him and presented him with a photograph of the 1868 Australians which had hitherto never seen the public light of day. The meeting coincided with an article on the 1868 Australians which had just been published in *The Cricketer*. Grimmett, history thanks, was a bower bird. He kept everything and he looked after everything he possessed. The photograph was in mint condition the day in 2000 it was auctioned in Melbourne.)

O'Reilly kept the Graham ledger for sixteen years. Perhaps he was thinking of writing the story of the 1868 tour, or perhaps he was waiting to ensure that it fell into the right hands. He presented the ledger to the Melbourne Cricket Club in January 1978 where it is carefully preserved; people wishing to peruse it must don white gloves. The ledger tells us that the 1868 tour returned a reasonable profit, £2176–3–10 to be precise. The profit came after all expenses were accounted for, so the players could have reasonably asked for some payment, other than funds for food and travel, for their part in the tour. A figure of 50 pounds for each man was spoken about: 'We believe we are justified in saying that besides their weekly wages, and ordinary expenses allowed them in England, they will each receive

50 pounds upon their return home.'[11] However, not one of the Aboriginal players received a penny at the end of the tour.

Some of the players may have been billeted at the New Falcon Hotel, as there is a separate account for £3.10.5 shown in the ledger as having been paid to that hotel. Graham's details of match income and expenditure were complemented by cuttings of newspaper reports on the match relating to the account details, pasted on the same page. There is Graham's handwritten notation of 'Blackguard' alongside Mr T.R. Elt's name in a brief newspaper report of Elt's claim for the Board of Guardians to supply him with 'extra bedding'. It seems that Mr Elt was the sort of fellow the captain of the *Parramatta*, John Williams, warned the players about as they approached the shores of England in May. Mr Elt, it seems, fleeced the Australians.

The Kent side proved too strong for Lawrence's men, although in the Kent total of 298 Mullagh took 6/125 off a marathon 59.2 overs. The Aborigines failed with the bat, replying with only 123, of which Dick-a-Dick hit 27 and King Cole a 'steady' 18, and 106. In the first innings William Norton took an incredible 5/2. King Cole took his only wicket on the tour, that of Captain Boycott (caught at slip by Lawrence) in what sadly turned out to be one of King Cole's last cricket matches.

The fourth match of the tour was against Richmond at Deer Park (5–6 June 1868). Cuzens was only a shade over 150 centimetres tall, but he was strong and stocky and had boundless enthusiasm. From what I have read of him I imagine that he had the bustle of a Malcolm Marshall and the slingshot power of a Jeff Thomson. His arm was higher than most and allowed him to gain steepling bounce and worry the best of the English players he bowled against. He didn't achieve a consistent batch of shooters, as did one or two of the others, for his high arm action encouraged greater bounce, which, in itself, one suspects, worried opposing batsmen more than the round-arm-type deliveries. Cuzens took 5/28 off 23 overs to skittle Richmond for 74, then he hit 24 to top score for the Aborigines in their first innings total of 97.

Sir William Dennison, who was the Governor of New South Wales in 1856 and the first governor to allow cricket to be played on the Domain in Sydney, asked to be introduced to the Aboriginal players.

They lined up in ceremonial fashion on the ground during a break in play and Sir William shook hands with each man, spoke to them with genuine enthusiasm and affection, and presented every player with a gift in the form of a crisp new 10 shilling note.

In Richmond's second innings of 236, Mullagh bowled 39 overs to take 4/65 and Cuzens followed up his first-innings triumph with 3/49 off 36 overs. Batting a second time the Aborigines scored 3/82 (Lawrence 42, Bullocky 15) to play out an honourable draw.

Against the strong Sussex XI at Brighton record crowds enjoyed the cricket and the Aboriginal sports, with 3000 people watching the first day and 4000 the next. The players stayed at the Olive Branch Inn at Brighton and the party were full of praise for their hosts, Mr and Mrs Haselden. A local writer observed the scene at the start of the match: 'A galaxy of beauty and fashion graced the subscribers' [sponsors] marquees. A more animated scene we have never witnessed on that ground.' Dick-a-Dick again starred with his parrying shield and leangle, but Charley Dumas provided the most fascination for spectators with his art with the boomerang. The *Brighton Gazette* described it thus:

> The boomerang is propelled forwards, skimming and twirling through the air with a loud whirr and when it has touched the ground with one end, it instantly rises and continues to gyrate in the most wonderous manner at a great height, now sailing like a swallow, now poising itself like a skylark, and now flying in circles like a pigeon, til it swoops like a hawk and falls, sometimes near the man who has thrown it, sometimes a considerable distance behind him.[12]

The Aboriginal players were eventually outclassed by Sussex after a promising start. Lawrence (63) and Mullagh (39) batted superbly to help their side to a first innings 171. They then took a first innings lead after Mullagh took 5/55 off 33 overs to restrict Sussex to 151.

The Australians collapsed when batting a second time, to be dismissed for a paltry 89, and Sussex hit 1/112 to easily take the game. While there were good signs with the bowling and the fielding, the Australians depended on too few to give the batting any semblance of solidity. If, for instance, Lawrence and Mullagh and perhaps Cuzens missed out with the bat, the side struggled to be competitive. Too often the batting folded, and inconsistency among the batsmen probably accounts for Lawrence often changing the batting order, trying to find the right combination. On the other hand, the constant changes in batting order might well have contributed to the very inconsistency Lawrence sought to resolve, for drastic and sometimes radical changes in the batting order can have the reverse effect on a team, undermining individuals and reducing the confidence of the team as a whole.

King Cole was suffering from a chest cold, but he played in the sixth match of the tour, against Lewisham at Ladywell on 10–11 June 1868. Mullagh's bowling won the match. He took 6/24 off 23 overs in the first innings, helping Lawrence (3/36) to dismiss Lewisham for 60, and 4/20 off 16 overs in the second innings when he and Cuzens (3/18) blitzed Lewisham for 53. The Australians scored only 42 in their first innings, Redcap top scoring with 12 and King Cole, whose batting was steady throughout, hitting an unconquered 11. Lawrence (32), Tiger (14) and Cuzens (11) helped the team make a second innings 4/72 to cruise to a six-wicket victory — the team's first win of the tour. The batting was still a worry, but they were confident and eager for the next match — their most significant of the tour — against the MCC at Lord's.

At Sussex the Graham ledger records 'a good profit of £168–4–6' including £5 for 'Lawrence incidentals'. At Ladywell expenditure included 'man at gate 17/–'.

Initially the MCC membership had voted not to meet the Australian team in a match at Lord's, but later reversed their decision, due mainly to lobbying by the various noblemen friends of Charles Lawrence and especially by the influential Surrey Cricket Club secretary, William Burrup. The powerful influence of the MCC meant that as soon as news of the MCC versus Australia match became known dozens of clubs contacted the Aboriginal team. The MCC took the lead and the others fell in line. In fact, without the full support of Lord's in this way, the Aboriginal tour of 1868 could well have been an absolute fizzer. The sketchy history of the MCC match alludes to behind-the-scenes resistance to the Aboriginal athletic displays and sports, but there is no evidence of official resistance. In terms of a meeting of the cultures, this match at Lord's was perhaps the most significant match played between an English eleven and a visiting Australian team in the 19th century. Here were tribal men from the western districts of Victoria — men perceived as savages — rubbing shoulders with the nobility of the country that had sailed to the great southern land and effectively stolen their land and transformed it, so that the Aborigine's traditional way of life, going back more than 40,000 years was irrevocably changed. The European 'settlement' of Australia was never anything other than an invasion. However, although Aboriginal resistance to the British invasion of Australia amounted to a fundamental repudiation of the British claim to sovereignty, there was never any formal declaration of war. When the Aborigines opposed the occupation by word or deed their resistance was regarded as criminal activity or open rebellion against the Crown.

In the MCC match the Australians were playing against a side which included the Earl of Coventry (MCC president in 1859), Viscount Downe (MCC president in 1872) and some former first-class players, including Harvey Fellows who in the summer of 1848–49 was considered to be one of the fastest bowlers ever. Fellows had slowed considerably by 1868, but he got one through the defence of Lawrence in the Australian first innings. Middlesex stalwart Charles Buller, stylish right-hand batsman, slow round-arm bowler and excellent deep fieldsman, was probably the best bat in the MCC line-up, although Robert Fitzgerald, who played 46 first-class matches for Middlesex and the MCC and took a team to North America in 1872, proved a stumbling block for the Aborigines in this match with a solid score of 50 in the MCC first innings. Other former first-class cricketers in the MCC lineup were Alfred Fitzgerald (brother of Robert), Frederick Trevor (in the scorebook as Captain F. Trevor) and Sir Frederick Hervey-Bathurst. In the scorebook the latter was listed as Lieut-Col F. H. Bathurst. He first played for the MCC in 1852, and became a Member of Parliament for Wiltshire after a stint fighting in the Crimean War. His father (also Sir Frederick) played for Hampshire from 1842 to 1861 and was regarded as one of the finest of all fast bowlers.

The Australians did well, scoring 185 in their first innings with Mullagh batting brilliantly to score 75. Lawrence hit 31, but the next best was Redcap (13). King Cole was run out for 7, having again shown great poise with the bat, and the rest fell cheaply. Lawrence's men held a deserved 21-run lead and Cuzens bowled magnificently to take 6/65. He clean-bowled the Earl of Coventry (0), Lieut-Col Bathurst (0), Robert Fitzgerald (3), Captain Trevor (13) and Alfred Fitzgerald. The Australians were all set to win the match, but fate took a hand. Bullocky failed to turn up, for no apparent reason, so he appeared in the scorebook thus: 'Bullocky, absent, ill ... 0'.[13] Lawrence was run out for one and Mullagh was caught by Viscount Downe off Charles Buller for 12. Cuzens hit a brave 21, but the team collapsed lamentably for a mere 45 and fell short of the target by 55 runs. The slow man Buller bamboozled and defeated the Aborigines just as the Victorian slow men Handfield and James had done at the MCG in 1866. While Lawrence was at the crease there was a faint hope. He had a badly strained leg and needed a 'traveller' (a runner).

Cuzens was Lawrence's runner. Lawrence played a ball from Buller to Harvey Fellows, who had lost much of his youthful zest but not his rocket arm from cover point. Lawrence moved a few paces, then said 'no' and moved back to safety. However, Cuzens had also moved out of his ground on the shot and was tardy in retrieving his ground. The wicket-keeper received Fellows' deadly throw over the bails from cover point and removed the bails. Lawrence had made well his ground, but his runner was out of his crease when the wicket was broken. Whether Lawrence was out because of Cuzens' poor running and judgment or his ignorance of the laws of the game is not known. It was possibly a combination of these factors.

The loss at Lord's did not dampen the Aborigines' enthusiasm for the sports held immediately after the end of the match. Again it was Dick-a-Dick who held the crowd in awe. Lord's had never witnessed anything quite like it, certainly nothing since August 1844 when the Ioway Indians encamped at Lord's. Members discarded their cloaks and top hats, paid their shilling and threw themselves into the fray. Here was a man holding a narrow shield, no wider than one of James Dark's celebrated cricket bats, and a thing which looked like a hockey stick, albeit longer at the 'leg', challenging members to hit him with a cricket ball thrown full force from a distance of up to 10 metres. The man must be stark, raving mad! It was the members themselves

Cricket Match played at Lords Grounds between .... Clubs

First Innings

Order of going in	Name of the Batsman	Figures as Scored	How Out	Bowler's Name	Runs
1	Tylor		Bowled	Long	0
2	Billesley		Bowled	Buller	11
3	Guy		Bowled	Buller	0
4	Red Cap		Bowled	Buller	13
5	Mullagh		Bowled	Buller	45
6			Bowled	Tollard	31
7	King Cole		Run out		7
8			ct & Bowled	Buller	8
9			Bowled	Sylley	6
10	Peter		Bowled		63
11	Dumas		Not out		0
	Byes				18
	Leg Byes				3
	Wide Balls				
	No Balls				3
				Total of First Innings	186

| Runs at the fall of each Wicket | 1 for 1 | 2 for 6 | 3 for 24 | 4 for 43 | 5 for 144 | 6 for 126 | 7 for 136 | 8 for 168 | 9 for 175 | 10 for 186 |

Cricket Match played at _Lord's C.G._ between _Marylebone Marybone Club_ ... ...

First Innings

Order of going in	Name of the Batsmen	Figures as Scored	How Out	Bowler's Name	Runs
1	Earl of Brantley(?)	4 11 2 1 2 2 1 11 25	Bowled	Mullagh	25
2	Dr Weir Esq.	1 3 2 4 1 2 2	Bowled	Mullagh	20
3	... Gee Esq.	1 1 1	Bowled	Mullagh	5
4	F. Butler Esq.	1 2 1 1	Bowled	Mullagh	14
5	... R. Bethune		Bowled	Cuzens	0
6	R.A. Fitzgerald ...	2 1 1 3 1 5 2 2 1 1 1 5 1	Bowled	Cuzens	50
7	W.W. Elliot Esq.	3 1 1 1	Run out		6
8	Capt Trevor	1 1 1 1 5	Bowled	Cuzens	10
9	W. Fitzgerald E.	2 1 2 1	Bowled	Mullagh	6
10	Deleval Astley	1 1 1 1 1	Run out		1
11	... Smith E.	1 1 1 1 1 1 1 1 2	not out		3
				Byes	12
				Leg Byes	3
	Byes	111			
	Leg Byes				
	Wide Balls				
	No Balls				
				Total of First Innings	164

Runs at the fall of each Wicket	1st 44	2nd 0	3rd 67	4th 72	5th 0	6th 107	7th 157	8th 142	9th 160	10th 164

The scorecards of the first innings for each side in the match at Lord's on 12–13 June 1868. This match was the catalyst for a successful tour.

who ranted and raved and became decidedly maddened with the frustration of not getting one ball to find its mark. After an exhaustive half hour (for the chuckers), Dick-a-Dick walked jauntily away with a decided bulge in his pocket, another cache of shilling pieces.

The Times, England's most influential newspaper, was dismissive of the tour. The newspaper's correspondent watched the match against Surrey and concluded that the team had 'second-rate bowling, the batting was sadly lacking in power, while the running between wickets was slow and hesitant'. The newspaper mentioned hardly a word about the Australian team after the first month of the tour, which included the Surrey match and the historic game at Lord's. Britannia ruled the waves in 1868 and sometimes she shoved bad news under the covers. In July when the Australians defeated the Gentlemen of Swansea by an innings and 33 runs the brief reports of the match gave little credit to the Australians. Local newspapers stressed that luck played a greater part than sheer skill in the visitors' victory.

In 1868 there was almost blind allegiance to the Crown and all it represented. Black people in Australia did not count: literally. In 1868 the population of European Australians was 1,539,552. How many Aboriginals were there? No one knew and few cared. They were not counted and, in effect, did not count. Few white people in Tasmania would have known that William Lanney ('King Billy'), the last full-blood Aborigine in Tasmania, was living out his last days. He eventually died of choleraic diarrhoea on 3 March 1869, but outside of Tasmania few knew of him, and he would not have been known to the Australian team. Other English publications, such as *The London Illustrated News* and *Punch* did as *The Times* did and virtually ignored the Aboriginal tour. The potential for rich copy and fascinating sketches were opportunities lost. The Australians were not great cricketers, nor were they a great cricket team, but they were skilled and they were unique and they were an important Australian sports team in history.

Reynold's News reported that the Australians were 'a new epoch in the history of cricket. There is not a third-rate batsmen among them!' Obviously the *Reynold's News* cricket writer had not yet set eyes on the batting prowess of Sundown, whose tour performance we have already discussed. One cricketer of the day, Fred Gale, who later won fame as a cricket writer, with the nom de plume of 'The Old Buffer', and who wrote a biography of the single-minded MCC stalwart Robert Grimston, wrote glowingly of the Aboriginal team:

I can 'speak a piece,' as poor Artemus said, regarding the Aboriginal cricketers. I played against them twice, at The Oval and at Eastbourne — and fielded 'point' on each occasion. Mullagh, in the opinion of many good judges, was a good enough player to play on the Players' side in the Gentlemen versus Players, England's premier challenge of the time. He played forward with a bat as straight as Fuller Pilch, and he was not to be got by a shooter, as, without being a 'potato digger', every time he played a ball he knocked an atom of turf or soil not bigger than half your little finger-nail, and not thicker — he was so true to the ground. He was really a very fine bat, and a good wicket-keeper. Moreover he is very intelligent, which was not the case with all the team.

Cuzens, who stood five foot three inches (who, I think, threw) was as fast as any bowler almost I ever saw, and very straight: it was easy enough on a good wicket, as there was no 'break'. Twopenny was a tremendous off-hitter, and as he ground his teeth every time he hit it, it added to the terror of standing 'point' to him. Dick-a-Dick was a wonderful field, and could throw an immense distance. All of them were fine fieldsmen, and some of them had a very peculiar way of fielding — they would grab a ball like a cat nailing a mouse, with the left hand, pass it like a flash of lightning to the right, and they could throw very straight and well.[14]

The tenth match of the 1868 tour was against the Gentlemen of Hastings on the Central Ground — a far cry indeed from the Battle of Hastings fought nearby nearly 800 years earlier. When I first ventured to the region, as a member of the 1968 Australian team, I experienced a strange sensation that I had been in Sussex before, yet I had never seen a photograph or a television documentary of the Hastings region. This is not an uncommon phenomenon. Many people experience a feeling of having been somewhere, sometime in the past, and have then discovered that generations earlier an ancestor or ancestors were prominent in that area. Perhaps the spirit of our ancestors lives in the blood line, each succeeding generation feeding the lifeline. The landscape struck a chord, as did the well-maintained ancient buildings, yet none of the ruins. The coast was also familiar.

Years later I found a possible explanation. An ancestor, William Malet, fought side by side with William the Conqueror at the Battle of Hastings. My father's cousin, Gordon Mallett, whose great grand-father was a convict (transported to Sydney on the *Bufsorah Merchant* for 'seven years across the seas' in 1828 for stealing a hatchet, a frying pan and some bedding), spent years researching the Mallett family history and he enlisted the help of Debretts. By the time Gordon died he had compiled an extraordinary profile of our famous ancients.

In Normandy, William was known as William Sire de Graville Deuxierne du mon. Researchers, in collaboration with Debretts, have translated the archaic French of Roman de Ron:

> William whom they call Malet boldly throws himself among them; with his flashing sword against the English he makes furious onset; but his shield they clove, and his horse beneath him killed, when came the Sire de Montfort and Lord William de Vez-Pont with the great force that they had, Him they bravely rescued. Many of their men he lost; Malet they remounted on the field on a fresh war-horse.[15]

It is said that when King Harold's body was found after the battle, the Conqueror entrusted it to William Malet for burial near the sea. It is believed that William Malet first buried King Harold in a cairn on the cliff near Hastings. When the air had settled after the battle, the body was removed and, with such honors as the period allowed, buried in Harold's own Abbey of Waltham. William Malet was made Sheriff of York, and given large grants of land in the county. Along with two others, Robert Fitz-Richard and William of Ghent, and 500 hand-picked knights, William was entrusted to care for the castle at York. In January 1069, the King sent Robert de Comines to take possession of the earldom, but his passage was via Durham and his whole force was ambushed and slain. This led to an immediate revolt in Yorkshire. The citizens of York slew Robert Fitz-Richard and many of his men. William, however, displayed superior strategic powers. He summoned the King's forces and routed the revolters. A second castle was built, which William Malet entrusted to William Fitz-Carborn, Earl of Hereford. William Malet was among the very few nobles privileged to build castles. He had permission to construct one at Eye, where he also established a market. In 1069 the Danes invaded. They sacked York. They killed and they pillaged. They broke down the Norman castles and took few prisoners, but among the fortunate few were William Malet and his wife and their two terrified children. Their captivity did not last long, for William Malet lived to fight another day. He died about 1071, during William the Conqueror's campaign against Herewaed in the marshes in the east of England. If there is such a phenomenon as the spirit of the blood it may well explain my love of England, especially the area around Yorkshire.

Unlike the Normans and the Saxons, the Aborigines were generally a peaceful and peace-loving people. The touring Aboriginal cricketers also respected authority and perhaps that is why they were so embraced by the English people in 1868. When they stood and cheered the opposition opening batsmen before the first ball of the historic Surrey match at The Oval, English cricket stood up and took notice. The English realised that this was indeed a special group of men.

Their cricket wasn't always top-notch, but individual efforts from Mullagh and Cuzens, especially, and others, including the cool, guiding hand of Lawrence, enabled the team to compete against teams which ranged in quality from ordinary to good. That they could mix it with these teams, which often included players of first-class quality, speaks volumes for their skill and their courage. It also tells us much about Lawrence's teaching skills. Perhaps too we should not ignore the early coaching of Tom Wills, whose tuition of the Aborigines in the 1866–67 period set the pattern for Lawrence to follow and to enhance. After nine matches the Australians had not fared well: they had won only one match (against Lewisham at Ladywell) and had lost six matches. The other two games had been drawn. Now this band of warriors from an ancient land a world away ventured upon the battleground that is Hastings. Lawrence withdrew from the game, due to what the scribes called a 'cut finger', apparently sustained during the MCC match at Lord's, although in fact his injury in that game was a strained muscle in his leg. Could the real reason have been that King Cole's heavy cold had developed into a more serious health threat? Lawrence was in London, by King Cole's side, in Guy's Hospital, London.

The Hastings match began on Monday, 22 June. As the first ball was being bowled, Lawrence sat on a chair by King Cole's hospital bed. (William Norton had agreed to replace Lawrence as captain.) King Cole was weak and breathing rapidly. His condition was deteriorating by the hour and the doctors feared that they would be unable to save him. His heavy cold was now diagnosed as tuberculosis, although pneumonia soon developed. Nature's cruel die had been cast. King Cole died in the early hours of Wednesday, 24 June 1868, the final scheduled day of the match at Hastings. During that long, last night, Charles Lawrence sat on a chair beside King Cole's bed and tearfully began a written tribute to the man. He wrote with a pencil on parchment. (The full text of the poem is in Chapter 6.)

Charles Lawrence returned for the eleventh match of the tour, against Halifax at Halifax. He celebrated with a first-innings haul of 6/36 with his round-armers to help Johnny Mullagh (4/20) rout Halifax for 64. Mullagh (56), Cuzens (42) and Redcap (33) all batted positively to steer the Australians to a score of 166. Then Mullagh (5/35 off 37 overs) and Lawrence (3/53) combined once again to take the lion's share of the Halifax wickets. Halifax fell for 130, and the Aborigines lost three wickets in achieving the target of 29 runs needed for outright victory. It was the second win of the tour. It was also an extremely emotional period for Lawrence and his men. The trauma of King Cole's death and subsequent funeral took its toll. (One hundred years later, in 1968, during the Second Australia–England Test at Lord's, and the occasion of the 200th Test match between the two countries, former prime minister and cricket buff extraordinare Sir Robert Menzies spoke of how illogical it was that there was an election in France during the very time a Test match was being played at Lord's. Menzies didn't mention King Cole and the first Australian cricket team. Perhaps he didn't know about them. Perhaps he did, but attached little importance to them. It was only in the previous year — 1967 — that the Aboriginal people had been given the right to vote.)

The players mourned the death of King Cole, but the caravan moved on. The side played East Lancashire at Blackburn, giving a good account of themselves, after East Lancs hit a formidable 234. Again Mullagh starred with the ball (6/84 off 42 overs). The Australians scored 144 in their first innings (Mullagh 41, Lawrence 25) and

97 in the second dig, with Bullocky scoring 24 and Lawrence 17. The match was drawn.

Against Rochdale their batting folded badly. After they dismissed the Gentlemen of Rochdale for a moderate 105 (Johnny Mullagh 7/58), Lawrence's men collapsed for 27, of which Lawrence scored 12 not out. Mullagh (4/23 off 34 overs) and Lawrence (4/40) bowled manfully to dismiss their opponents for only 91 in their second innings. However, the first innings deficit proved too much. The Aussies scored 92 in their second dig, but fell short of victory by 77 runs. Rochdale won the match, but again the Aboriginal Australians won the hearts of the crowd with their athleticism and their sense of fun.

However, one man in a straw hat may have had a different view of the visitors, for Mullagh's boomerang was on its way back to the thrower when it swooped rather crazily towards a section of the crowd, slicing a hole in the man's hat and inflicting a small cut on his forehead. Happily it was only a minor wound. Mullagh seemed capable of hat-tricks even with the boomerang. During a break in play the cricketers were paraded in front of the main pavilion, where Hamlet Nicholson, manufacturer of the famous composition cricket ball, met the players. He spoke to each man briefly, shook his hand warmly and then presented him with a composition ball. The players beamed, for it was the very brand of 'compo' ball they had used in Australia. There is no evidence that Nicholson ever used the 1868 Aborigines to promote his product. However, we do know that they all signed a ball and presented it to Nicholson after the end of the match. That signed cricket ball may still lie in a trunk or a drawer in someone's household somewhere in England. What a prized trophy that would be for Australian history.

The fourteenth match of the tour was against South Wales at Swansea. Here the Australians again proved themselves to be a strong unit when things gelled. Mullagh (6/17) and Lawrence (4/38) destroyed the South Wales batting, knocking the Welshmen over for 68. Then Johnny Cuzens flayed the South Wales attack to score a quick-fire 50. Redcap continued his recent improvement with 37 and Mullagh hit 25 in the Australians' 193. Mullagh (4/23 off 34 overs) and Lawrence (4/40) again did their double-act to dismiss

South Wales for 92. The Aboriginal team had won by an innings and 33 runs.

At Bradford the Aborigines could muster only 40 in their first innings in reply to Bradford's 154 (Cuzens 4/21 off 14 overs), but the game was salvaged into honourable draw by the batting of Mullagh (55), Twopenny (32) and Tiger (23).

Match sixteen was against the Gentlemen of Yorkshire; it was not a full-strength representative Yorkshire Eleven, but a very tough side. What Yorkshire side isn't tough? The Aboriginal team batted second and scored a meagre 92, Cuzens top-scoring with 32. Mullagh batted low in the order, at number eight, and he was stumped for just 8. Mullagh's batting so low in the list may have stemmed from a misunderstanding over the lunch arrangements on the first day, when the Aboriginal players were excluded from the lunch tent. Mullagh vowed that he would not take the field again, but he did bat in the second innings, offering little more than token resistance and walked off with a duck under his belt. Certainly without Mullagh in the attack the Yorkshire batting was allowed a certain freedom. Redcap filled the breach with a superb display of bowling, taking 7/34 off 21 overs, and Johnny Cuzens, bowling like the wind, knocked Roper's off-stump out of the ground with a trimmer of a leg-cutter. Pritchett (84) restored the innings and played the perfect sheet anchor. He was well-supported by Cookson (26) and Irvine (21). Yorkshire won by an innings and 51 runs. The *Yorkshire Gazette* reporter was none too keen on promoting the ability of the Aboriginal players.

The fielding and bowling of the Australians was only of a mediocre character, and this accounts to a considerable extent for the large score the Yorkshire Gentlemen obtained in their first innings. In the course of the play the 'darkies' missed several points, which, by the exercise of greater professional skill, they would have gained; and the byes would not have reached to so high a figure had there been an efficient long-stop at his post ... They were 109 below the Yorkshire Gentlemen as they went in for their second innings, and they were exceedingly unfortunate, gaining a score of only 58, out of which number 42 runs were obtained by Cuzens, who is the only good batter in the team, he securing several times four hits, amidst the applause of the spectators. Speaking of the Australians in general terms, it may be stated that they have much to learn ere they become good cricketers, their fielding and bowling is indifferent, their batting (with the exception of Cuzens) is devoid of science and they seldom succeed in stopping the ball when their opponents have possession of the bat ...[16]

The lunch snub brought forth a variety of sentiments in the press. The *Yorkshire Gazette* was typical:

On the first day a very disagreeable incident occurred. On luncheon being announced the Aboriginals found themselves excluded, nearly all the seats being filled. At this they took offence and left the tent, one of them [Mullagh] declaring that he would not play again. This untoward event was the cause of much criticism and many comments.[17]

The *York Herald* came out strongly on the side of fair play:

Cricket has hitherto owed much of its popularity as a national pastime to the perfect equality on which all who indulge in the game have met at the wickets, and it were a pity therefore that a breach of the good old custom should have taken place in the case of a team representing those under the same rule as ourselves at the antipodes.[18]

The Runcy Club supplied a ground staffer, William Shepherd, to accompany the Aboriginal team as occasional player and umpire. At this Yorkshire match Shepherd was standing in as team captain in the absence of Charles Lawrence. The Aboriginal players were unlucky to have Shepherd and not Lawrence to negotiate for them when they were snubbed in the lunch tent. On 25 July 1868, eleven days after the match ended, a letter to the editor appeared in the *Yorkshire Gazette*. The letter was written by William Prest, a man who batted at number 9 for Yorkshire, scoring 7 not out, and also collected two cheap wickets (Dick-a-Dick for 1 and Twopenny for 6) in the Australians' second innings of just 53. Prest wrote passionately in defence of the Yorkshire club over the lunch snub to the Australians.

Either just before, or immediately after, we commenced play, I happened to inquire as to what arrangements had been made about luncheon for the Australians, and was told that nothing special had been done, when I suggested that we ought to give them one; in which suggestion the secretary and the gentleman to whom I spoke at once concurred, and it was forthwith ordered.

I may mention that it is most unusual now to provide luncheon for professional players as they scarcely ever take any, preferring to have a tea-dinner when the game is over for the day — a biscuit or a sandwich by way of lunch satisfying all their requirements.

This is also the case with the Australians, as *before luncheon had commenced*, or I think anyone had sat down, I went with another gentleman to their dressing-room, called out Shepherd (on this occasion their captain and manager), told him luncheon was provided for his side, asked him what their custom had been in previous matches, and what they would wish to do. He said at once they much *prefer* having a sandwich and a glass of beer, as they were accustomed to do, and had arranged tea at seven p.m. as usual. He also gave us other reasons why he should himself prefer this course. We told him to do just as he liked, that he was to look after his men, see they had what they wanted, and what they had we would pay for. During lunch one or three of the Australians left the ground, went to Ferrand's House, where they were staying, and had not returned when the hour to recommence play had arrived.

I certainly did hear the reason given was, that they had not been asked to lunch, and it may be that Shepherd did not inform them of the invitation; but this is a matter between him and them — not us and them. I may, however, say that Mullagh's reason next day for absenting himself was on the score of illness.

To avoid any misunderstanding, at the end of the day's play, Mr Leonard Thompson, the chairman of the committee, formally invited the whole of the eleven to lunch with us next day, an invitation they accepted, and lunch was ordered, and, to allow more room, in one of the tents. On the Tuesday morning, to prevent any possibility of a mistake, I went with Mr Thompson to Shepherd to speak about the lunch when he informed us the Australians (though they had each individually accepted the invitation the night before) had arranged to have one by themselves in Ferrand's booth. We told him we wanted them to please themselves; that he was to see they had all they wanted and (not to be baulked of our hospitable intentions) we *would pay for it*.

To sum up, then, we had lunch provided on the first day for our opponents, and for several reasons (many of which I don't think it advisable to mention) their captain asked us not to press the invitation thereto. We specially asked them the night previous for the second day; they accepted it and didn't come, and we paid for their luncheon both days. What more could we do?

I think when the above circumstances are known, your readers will readily acknowledge that the well-earned and highly prized character for hospitality which the county has acquired has suffered no diminution of its lustre at the hands of the Yorkshire Gentlemen's Cricket Club. I am, Sir, your obedient servant. William Prest, Sheffield, 22 July 1868.[19]

The seventeenth match of the Aborigines' summer was against Longsight at Manchester. Again the Australian batting struggled, managing only 53. But the two bowling heroes Lawrence (5/49) and Mullagh (4/26) operated unchanged throughout the Longsight innings to dismiss the home side for 78. Only the wicket-keeper Ted Bousefield, with a punishing 33, took anything like a toll on the Australian bowling. The Australians fared better when they again batted, scoring 123. Lawrence top-scored with 37 and Cuzens, whose batting began to blossom, hit an adventurous 31. On the morning of the last day, the local newspaper reported the inevitability of a Longsight win:

> ... Longsight, with seven wickets to go down and several of their best players to go in, having only 30 runs to get to win, barring accidents this ought to be successfully done within an hour, in which case it is proposed to spend the rest of the afternoon in witnessing a variety of performances by the Aboriginals, illustrative of their mode of using their native weapons of war or the chase. No doubt this feature in the day's sports will prove far more interesting than their skill — no matter how creditable — in a game to the manner of which they were not born.[20]

The side then travelled to Bury where they faced the Vulcan United outfit. It was a closely contested match and, when stumps were drawn at 7 pm on 21 July, the Australians were 5/128, just 12 runs short of outright victory. They had outplayed their opponents but could not quite deliver the killer blow. The correspondent for the *Bury Times* wrote:

> ... the blacks, as they are generally termed, are on the whole a stoutly built act of men, but rather under the average stature of Englishmen. By some their play has been spoken of as a burlesque upon cricket, but it is by no means that. It is true there are one or two who are awkward in the field, but the play on Tuesday evidenced that many of them have considerably profited by their excellent captain's tuition, and we may

mention Mullagh as a remarkably fine bowler and cricketer and Cuzens and Twopenny — for they are known by some curious and amusing names — as equal to many members of provincial elevens, the former being a really clever batter and bowler.[21]

During Vulcan United's first innings of 99 Mullagh delivered 12 consecutive maiden overs in his 5/35. Mullagh was again the star all-rounder. He took a second-innings haul of 4/23 off 35 overs and hit an impressive 49 in the Aborigines' second innings of 5/128. In the first dig, Lawrence's men scored just 53, of which Twopenny hit 23. Needing 140 for victory, it was Mullagh with 49 and Lawrence with 41 who gave the team a chance. Mullagh was described as 'the best bat of the eleven, played as steady, careful and beautiful play as any cricketer need desire to see'.[22]

Mullagh was an extremely versatile cricketer. He frequently kept wicket as the substitute for Bullocky. (His bowling was not quite as slow through the air as that of J. M. Barrie, the author of *Peter Pan*. Barrie once confessed to Bill O'Reilly that his slow leg-breaks were often so slow he could either run after the ball and retrieve it a few paces down the pitch if he didn't like the ball's flight, or he could bowl it and have ample time to get down the other end and keep wicket to his own modest offerings.) Mullagh's bowling was out of the old school of round-arm merchants — fast and straight. In his follow-through Mullagh moved swiftly towards the batsman as he finished his delivery. W. G. Grace did a similar thing, trotting towards silly mid-off at the completion of a delivery. It was an intimidatory ploy by WG. Mullagh's follow-through surprised a number of quality batsmen and he often collected a scalp: caught and bowled.

But usually the danger for batsmen came with Mullagh's penchant for throwing down the wicket as the batsman began to advance down the wicket after hitting the ball. Mullagh was deadly accurate on the throw. He often ran an opponent out in this manner. There was a quizzical air of majesty and menace about Mullagh's cricket, for he played the game with an intensity which was at odds with the way his team-mates played. They played without care. They laughed and joked when running between wickets. Sometimes when a team-mate was clean-bowled a howl of delight emanated from the Australian dressing-room.

Dick-a-Dick was the ultimate showman. He used to frequent the bazaars and fairs, spending his money on seemingly useless items. He was fascinated by the magic of the fair, with its side-shows, hoop-la stalls and wheel of fortune. At every match Dick-a-Dick found himself with a bulging pocket full of shilling coins, but he squandered his small fortune at the fairs. He was neither streetwise nor particularly smart in the ways of Europeans. He could be easily conned in side-show alley, for what was cheap and nasty to others was a valued prize to Dick-a-Dick. He believed that all that glittered was pure gold and he bought some extraordinary material, including a painting of an old woman that was so lacking in class that even his team-mates rallied against him in an effort to off-load the painting and remove its ugliness from their presence. He collected an amazing array of rings, watches and other cheap jewellery. He bestowed the cheap jewels upon his fellows, but the ugly painting, created in oils and framed in oak, became a burden on the entire party. Team management hit upon an idea. They decided to raffle the oil among guests at the hotel. Tickets were set at half a crown. Dick-a-Dick took a ticket himself. He got number seven, but two other guests also got number seven, the winning number, so the raffle was thrown into chaos. The three "number sevens" decided to settle the issue with a throw of the dice. Dick-a-Dick threw a big number and was set to win his own prize, but luck came to the rescue in the form of a portly and benevolent old gentleman who offered Dick-a-Dick ten shillings for his ticket. Dick-a-Dick promptly released the ticket and the painting changed hands.

The nineteenth match of the tour was against Carrow, at the Lakenham Ground in Norwich. Mullagh and Lawrence combined to rout the home side for 82; Mullagh took 4/18 and Lawrence 4/57. The Australians then belted 235, of which Johnny Cuzens hit a brilliant 87, Mullagh 42, and Lawrence and Red Cap each 20. Batting again, Carrow fared only marginally better than they had in the first innings. Lawrence took 8/50 to rout Carrow for 101, presenting the Australians with a resounding victory by an innings and 52 runs. The *Norwich Mercury* of 29 July 1868 made the observation:

The noted Australian Eleven have been creating a little sensation in many parts of the country since their introduction here, by their play, appearance and their novel performances with some of their native weapons and implements of the chase, and the enterprising gentlemen who conceived the idea of this visit have proved that they had a tolerably shrewd appreciation of the characteristics of John Bull.[23]

Against Keighley at Yorkshire, it was Redcap, not Mullagh, who teamed with Lawrence to dismiss the opposition for a moderate 118. Redcap took 5/54 off 22 overs. Lawrence took 3/55 off 23.1 overs and Keighley scored a total of 118. The Aborigines replied with 101, with Lawrence 28, Twopenny 18 and Dick-a-Dick 18. The Keighley openers — Smith and Waring — were stunned by the enthusiasm and spontaneity of the customary Aboriginal war-cry, which 'somewhat resembled a broken English cheer'.

(In the mid-1970s I found the nearest thing to a war-cry in Sheffield Shield cricket to be the odd, albeit furious, approach to the wicket by New South Wales paceman Lennie Pascoe. When his Irish was up, Pascoe rushed in to bowl, yelling 'killer ball' and other extraordinary one-line threats.)

It was during a break in play at Keighley that Mosquito, demonstrating his skill with his stockwhip, was being heckled by a large, rotund member in the stand. The man sported a top hat above a ruddy, puffed and blotchy countenance. A huge cigar rested uneasily in the man's mouth and it jerked crazily as the man continued to hurl abuse at Mosquito. After a good five minutes of vitriol from the stand, Mosquito invited the man to hold a coin. The man scoffed, but the very hint of a loss of face obviously gave him a sort of courage. He shed his long coat but retained his top hat. He stood like a statue, the shilling held between a trembling forefinger and thumb. The cigar sat motionless between the man's fat and quivering lips. Mosquito put on his show. He bowed to the crowd, broke into a huge grin and gave the whip a crack. Then he again raised the whip and cracked it, missing the man's coin by a long chalk but not the cigar. He cut it clean in two and in so doing the tip of the whip just nicked the man's nose. The man had literally 'lost face', or, more to the point, he was skinned. The sheer justice of it tickled Mosquito's sense of fair play. The crowd, too, enjoyed a collective belly laugh.

The caravan moved on. This time the team turned out against

Bootle at Liverpool. The Australians won the match comfortably, by nine wickets. Lawrence starred with bat and ball, taking 5/62 and 5/26, plus a first-innings knock of 50 not out. Redcap took 4/37 in Bootle's first innings of 110 and Cuzens, whose recent form was outstanding, scored an unconquered 54 as the Australians powered to 1/87 and an easy win. The local press wrote in glowing terms of the visitors:

> All the Bootle men are good cricketers, and many of them old stagers in the game, but they were fairly over-matched by the Antipodeans. We were surprised to find that the majority of the Aborigines are fine, tall, well-made and not bad-looking men. Lawrence, their trainer and captain, is a finished cricketer. He is thoroughly at home in every department of the game, and the way he has coached his black friends is highly creditable to his powers as a tutor. Mullagh and Cuzens are right-hand men, and Dick-a-Dick is also improving rapidly.[24]

Dick-a-Dick, who hit 23 in the first innings and was not asked to bat in the second, spent all of his time in the field at long leg. The crowd was brought to its feet in hushed amazement as a young boy nonchalantly strolled on to the field and looked quizzically at the tall Australian. The crowd watched the boy's every move.

> Dick-a-Dick seemed much amused, and pointed out to the little man the danger he was in from the ball, but to no purpose, for his little admirer followed him from point to point, until he had thoroughly satisfied himself upon some momentous problem in Dick's economy which had evidently puzzled him; and then quietly returned to his friends.[25]

The little boy approaching Dick-a-Dick at Bootle was a magic moment. The team's Artful Dodger had powerful arms and legs and the hand-eye co-ordination of a Don Bradman. He was also a warm and caring human being. When he smiled at the little boy Dick-a-Dick won the crowd. The applause was spontaneous.

Dick-a-Dick's impressive physique did not go unnoticed either:

> Dick-a-Dick is a very powerful man. During the recess for dinner, one of the Bootle gentlemen was exhibiting his biceps, of which he was evidently proud. Dick saw and felt the muscle and said, 'Too soft — feel this', and exhibited an upper arm which we venture to say not many

English athletes can equal; it was literally as hard as a solid ball of indiarubber and of immense size.[26]

There must have been a tinge of nostalgia for Charles Lawrence when he turned out for the Australians against Nottingham Commercial Club at Trent Bridge, for this ground was the one laid out by the redoubtable William Clarke, one of Lawrence's early mentors. It was Clarke who helped Lawrence get a coaching and playing job in Ireland, and he played in that All England match at Edinburgh in 1849 when Lawrence took all 10 wickets. Some of the great names of Nottingham cricket were absent, playing for an All England Eleven, such as George Parr who scored a duck on that same day, 3 August 1868. In the second innings he also got a duck, so the seeming immortals are vulnerable after all. Tom Hayward and Richard Daft also played that day for the All England Eleven. Meanwhile, the Australians bowled manfully to dismiss the Commercial Club for just 91, Brittle top-scoring for the home side with 27. Mullagh (4/47) and Lawrence (5/37) did the bulk of the bowling toil, but soon after the side's batsmen again struggled. Australia fell for 76, Cuzens getting 43 of the runs. Then the men of Nottingham flayed the Aussies. Royal got an undefeated 100, Brittle was not so brittle with 47, and only Cuzens, among the bowlers, got cracking. He took 5/82. Nottingham scored a second innings 372 and perhaps it was as well that the side batted for such a long time, for the Australians were 4/57 in their second innings (Lawrence 28, Mullagh 18) when time ran out and they escaped with a draw.

Against Longsight at Manchester, Mullagh and Lawrence combined to take all 19 Longsight wickets to fall to a bowler. John Shawcross broke the pattern by getting himself run out for a duck in the team's first innings. Mullagh's bowling double comprised 6/18 and 2/14, while Lawrence did even better with 3/25 and 8/48. The Australians scored 75 and 151 to easily defeat Longsight who could only put together paltry totals of 47 and 74. The Australians' second innings saw Cuzens (25) and Mullagh (33) lead the way before Twopenny hit out at everything to notch 29.

The twenty-fourth match of the tour was against the Gentlemen of Sheffield at Brammall Lane, played on 10–11 August. Sheffield batted first, scoring 233, the captain, Williams, top-scoring with 54. William Prest, who defended his beloved Yorkshire in the *Yorkshire Gazette* of 25 July, hit a solid 47, and Mullagh took 6/95. The Australians replied with 185, of which Mullagh scored 55 and Twopenny 22. Rain ruined any further play, but the match belonged almost exclusively to Twopenny. Not, of course, for his score of 22, but for scoring nine runs (all run, with no overthrow) in one hit. Such a feat has not been achieved by even W. G. Grace, Don Bradman, Len Hutton or Ricky Ponting.

The cricket correspondent for the *Sheffield Independent* told his audience of Twopenny's extraordinary accomplishment:

> Twopenny made the sensational hit of the match, accomplishing a feat which has no parallel on Brammall Lane, and we should say on no other ground, and Mr Foster, who was well up, did not offer for some time to go for the ball, and when started it was at a slow pace, the result being that nine was run for the hit amidst vociferous cheering.[27]

Mullagh's knock of 55 was well-received. He was cheered all the way to the pavilion after being caught at the wicket. Mullagh stayed at the wicket for two hours, his innings a further illustration of Mullagh's consistency throughout the tour. He cut and drove with power and precision; no one doubted that Mullagh could mix it with anyone on cricket's first-class stage. The match was infamous for Tiger having a heated clash with police. Tiger batted in the coveted number three position, but he managed to score only 5 runs and he wasn't asked to bowl. After the match Tiger found himself in a nearby pub with a few of the opposition players. As the night wore on, the Sheffield players began to wander off, but Tiger stayed and stayed. At 2 am he was found to be drunk in King Street, Sheffield, by Constable Capel of the Sheffield constabulary. Constable Capel approached Tiger and advised him to go home, but the Australian resisted and the inevitable scuffle broke out. During the scuffle, Tiger 'got his head broke'. Capel used his truncheon to keep order and lay down the law in a heavy-handed way. However, Tiger fought like his namesake and Constable Capel was forced to blow on his whistle and summon help. Assistance soon arrived in the personage of Constable Bracket. The pair laid into Tiger, who knocked Bracket down in an instant and was allegedly trying to strangle him when Constable Capel brought down his truncheon a final time, knocking the Australian out. The police half-carried, half-dragged Tiger to the Sheffield Town Hall, where a doctor was called 'to dress his wounds'. Tiger was given a makeshift bed in one of the Town Hall meeting rooms and appeared before the magistrate the next morning. He was charged with assaulting Police-Constable Capel. The newspaper reported:

> Early yesterday morning Police-Constable Capel attempted to take the prisoner [Tiger] into custody for being drunk and creating a disturbance in King Street, but Tiger stoutly resisted his apprehension. Another policeman came to the assistance of Capel, but the 'black' assaulted both the officers very violently. He knocked one of them down and attempted to strangle him whilst on the ground. Eventually, and after a good deal of force on the part of the constables, he was removed to the police station. Mr Phillips asked if Tiger understood the nature of the charge. — The secretary of the cricket ground here stepped forward and … communicated with the prisoner by word, after which he informed the magistrate that Tiger had an indistinct recollection that he had knocked somebody down. The gentleman also said that he had rather a weak mind, and in the state of intoxication he would no doubt be very violent. Mr Phillips then administered to the black a severe reprimand, telling him that if he committed an offence like that again they would be compelled to send him to Wakefield, which would bring his cricketing career to an abrupt termination. However, taking into account the peculiar circumstances of the prisoner's case, and considering he was a man of weak intellect, they would not send him to prison, but would fine him 20s. and costs. The money was immediately paid. It appears Tiger occupied the post of long slip and the secretary explained that he [Tiger] had given them the slip (laughter in the court) — as they were under the belief he was at his lodgings at the time the assault was committed.[28]

Tiger's clash with the two police constables at Sheffield was one of the few player problems of the tour. A drunk and disorderly Aboriginal man in England was just the sort of 'evidence' the anti-tour brigade could hope for back home as they planned and schemed to establish the Aboriginal Protection Act. Twopenny's 'niner' and Tiger's punch-up held most interest in the wake of the match, although there were some fabulous performances in the sports events. The running high jump, clearly the most contested event on the sports program, was eventually won by Johnny Cuzens, who cleared 5 feet 8 inches, just shy of the then world record and 1 inch higher than he stood in his boots. Mullagh cleared 5 feet 6 inches, and Mosquito an inch higher. Dick-a-Dick again excelled with his dodging and he also won the long throw, throwing the cricket ball some 108 yards 2 feet 6 inches. Redcap threw 102 yards to come second and Charley Dumas threw 101 yards. Dick-a-Dick showed his amazing versatility by winning the 100 yards running backwards race, then the 150 yards steeplechase. He knocked down the first hurdle, but he ran on strongly to blitz the field, and 'won in a common canter in 19 seconds'.[29]

Peter turned on a wonderful display with the stockwhip, 'easing' the shillings from the forefingers and thumbs of willing participants from the crowd. He revealed a practised skill with the whip which rivalled the brilliance of Mosquito.

By now the tour was more than halfway along its course. George Parr himself may have been the man to consult about travel arrangements given his extensive experience in arranging the All England wandering elevens. The Australians found themselves taking train and coach for extraordinarily long distances — going from Rochdale to Swansea, then Swansea to Bradford. It is reflective of the itinerary not having been arranged at the outset of the tour. Their fixture list hung fire at first because of prejudice, not due to colour but to the sheer strangeness of the visitors. The tour management accepted invitations as they rolled in, not paying attention to the distance between each venue.

Eventually the team would play 47 matches. Lawrence's men played their 25th match of the tour against Savile at Dewsbury. This was Jim Crow's last match, before he and Sundown returned early to Australia due to ill-health. The Australians were strongly criticised by a local cricket writer, whose pen was dipped in smug superiority:

It was natural that the arrival of these sable cricketers in England should produce quite a sensation among the admirers of that skillful exercise, and anticipations were prematurely formed which have never been realized. In Australia, where the game cannot have obtained to any great extent, the performances of the present representatives in England may have been regarded as something more than ordinary, but to contest them with good English cricketers, or to place them before a discriminating public, is simply excepting for the novelty of the thing, a farce. The lookers on would watch in vain for such men as the veteran Parr, the superb Daft, the good 'all-round' Freeman, or for such a practioner at 'point' as Carpenter. We are so used to good cricket in Yorkshire that it is madness to bring before us an indifferent team, and it will never be a profitable undertaking to him who may attempt to make money out of it. These men who paid us a visit on Thursday, and will remain over this day [Saturday] are a highly colored race, but their features are in every respect distinctive from either the American or African negro. Although speaking the English language in broken accents, yet they are moderately intelligible, and converse with great cheerfulness.[30]

Savile gave Lawrence's men a right royal hiding, scoring 217, then dismissing the Australians for moderate totals of 73 and 86. Mullagh scored 48 of his team's 86 in the second innings.

Preparations got under way almost immediately the match ended for Sundown and Jim Crow to return home. Both men were physically ill and depressed. The team management were taking no chances this time, for the tragedy of King Cole's death weighed heavily on the minds of Lawrence, Hayman, Graham and Smith. Great care was made to ensure that Sundown and Jim Crow returned on the *Parramatta*, once again under the care of Captain John Williams. The *Parramatta* set sail from Plymouth at 10 pm on 5 September. They sailed late on the second day of the team's 32nd match, against Lincoln on Nettleton Road Field, Lincoln.

A ship's passenger, Duncan Brown, created an illustrated journal of the voyage, but, like the Reverend Henry Nisbett, Brown makes no reference to an Aboriginal person on board ship. There is also no reference to either Sundown or Jim Crow in the passenger list. They must have been listed among the '10 second-class or 10 third-class passengers'.

The *Parramatta* arrived in Sydney on 24 November 1868. It was hot. Brown wrote that he could hear the locusts from the anchorage. Sundown and Jim Crow also heard the locusts. They were home; they could not wait to touch and caress the precious earth. The two Aboriginal cricketers left England without so much as a word in the

Sketch of the *Parramatta* from Duncan Brown's journal.

SHIPPING.

ARRIVALS—NOVEMBER 24.

Parramatta, ship, 1521 tons, Captain Williams, from Plymouth 5th September. Passengers—Judge Owen, Mrs. Thomas Holt, Miss Holt, 3 children, 2 governesses, and 1 servant, Mrs. Christopher Rollecton and child, Mrs. Adam and servant, Miss Fisher, Miss Robinson, Miss Hargrave, Miss Shephard, Mr. and Mrs. B. Palmer, 4 children, and servant, Miss Palmer, Mrs. and Miss Conelly, Mr. J. W. Abbot and son, Mrs. M'Vitie, Mr. and Mrs. Dickens, and 5 children, Mrs. John Williams (3), and Master Williams, Messrs. A. . Tooth, Duncan Brown, A. J. Waring, and H. C. Spackman, Master Gough, 10 second cabin, and 10 third-class passengers. Gilchrist, Watt, and Co, agents.

THE PARRAMATTA.—Captain Williams and his fine vessel have again arrived safely in port, bringing a full complement of passengers, including many old residents of the colony, after a most prosperous passage of 79 days. The trip throughout has been pleasant in the extreme, fine weather, as a rule, having been experienced; and her passengers are unanimous in expressing their appreciation of the kidness and forethought that has been bestowed on them during the voyage, Captain Williams relates of his passage as follows:—The pilot left the ship off Plymouth on 5th September, at 10 p.m.; sighted Madeha September 15th; on October 4th, was in latitude 0-4 8., longitude 24-30 W.; on 25th October, the ship's position was latitude 45-8., longitude 23. E; November 12th, she was in latitude 43-8; longitude 117-35 E.; November 19th, in latitude 44-8., longitude 150-25 E; November 22nd in latitude 35-24 S., longitude 152-52 E., and yesterday, at 9 a.m., got sight of the South Head lighthouse. The topsails were never reefed until she reached the meridian of St. Paul's and Amsterdam. Unsettled weather, with low barometer, prevailed all the way from the meridian of Cape Leuwin to latitude 36-8., and longitude 153 E. The ship passed south of Tasmania November 17th, exchanged signals with the brig Princess Alice, bound to the westward. This is the only vessel met with connected with the colony. This ship has on board two very superior merino rams for sale.

Notice in the *Sydney Morning Herald* of 25 November 1868 heralding the arrival of the *Parramatta*. Two members of the 1868 team — Jim Crow and Sundown — sailed home early on this ship, as a result of illness.

English press. And so they arrived in Sydney, unannounced, unsung, back to the stark reality of being virtual prisoners in their own land. Within a few months the *Aboriginal Protection Act 1869* would come into force. The Act effectively determined where an Aboriginal person could live. It allocated funds granted by Parliament and was paternalist as well as protective. The Act was a disaster for the Aboriginal people, for they were often forced off their traditional lands and placed in reserves. For a people who had much strong emotional and physical ties to the land, the removal from the land of their birth was devastating.

Jim Crow and Sundown seemed to have coped with the tour remarkably well, although after King Cole's illness and subsequent death they both suffered fits of depression. The decision to send them home with the caring and benevolent Captain Williams aboard the familiar *Parramatta* was a sensible decision by the team management. Although there is no definitive entry in the Graham 1868 tour ledger which deals directly with fares for Sundown and Jim Crow on the *Parramatta*, there is an amount for £22.7.6 listed in the expenses for the match against Savile at Dewsbury. This was Jim Crow's last match. He batted last and got a duck and did not get a bowl.

Sundown and Jim Crow trusted Captain Williams. Their trip from Plymouth to Sydney, which took 79 days, was generally plain sailing, with good weather and fair seas. Seven days out from Sydney, the *Parramatta* exchanged signals with the brig *Princess Alice* as they passed in opposite directions to the south of Tasmania. Captain Williams noted that the *Princess Alice* was the only vessel with a connection to the colony that they had met during the entire voyage.

Back in England, the Australians beat Tynemouth at North Shields by two wickets and drew with Northumberland at Newcastle. Johnny Cuzens was really starting to come into his own as a genuine all-rounder. He hit 59 against Tynemouth and combined with Lawrence to dismiss Northumberland for 162, Cuzens getting 4/28 off 22 overs and Lawrence taking 5/89 off a marathon 36 overs. Cuzens was a remarkable athlete. He topped 1000 runs and 100 wickets for the tour and he seemed to be getting better as the tour wore on. Cuzens was the team's most brilliant sprinter, but he always ran barefooted. William Shepherd thought that a special pair of

The Aboriginal team of 1866 under the captaincy of Tom Wills formed the nucleus of the side that toured England in 1868. Back row (standing, left to right): Tarpot, Tom Wills, Mullagh. Front row (left to right): King Cole (with leg on chair), Dick-a-Dick, Jellico, Peter, Redcap, Harry Rose, Bullocky, Cuzens. (Tarpot, Wills, Jellico and Harry Rose did not tour England in 1868.) (Original photograph — National Library of Australia)

The celebrated All England XI, 1847: Joseph Guy, George Parr, William Martingwell, Alfred Mynn, William Denison (the first eminent cricket reporter), James Dean, William Clarke, Felix, Oliver Pell, William Hillyer, William Lilywhite, William Dorrington, Fuller Pilch, Thomas Sewell. Lawrence took all 10 wickets against Clarke's All England Eleven when he played for Scotland in Edinburgh in 1849. (A painting by Felix, 1847)

Under Noble and Distinguished Patronage.

ENCAMPMENT
OF THE
Ioway Indians!
AT
LORD'S CRICKET GROUND,
St. John's Wood Road,
FOR ONE WEEK ONLY.

FIRST TIME IN EUROPE.
Indian Archery Fete & Festival!

Twenty-six Thousand Persons crossed the River from the city of New York to Hoboken, in one Day, to witness the Ball-Play and other Amusements of the Ioway Indians.—*NEW YORK HERALD.*

The celebrated party of IOWAY INDIANS, amounting to Fourteen persons, including the principal chiefs, "Braves" or Warriors, and the Great "Mystery" or "Medicine Man" of the Tribe, with their "Squaws," their Children, and a "Papoose" (or infant), who have been brought to this country at an enormous expense, and who lately arrived from New York,

WILL, ON MONDAY AUGUST the 26th, AND FIVE FOLLOWING DAYS,
BE ENCAMPED
AT LORD'S CRICKET GROUND,

when they will display their skill in shooting with Bows and Arrows, in a grand archery *fete*; also will give their extraordinary and amusing Ball-play; and exhibit several of their peculiar and characteristic Dances, the programme of which is subjoined.

The Editors of the public press (whose opinions are quoted on the other side) have universally pronounced the IOWAY INDIANS to be the finest specimens of the "Red Men," the denizens of the forest and lake, ever seen in England. The party are thus described :—

THE DELEGATION.
CHIEFS.
MEW-HU-SHE-KAW—(White Cloud) first Chief of the Nation.
NEU-MON-YA—(Walking Rain) third Chief.
SE-NON-TY-YAH—(Blister Feet) great Medicine Man.

WA-TA-WE-BU-KA-NA—(Commanding-General). The Son of
        Walking Rain, 10 years old.
JEFFREY—(The Interpreter).

WARRIORS AND BRAVES.
WASH-KA-MON-YA—(Fast Dancer).
NO-HO-MUN-YA—(One who gives no attention).
SHON-TA-YI-GA—(Little Wolf).
WA-TA-WEN—(One always foremost).

SQUAWS.
RUTON-YE-WE-MA—(Strutting Pigeon) White Cloud's wife.
RUTON-WE-ME—(Pigeon on the Wing).
OKE-WE-ME—(Female Bear that Walks on the back of another).
KOOS-ZA-YA-ME—(Female War Eagle sailing).
TA-PA-TA-ME—(Sophia) Wisdom ; White Cloud's daughter.
CORSAIR—(A Papoose).

This, it should be remembered, is the first time that ever a party of Indians have appeared encamped in an open plain in Europe ; they will appear in their tents as in their native village, and will enable the public to form a correct idea of their peculiar habits, manners, and customs : exhibiting a perfect representation of Indian forest life, and will form a most romantic and beautiful scene.

[TURN OVER.

Advertisement that appeared in *The Times*, London in 1844. A tribe of Ioway Indians camped at Lord's Cricket Ground. They displayed their lifestyle, complete with pitched wigwams, their hunting and cooking skills and generally enthralled the English people.

Part of Duncan Brown's diary. Brown wrote of and sketched life aboard the *Parramatta* enroute from England to Australia in 1868. Aboard were two of the Aboriginal cricketers — Jim Crow and Sundown — who returned to Australia a few months before the main party due to illness. (Duncan Brown Diary, courtesy of Elizabeth Dunbar-Naismith).

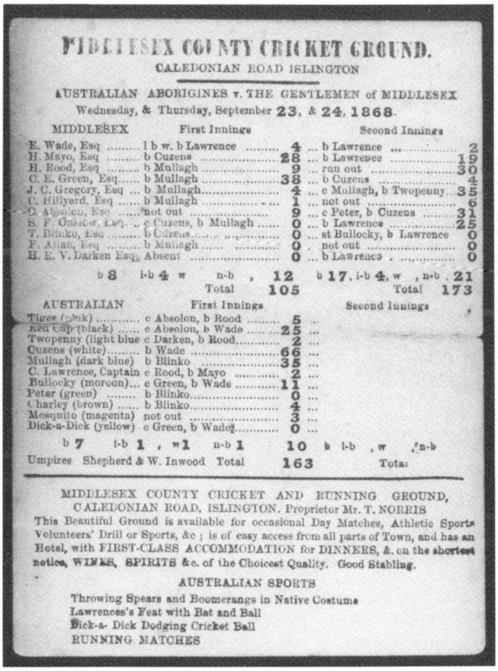

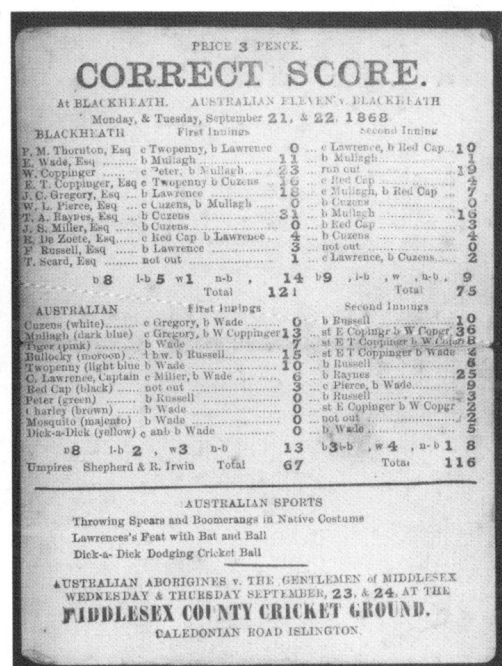

MIDDLESEX COUNTY CRICKET GROUND.
CALEDONIAN ROAD ISLINGTON

AUSTRALIAN ABORIGINES v. THE GENTLEMEN of MIDDLESEX
Wednesday, & Thursday, September **23, & 24, 1868.**

MIDDLESEX	First Innings		Second Innings	
E. Wade, Esq	l b w, b Lawrence	4	b Lawrence	—
H. Mayo, Esq	b Cuzens	28	b Lawrence	19
H. Rood, Esq	b Mullagh	9	run out	30
C. E. Green, Esq	b Mullagh	38	b Cuzens	4
J. C. Gregory, Esq	b Mullagh	4	c Mullagh, b Twopenny	35
C. Hillyard, Esq	b Mullagh	1	not out	6
G. Absolom, Esq	not out	9	c Peter, b Cuzens	31
S. F. Onslow, Esq	c Cuzens, b Mullagh	0	b Lawrence	25
F. Blinko, Esq	b Cuzens	0	st Bullocky, b Lawrence	0
F. Ainse, Esq	b Mullagh	0	not out	0
H. L. V. Darken Esq	Absent	0	b Lawrence	0
	b 8 l-b 4 w n-b	12	b 17, l-b 4 w , n-b	21
	Total	105	Total	173

AUSTRALIAN	First Innings		Second Innings
Tiger (pink)	c Absolon, b Rood	5	
Red Cap (black)	c Absolon, b Rood	25	
Twopenny (light blue	c Darken, b Rood	2	
Cuzens (white)	b Wade	66	
Mullagh (dark blue)	b Blinko	35	
C. Lawrence, Captain	c Rood, b Mayo	2	
Bullocky (moroon)	c Green, b Wade	11	
Peter (green)	b Blinko	0	
Charley (brown)	b Blinko	4	
Mosquito (magenta)	not out	3	
Dick-a-Dick (yellow)	c Green, b Wade	0	
	b 7 l-b 1 , w 1 n-b 1	10	b l-b , w , n-b
Umpires Shepherd & W. Inwood	Total	163	Total:

MIDDLESEX COUNTY CRICKET AND RUNNING GROUND, CALEDONIAN ROAD, ISLINGTON. Proprietor Mr. T. NORRIS
This Beautiful Ground is available for occasional Day Matches, Athletic Sports, Volunteers' Drill or Sports, &c ; is of easy access from all parts of Town, and has an Hotel, with FIRST-CLASS ACCOMMODATION for DINNERS, &. on the shortest notice, WINES, SPIRITS &. of the Choicest Quality. Good Stabling.

AUSTRALIAN SPORTS
Throwing Spears and Boomerangs in Native Costume
Lawrences's Feat with Bat and Ball
Dick-a-Dick Dodging Cricket Ball
RUNNING MATCHES

PRICE 3 PENCE.
CORRECT SCORE.
At BLACKHEATH. AUSTRALIAN ELEVEN v. BLACKHEATH
Monday, & Tuesday, September **21, & 22, 1868.**

BLACKHEATH	First Innings		Second Inning	
P. M. Thornton, Esq	c Twopenny, b Lawrence	0	c Lawrence, b Red Cap	10
E. Wade, Esq	b Mullagh	11	b Mullagh	0
W. Coppinger	c Peter, b Mullagh	23	run out	19
E. T. Coppinger, Esq	c Twopenny b Cuzens	19	c Red Cap	0
J. C. Gregory, Esq	b Lawrence	18	c Mullagh, b Red Cap	7
W. L. Pierce, Esq	c Cuzens, b Mullagh	0	c Cuzens	0
T. A. Raynes, Esq	b Cuzens	31	b Mullagh	19
J. S. Miller, Esq	b Cuzens	0	b Red Cap	3
R. De Zoete, Esq	c Red Cap b Lawrence	4	b Cuzens	3
F. Russell, Esq	b Lawrence	3	not out	2
T. Scard, Esq	not out	1	c Lawrence, b Cuzens	0
	b 8 l-b 5 w1 n-b	14	b 9 , l-b , w , n-b	9
	Total	121	Total	75

AUSTRALIAN	First Innings		Second Innings	
Cuzens (white)	c Gregory, b Wade	0	b Russell	10
Mullagh (dark blue)	c Gregory, b W Coppinger	13	st E Coppinger b W Copger	36
Tiger (pink)	b Wade	7	st E T Coppinger b W Copger	8
Bullocky (moroon)	l b w. b Russell	15	st E T Coppinger b Wade	4
Twopenny (light blue	b Wade	10	b Russell	6
C. Lawrence, Captain	c Miller, b Wade	0	b Raynes	25
Red Cap (black)	not out	3	c Pierce, b Wade	9
Peter (green)	b Russell	0	b Russell	0
Charley (brown)	b Wade	0	st E Coppinger b W Copger	2
Mosquito (majento)	b Wade	0	not out	2
Dick-a-Dick (yellow)	c & mb b Wade	0	b Wade	0
	b 8 l-b 2 , w3 n-b	13	b 3 l-b , w 4 , n-b 1	8
Umpires Shepherd & R. Irwin	Total	67	Total	116

AUSTRALIAN SPORTS
Throwing Spears and Boomerangs in Native Costume
Lawrences's Feat with Bat and Ball
Dick-a-Dick Dodging Cricket Ball

AUSTRALIAN ABORIGINES v. THE GENTLEMEN of MIDDLESEX
WEDNESDAY & THURSDAY SEPTEMBER, **23, & 24,** AT THE
MIDDLESEX COUNTY CRICKET GROUND.
CALEDONIAN ROAD ISLINGTON.

Scorecard: Australian Aborigines versus The Gentlemen of Middlesex, Islington, 23 and 24 September 1868. (MCC Museum, Lord's)

Scorecard: Australian Eleven versus Black-heath, 21 and 22 September 1868. (MCC Museum, Lord's)

Dignified band of Victorian Aboriginal people, photographed by A. J. Fauchery in 1858. (Museum Victoria)

ARRIVAL OF THE BLACK CRICKETERS.

Since the late ingenious George Martin brought Deerfoot from America to contend against English pedestrians no arrival has been anticipated with so much curiosity and interest as that of the Black Cricketers from Australia. It has been already stated that the team had sailed from Sydney in the Paramatta, and that they were expected to reach our shores in May. We have now to record the fact that they landed at Gravesend last Wednesday, and on the following day exhibited their cricket prowess at Town Malling, in Kent, in the presence, among others, of Mr. W. S. Norton, the honorary secretary of the Kent County Club, and we hear that they gave great satisfaction to a critical *coterie* of spectators. They are thirteen in number, and are captained by Charles Lawrence, late of the All-England Eleven, who has been for some time at the antipodes. We append their native names, and opposite is given their *soubriquets*, under which they will doubtless be known here :—

Jungunjinanuke	Dick-a-Dick
Arrahmunijarrimun	Peter
Unaarrimin	Mullagh
Zellanach	Cuzens
Ballrinjarrimin	Sundown
Brippokei	King Cole
Bonnbarngeet	Tiger
Brimbunyah	Red Cap
Bullchanach	Bullocky
Grougarrong	Mosquito
Jallachmurrimin	Jim Crow
Murrumgunarriman	Twopenny
Pripumuarraman	Charley Dumas

They are the first Australian natives who have visited this country on such a novel expedition, but it must not be inferred that they are savages on the contrary, the managers of the speculation make no pretence to anything other than purity of race and origin. They are perfectly civilised, having been brought up in the bush to agricultural pursuits as assistants to Europeans, and the only language of which they have a perfect knowledge is English. Monday in the Derby week (May 25) is to witness their *début* in London, arrangements having been made for them to play their first match against Eleven Gentlemen of the Surrey Club, at the Oval, on May 25 and 26; and on the Thursday after the Derby they will go through a series of athletic exercises on the Surrey ground. The following gentlemen of the Surrey Club have been selected to play against the Blacks in their first match :—

I. D. Walker	W. L. Holt	C. Noble
R. Baggallay	R. Boultbee	W. Hibberd
G. M. Kelson	R. Burton	— Waitson
R. Troughton	H. Jupp	

In addition, the Blacks are engaged to play Eleven Gentlemen of Kent, at Gravesend, on Whit Monday, Tuesday, and Wednesday, the following being the Kent names selected :—

W. S. Norton	C. B. Griffith	E. A. White
M. A. Troughton	W. Lindsay	F. Ray
G. M. Kelson	R. Lipscomb	Captain Boycott
P. Hilton	R. B. Cooper	

Matches have also been arranged to take place at Nottingham, Sheffield, Manchester, Bradford, Halifax, Dewsbury, Portsmouth, and Hastings. With respect to their prowess as cricketers—that will be conclusively determined by their first public match. We hear, however, that Cuzens and Mullagh show considerable talent and precision in bowling, but, to use a homely phrase—the proof of the pudding will be in the eating.

Press report of the arrival of the Aboriginal cricket team of England in May 1868. (*Sporting Life*, London, 16 May 1868)

'Found, Mr Duncan, Roderick, Bella and David', c 1876 by William Struitt (1825–1915), pencil and wash drawing, National Library of Australia. The drawing accompanies the fictional account of the real saga of the missing Duff children in the Wimmera in 1864. Dick-a-Dick and Redcap were the black trackers who saved the children. (National Library of Australia)

This is how the 1868 team would have seen the entrance to The Oval when they played Surrey in the first match of their tour.

Charles Lawrence bowling. (Charles Lawrence Collection)

Dick-a-Dick's leangle or killer boomerang. Note the honeycombed markings on top of the handle. They trace Dick-a-Dick's life, his home, his village, his dreaming. (MCC Museum)

John McGuire, who led the 1988 re-enactment of the first tour of England, with Ashley Mallett and Charles Lawrence's great grandson Ian Friend at the MCG in 2000. Mallett is holding the bat Lawrence used on the 1868 tour of England. (Photograph Jenni Meany. James McCaughey Collection)

The fully-rigged wool-clipper, *Parramatta*, aboard which the 1868 team sailed to England. Sporting a painted hull of black (mostly) and gold, the *Parramatta*, laden with a cargo of wool, completed the trip from London to Sydney in just 79 days. (Mitchell Library, State Library of NSW)

Charles Dickens' fictional cricket match between Dingley Dell and All Muggleton is illustrated on the reverse of the current English ten-pound note.

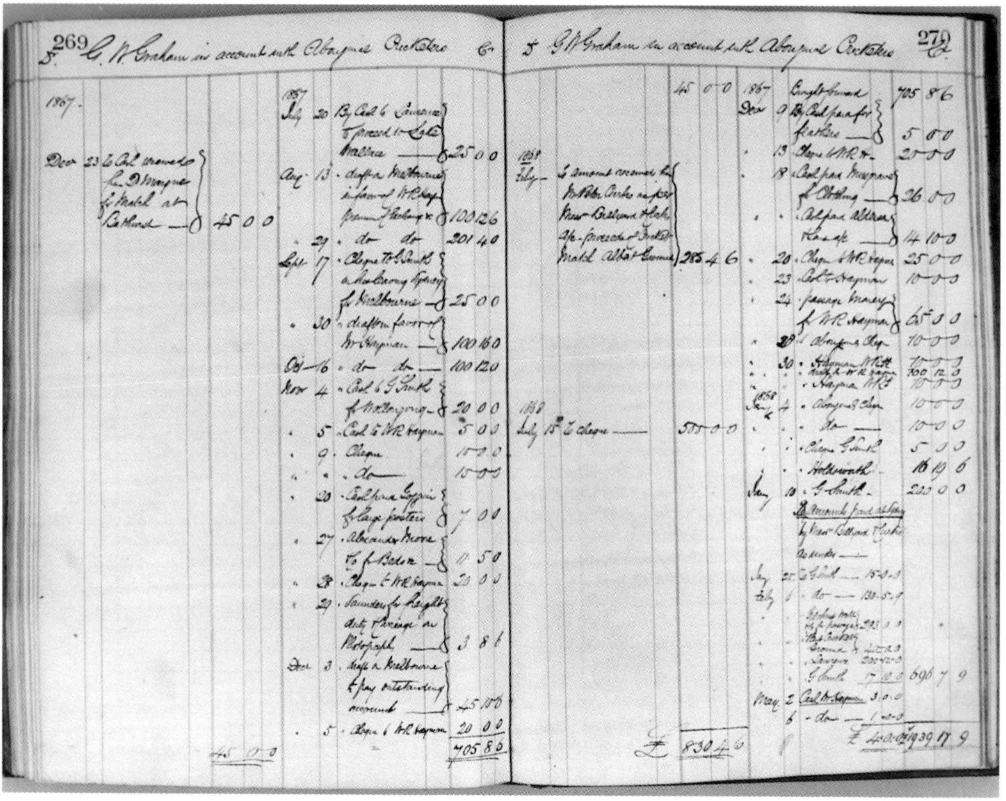

269 Dr G. W. Graham in account with Aboriginal Cricketers Cr

Dr G. W. Graham in account with Aboriginal Cricketers 270 Cr

705 8 6

£ 830 4 6

£ 1939 17 9

Two pages from the Graham Ledger. They are an 'official' record of takings and expenditure on the 1868 tour. (Melbourne Cricket Club Museum)

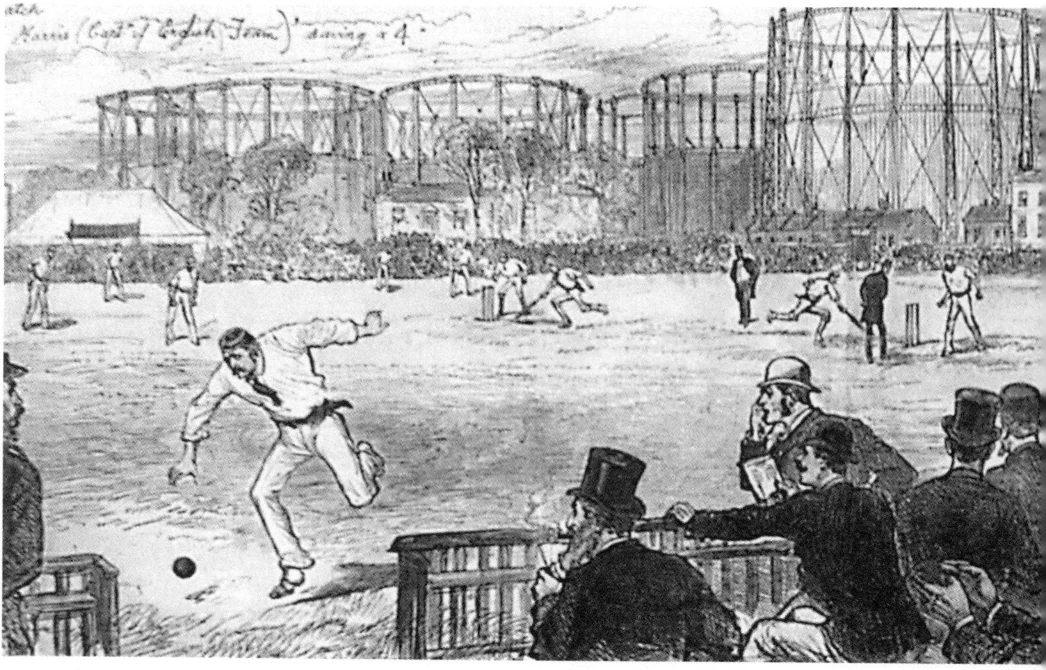

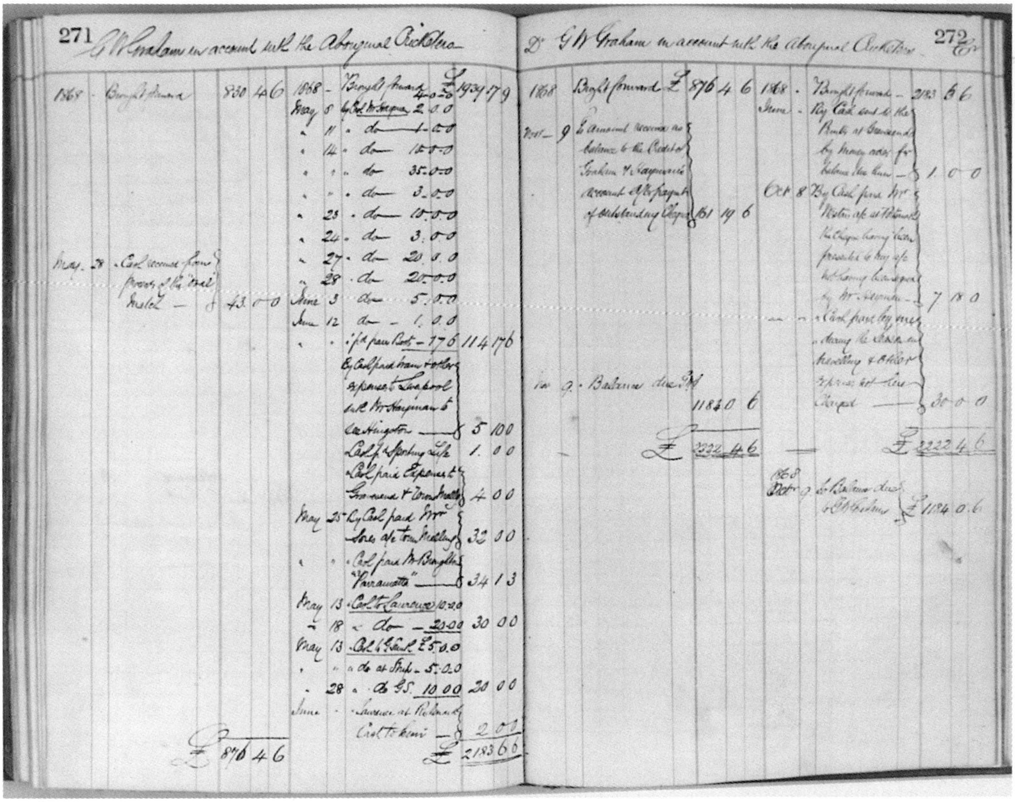

Famous painting of The Oval, c 1880.
The ground in 1868 would look much
like the one depicted here.

Searching for 1868 originals

Sir, I am researching the 1868 Australia tour of England. This team, captained by Charles Lawrence, once of Surrey, comprised mainly Australian Aboriginals from the western district of Victoria.

In 1930 a chap approached Clarrie Grimmett and gave him a photo of the 1868 Aussies, an image until then thought to be lost. Then in 1966 (or thereabouts) a fellow turned up at Bill O'Reilly's favourite pub in Blakehurst (New South Wales) and plonked the 1868 ledger on the bar. He said to Bill, Australia and the world's greatest leg spin bowler, "You'll know what to do with this..."

These are two examples. Could there be other jewels in the crown? I ask your readers and lovers of cricket to search their attics for Great-Grandad's effects and see if they have a photo, artefact or important document relating to this tour. I have been involved in a documentary film about the tour and am working on a book on the subject. Some of your readers may know me as an Australia Test cricketer touring England in 1968, 1972, 1975 and 1980.

Yours,
ASHLEY MALLETT,
PO Box 66, Angaston,
South Australia 5353.

Left: Charles Lawrence, as he looked in 1861–62, as a member of H. H. Stephenson's first England tour of Australia. (Melbourne Cricket Club archives)

Above: Twopenny: warrior fast bowler and big hitter. (Taken from the composite team picture by P. Dawson of Hamilton, Melbourne Cricket Club Archives).

Above right: Rear Admiral David Dunbar-Naismith discovered Duncan Brown's diary of his voyage on the *Parramatta* (Elizabeth Dunbar-Naismith Collection)

Left: Author's Letter to the Editor of *The Times*, London, published on 12 May 2000.

At LORD'S, June 22 and 23, 1840.

SLOW BOWLERS.	1st Inn.	2nd Inn.
W. Lillywhite, b Redgate	1	c Taylor, b Redgate 13
J. Cobbett, c Kynaston, b Mynn	0	run out 9
N. Felix, Esq., c Redgate, b Dean	35	c Hawkins, b Mynn 27
F. Pilch, b Redgate	0	b Redgate 8
T. Box, b Mynn	11	run out 0
W. Clifford, b Redgate	19	b Mynn 5
W. Garrat, b Mynn	15	b Mynn 15
T. Sewell, c Mynn, b Dean	6	b Redgate 12
J. Bayley, b Mynn	0	not out 5
B. Good, not out	5	c Kynaston, b Redgate 5
Earl of Winterton, b Dean	1	b Mynn 0
Byes 14, wide 1, noes 1	16	Byes 15, wides 2... 17
	109	116

FAST BOWLERS.	1st Inn.	2nd Inn.
W. Hillyer, b Cobbett	5	b Cobbett 9
C. Hawkins, b Cobbett	20	b Cobbett 28
C. G. Taylor, Esq., c Lillywhite, b Cobbett	1	b Lillywhite 26
A. Mynn, Esq., c Cobbett, b Lillywhite	2	c Cobbett, b Lillywhite 11
J. Guy, b Cobbett	13	run out 7
H. Hand, Esq., b Cobbett	0	b Lillywhite 0
Hon. F. Ponsonby, not out	17	b Lillywhite 3
R. Kynaston, Esq., b Cobbett	5	b Lillywhite 26
J. Dean, c Felix, b Cobbett	2	not out 4
S. Redgate, b Cobbett	0	b Cobbett 5
Hon. Colonel Lowther, b Lillywhite	0	b Cobbett 0
Byes 5, wides 0	5	Byes 3, wides 0 ... 3
	70	122

The Slow Bowlers winning by 33 runs.

The scorecard of the match that 11-year-old Charles Lawrence watched at Lord's, when his hero Fuller Pilch was out first ball. (Frederick Lillywhite, *Cricket Scores and Biographies of Celebrated Cricketers from 1827–1840*, Vol. 11)

The team about to take to the field at Trent Bridge, Nottingham, August 1868. Standing (left to right): Dick-a-Dick, Tiger, Mullagh, Lawrence, Cuzens, Redcap, Bullocky, Twopenny. Seated (left to right): Mosquito, Peter, William Shepherd, Charley Dumas.

England's first overseas tour was in 1859 to North America. Pictured are John Wisden on the kitchen chair, John Jackson on the bench, Alfred Driver and John Lillywhite in front, and, standing, Robert Carpenter, William Caffyn, Tom Lockyer, H. H. Stephenson (crouching), George Parr, James Grundy, Julius Caesar and Tom Hayward. Caffyn toured Australia and stayed to coach in Sydney. He played against the 1868 team in Sydney. Julius Caesar umpired a number of the 1868 Aboriginal tour matches in England.

Members of the 1988 Aboriginal Australian cricket tour of England, a re-enactment of the 1868 tour. From left: Sean Appo, captain John McGuire, and team manager Mark Ella.

Fuller Pilch, England's batting hero of the 1820s and 1830s. (Lithograph by G. F. Watts)

AUSTRALIAN AND ENGLISH SPORTS

On the Trent Bridge Ground,

NOTTINGHAM,

ON WEDNESDAY, AUG. 5, 1868.

OPEN TO AMATEURS ONLY.

Judge, Mr. J. Billyeald.　　Starter, Mr. C. F. Daft.

	Value of Prize.
1. One hundred yards' Flat Race -	£1
2. Running High Jump -	10s.
3. Standing High Jump -	10s.
4. One hundred & fifty yards' Hurdle Race,	£1
5. Vaulting with Poles -	£1
6. Throwing the Cricket Ball -	New Ball
7. One hundred yards backwards -	10s.
8. Water Bucket Race -	10s. & 5s.
9. Throwing the Boomerangs and Spears, and Kangaroo Rats, by the Blacks.	
10. Lawrence's Feat with Bat and Ball.	
11. Dick-a-Dick Dodging the Cricket Ball.	

Entrance for the first eight events, ONE SHILLING each; to be made to Mr. C. F. Daft, Hon. Secretary, Angel Row, Nottingham, up to Six p.m. on the 4th of August.

The celebrated SAX TUBA BAND will be in attendance, and play a variety of popular Music.

George Richards, Printer, Greyhound Street, Nottingham.

Press advertisement to attract the Nottingham people to watch the Aboriginal cricketers run, jump, dodge and throw the spear and boomerang, 5 August 1868.

Johnny Mullagh: Aboriginal batting hero who became a legend in the Harrow area of Victoria.

The famous Bat & Ball Inn, Hambledon, where the cricketers found that foaming tankards of beer after a hard day's play were just the ticket.

The Players versus The Gentlemen annual cricket match at Lord's, c 1850. (MCC Museum, Lord's)

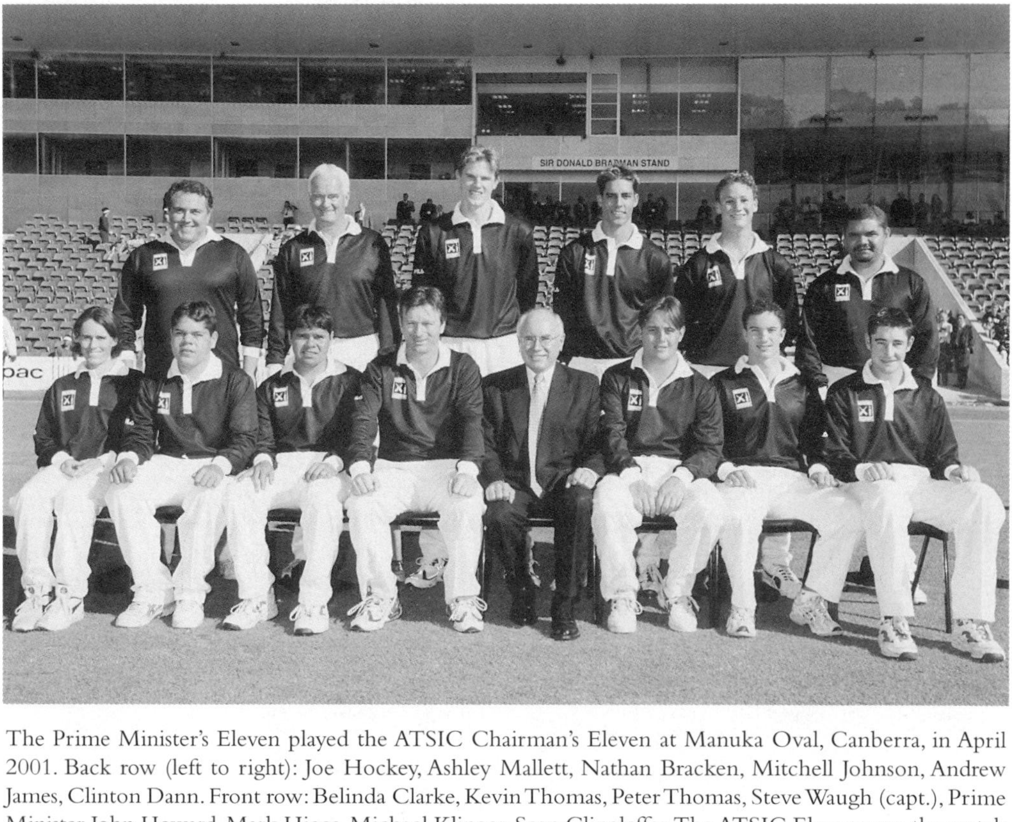

The Prime Minister's Eleven played the ATSIC Chairman's Eleven at Manuka Oval, Canberra, in April 2001. Back row (left to right): Joe Hockey, Ashley Mallett, Nathan Bracken, Mitchell Johnson, Andrew James, Clinton Dann. Front row: Belinda Clarke, Kevin Thomas, Peter Thomas, Steve Waugh (capt.), Prime Minister John Howard, Mark Higgs, Michael Klinger, Sean Clingleffer. The ATSIC Eleven won the match to notch the Johnny Mullagh Memorial Trophy. (Prime Minister's Department, Canberra)

One of the greatest Aboriginal fast bowlers of them all, Queensland speedster of the 1930s, Eddie Gilbert, the only bowler to knock the bat out of Don Bradman's hands. He also dismissed Bradman, that day at the Gabba in 1931, for a duck. (Pat Mullins Collection)

A composite photograph of the 1868 Australian Aboriginal Cricketers.

running shoes might provide Cuzens with even more speed. He bought him a pair and presented them to him in Sheffield. The Graham Ledger records 'expenses included "boy 5/-" and "spikes and cap 1/1/-" ', a clear indication that the shoes Shepherd bought for Cuzens did not come out of Shepherd's own pocket. Cuzens' shoes were not tested until the third day of the last match of the tour at The Oval.

A drawn match at Middlesborough was followed by further drawn games against Scarborough at Castle Hill and Hunslet at Hunslet. Mullagh again did the heavy track work and continued to get among the wickets.

In the 31st match of the tour South Derbyshire beat the Australians, with James Smith hitting 57 for Derbyshire, then taking 6/28 and 6/16 with his swift round-arm deliveries. Dick-a-Dick had a terrible match with the bat, bagging a pair. Then he suffered the first, and only, blow to his body during his dodging exhibition. Samuel Richardson, who became Derbyshire County Captain from 1871 to 1875, miraculously got a ball past Dick-a-Dick's guard. The Australian suffered more from loss of face than from the agony of the blow, for the ball just brushed his left shoulder. However, a hit was claimed and Dick-a-Dick, for a change, had to part with some of his loot.

Richardson was assistant County Secretary for Derby until 1890, the year he took flight with 1000 pounds stolen from the county coffers. Richardson's deceit was discovered by none other than Frederick Spofforth, the great Australian fast bowler, the man who claimed 14 wickets at The Oval in 1882 to start The Ashes legend. Spofforth identified Richardson as the culprit, but Richardson had long gone, fleeing England and finding refuge in Spain, where he became the official court tailor to King Alfonso. As for the Derby match, it was played out near the shadow of the Derby church with the crooked spire. Legend has it that the spire will only straighten when a virgin walks the inner stairway. Derby was Frederick Spofforth's last hurrah in cricket; he played there in 1890 and 1891, although his final first-class match was for the MCC at Scarborough in 1897. Known as 'The Demon', Spofforth was the first of the great fast bowlers. He was more than a tearaway quick: Spofforth has the artifices of change of pace and spin that one normally associates with the great spinners.

The Graham ledger records the notation 'Dick dodging 10/-'. Could this have been Dick-a-Dick's pay-out to Samuel Richardson? Perhaps Dick-a-Dick was so confident by September that he was offering 10–1 odds.

Against Lincoln at Lincoln, the Australians' batting again disappointed. After a first-innings score of 78, of which Lawrence hit 37, the Aborigines were set 66 to win, thanks to good all-round bowling from Mullagh 6/23 (off 22 overs) and 5/42 (off 41 overs), Lawrence 4/20 (off 23 overs) and Cuzens (4/30 off 33 overs). However, the batting collapsed again and the team was all out for 56, Twopenny top-scoring with a slogging 15. During the after-cricket sports, Dick-a-Dick managed to get more than his share of fun with a bunch of cricket-ball throwers.

Four or five cricketers (including Nicholls and Dale) did their best to throw the balls at the darkie, and one of the spectators, glorying in the name of 'Tommy' seemed confident of his own prowess, but Dick-a-Dick was 'one too many' for them all, and he merrily grinned at and defied them as the balls whizzed past him or were guarded off by the narrow shield which he held in his hand.[31]

Billed as the 'grand match between Burton & the black Australians', the local cricket correspondent wrote:

Never before was there such a concourse of people on the Burton Ground as on Monday and Tuesday, to witness our eleven play the Darkies, and a great success the match was in every way; had the match been closer everything would have been excellent, but the Darkies never let Burton get near them in either innings. They are, and may well be proud of their victory, as they defeated a very strong batting eleven. Monday's dawn betokened a beautiful cricket day and so it proved; the company was however not so great on this day as was anticipated.[32]

As beer and pubs were synonymous with cricket then and have traditional and commercial links today, Redcap's dismissal, 'caught Worthington, bowled Bass', in the Australian second innings, provides us with a sobering little aside. Bass took 5/46. Lawrence's men won the match, the 33rd of the tour, by 69 runs — a resounding victory.

Lawrence took 5/29 and 7/47, Cuzens took 4/28 and Mullagh top-scored with 42. Mullagh kept wicket for much of the time. He revealed his great versatility by stumping four batsmen and catching two behind.

The Australians demolished Bootle, near Liverpool, in what became the 34th tour match. Mullagh had a bumper game hitting 51 and 78, then taking 7/32 and 4/17 to virtually play a lone hand in the victory, which was by 154 runs.

While Mullagh's cricket skills gave him genuine star status, his efforts in the after-match sports were a concern, for when Mullagh threw his boomerang, it did not come back. In fact the whirring aerodynamic wonder had its flight-path drastically altered by a sudden squall of wind and the boomerang swung wildly off course and swooped towards the ducking crowd. It struck a spectator a severe blow to the head. It sliced through the man's top hat and inflicted a severe laceration to the side of the head. A doctor attended to the man immediately and he was soon patched up and considered well enough to make his way home. However, Mullagh's misguided boomerang did not damage his cricket reputation, for the Bootle captain, Mr Clegg, presented Mullagh with a purse containing 50 shillings, and said that he did not think that there was a better batsman in England than Mullagh.

In match 35 the Australians thrashed Witham by an innings and 43 runs. Cuzens hit a whirlwind 64 and Lawrence 48. Mullagh got a good bowling double with 5/27 and 3/18, while Cuzens took 3/5 in the first dig and Lawrence took 7/33 in the second dig.

In the return match against Sussex, the Sussex men found the Australians a very different proposition from the side they had faced at Hove in June, although they duly noted that the Aborigines still showed a lack of judgment in their running between wickets. Sussex was bundled out for 74 (Lawrence 6/33) after the Australians hit 96 (Lawrence 55). The Australians batted again and were 7/113 (Tiger 32) when time ran out. The next day was set aside as a special day of sports. Admission was set at an abnormally high rate of three shillings, to help provide prize money for the second and third place-getters.

Game 37 against Blackheath at Blackheath saw Twopenny take an extraordinary catch at long stop off Lawrence to set the Aborigines'

GRAND GALA AT WITHAM, ESSEX.

THE

AUSTRALIAN ABORIGINES

HAVE BEEN ENGAGED TO COME TO

WITHAM

On MONDAY & TUESDAY, SEPTEMBER
14th and 15th, 1868,

WHEN

A CRICKET MATCH

AND VARIOUS

AUSTRALIAN & ENGLISH ATHLETIC SPORTS,

Including Flat and Hurdle Races, Jumping, Throwing
the Boomerang, Sham Fight, Kangaroo Rats, &c., &c.,

WILL TAKE PLACE

On the Grounds of R. PARTRIDGE, Esq.

For further particulars see hand-bills, which will
shortly be issued.

TO PUBLICANS & OTHERS.

GRAND GALA AT WITHAM, ESSEX,
14th and 15th September, 1868.

THE AUSTRALIAN ABORIGINES.

TENDERS for supplying the LUNCHEON for the
CRICKETERS BOTH DAYS, and for HIRING
GROUND for the ERECTION of REFRESHMENT
BOOTHS on the above occasion, will be received on
or before the 1st of September, 1868.

Applications, in writing, for the above Tenders to be
addressed to C. Stevens, Esq., Witham, Essex, where a
Plan of the Ground may be seen and any information
afforded.

ball rolling. Twopenny caught a reckless slash by Peter Thornton, the ball careering high and to Twopenny's left. He timed his leap to perfection and thrust out his left hand at just the right instant and the ball stuck to his palm as if glued. Twopenny danced with glee. Blackheath, however, won a hard-fought battle by a margin of just 13 runs. Johnny Cuzens won a new ball for his feat in capturing three wickets in four balls — as near to a hat-trick as one might get without grabbing the ultimate prize. Cuzens' victims were Pickering, Westhall and Pickwick.

Successive drawn matches followed — against Middlesex at Islington, against Surrey at The Oval, against The Press and Critics at Maidstone, against Eastbourne at Eastbourne and against Turnham Green at Hammersmith.

A resounding innings and 72 runs victory against East Hampshire at Southsea capped the team's 43rd match. Twopenny, who had rarely bowled in the early stage of the tour, suddenly came to the fore with some devastating performances. He took 9/9 off 10 overs in the first innings of the East Hampshire clash and 6/7 off 16 overs in the second innings.

The Australians salvaged a draw against Hampshire at Southampton. Twopenny again grabbed a remarkable bowling double with 9/17 off 21 overs and 3/39 off 17 overs.

Then came the Aboriginal players' greatest tour victory, the match against Reading at Reading. The home side was no match for the rampaging Aborigines. Reading made 32 and 34 to the Australians' 284. Mullagh took 8/9 off nine overs then went out to hit 94, the highest individual score by his side on tour. Cuzens also hit out, making 66, and Bullocky made 37. Lawrence took 8/9 in Reading's second innings.

Match 46 was against Godalming at Godalming, a pleasant enough ground surrounded by smallish oaks in the heart of Surrey. Godalming fell for 37, due to Lawrence's 'dodgers' and the Aborigines replied with 79 (Cuzens 20). Then the home side steadied and hit 128 and Lawrence's men were struggling at 6/25 when play ended. In June 2000 I sat chatting with a friend in his house in Beech Lane, Guildown, Guildford. The late afternoon sun filtered through David Frith's lounge-room windows and we talked cricket. Then came the realisation that one should at least walk on the sacred turf where the side had played all those years ago. The last train to London was at 11 pm. We had the time. David drove purposefully and we soon arrived at the little ground in Godalming. Some of the oaks that were there in 1868 were still there in 2000. While I surveyed the ground, Frith plucked some leaves of an oak, the same blood of the tree that was there when Dick-a-Dick, Twopenny, Mullagh and Cuzens stood nearby. Maybe even Mosquito whipped off a leaf or two, or perhaps Charley Dumas threw his boomerang with such deadly effect it knocked over a squirrel, as indeed Redcap had done at Mote Park. I placed the oak-leaf prize between sheets of white paper and 'smuggled' the booty into Australia. As I write, the pressed oak-leaves adorn my pin-board. David Frith's gesture was greatly welcomed.

There was one more match to play. It was a case of The Oval revisited for the Australians. Cuzens got revenge on Thomas Baggallay, who hit a slashing 68 in the first game of the tour, by taking his leg-stump clean out of the ground with a searing yorker. John Constable Gregory, who played 23 first-class matches for Middlesex and Surrey from 1865 to 1871, hit a magnificent 121 not out, the highest score against the Aboriginal team on tour. Gregory played the bowling of Cuzens with great courage and skill for Cuzens was wiry and zestful and strong. He had an action which may have resembled that of Jeff Thomson, who turned out to be the fastest bowler to draw breath. Gregory's 121 was out of 173, so the rest of Surrey's batsmen failed miserably.

J. C. Smith might have played a lot more first-class cricket had he not ruptured an artery in his leg during a match. For many years Smith appeared in more matches in England than almost any other player and on some days he appeared in no less than three separate games, albeit most of them being matches of an inferior quality. In 1868 J. C. Smith belonged to no fewer than 18 London cricket clubs! The Surrey men struggled against the bowling of Twopenny, Cuzens, Mullagh and Lawrence. The Australians did not perform with the bat, scoring 56, of which Bullocky top-scored with 24. Mullagh got a rare duck in the first innings. In the second innings Cuzens batted magnificently, hammering the Surrey bowling to the tune of 63. Mullagh got 18, Redcap 22 and few of the others troubled the scorers too much. With the Australians falling for 143 in the second innings, Surrey needed only 27 to win; they achieved victory with only one wicket down.

In all, the Australians had played a remarkable 47 matches. They won 14, lost 14 and had the better of many of the 19 drawn games.

CHAPTER SIX

TRAGICALLY King Cole (Brippokei) died after a sudden and short illness. His death came just 11 days after he played in the Lord's match, which ended on 13 June. Soon after the match, King Cole began to cough. However, the cough was not considered sufficiently bad for King Cole to miss the match against East Hampshire at Southsea, a two-day game played on 15–16 June. King Cole didn't bowl and he batted at number nine, scoring 3 in the first innings and an unconquered 3 in the second.

He soon developed a heavy chest cold, which got rapidly worse, and it was decided to take him to London for treatment. Lawrence took him on the train. They drove from Paddington Station by cab to Guy's Hospital where King Cole's condition appeared much worse. His chest cold had developed into the dreaded pneumonia. Pneumonia in 1868 was tantamount to a death sentence. There were none of the antibiotics modern medicine might use to fight such an ailment. This was especially so for the Indigenous Australians. It was feared that the slightest cold could adversely affect the team, but especially the Aboriginal players. And so it turned out for King Cole. His immune system could not cope with pneumonia.

The side played Bishop Stortford over two days, 19–20 June, around the time that Lawrence and King Cole set out for London. For four days a distraught Lawrence sat at King Cole's bedside. We can only surmise what comforting words he might have offered King Cole.

A great sadness would have befallen King Cole. Death itself was not the great hurt, for King Cole knew, as all humankind knows, that death inevitably comes to us all. The sadness for King Cole was the reality that he was dying in a foreign land, on foreign soil far from his beloved home. He would never again watch a wallaby skip among the rocks, or shield his eyes from the sun to see the silhouette of an eagle in flight. He would never again hear the humorous chatter of a family of galahs or watch an inquisitive emu's unblinking stare. He would never again see an Australian sunrise or a sunset. Never again would he see a kangaroo lower its head to lick the early morning dew from the grass. He would never again hold a woman in his arms or watch the myriad stars under the heavens of the Southern Hemisphere. He would never have children, never get the chance to teach his sons to fashion a boomerang or throw a spear. He would never again have the chance to play cricket, the game of the white invader, a game which he grew to love.

Sadly there was not one of his Indigenous team-mates by his side as he lay in his hospital bed. In that poignant cultural context, King Cole died a lonely death in the early hours of Wednesday, 24 June 1868. It was the last day of the match against Hastings, at Halifax, the tenth match of the 1868 tour.

Brippokei was buried at Victoria Park Cemetery (now called Meath Gardens) in the borough of Tower Hamlets, one of London's thirty-two boroughs. He was buried in a 'pauper's' grave. The Surrey Cricket Club had offered to cover the costs to bury King Cole and it is not clear whether Lawrence, Hayman and Smith took up the offer or if they decided to pay the cost themselves. Either way the amount of money involved would have been insignificant. The cost of a funeral at Victoria Park Cemetery in 1876 was one guinea. A pauper's grave was much cheaper and in 1868 cheaper by far. None of King Cole's Indigenous team-mates attended the funeral. Lawrence was the lone Australian representative.

As Johnny Mullagh carried on the good work with a couple of wickets at Hastings in that drawn tenth match, Lawrence stood, head bowed, as King Cole was lowered into the ground. Lawrence held a piece of paper. He had written a poem. It is not known whether he adapted words from a well-known verse or created the entire piece. These are the words he uttered for King Cole that Wednesday so long ago:

To Britain he came from the land of the west
As a stranger for honour and glory
And now as a hero intrepid and bold
Will his name be recorded in story

For not with the sword did he covet renown
The battle he fought was at cricket
In lieu of grim weapons of warfare he strove
With the bat and the ball at the wicket

Still fortune was faithless and fickle to him
Not long in the strife he contended
And never did victory gladden his side
Whenever the fort he defended

Now run out for nought in the innings of life
By the grace of the good he is sleeping
Yet sad are his comrades, though reckon they well
How safe is their mate in our keeping

And, chieftans of England, give ear to the song
Of a minstrel with harp unromantic
You who have won laurels by Yarra's far shore
Or bays gathered over Atlantic

If ever you travel old ocean again
Take guard of the bloody uprooter
For death may be chartered to bowl in a match
And trundle you down with a shooter.

We know of nothing else that Lawrence might have uttered at the
ceremony for there are no reports of the occasion. There might have
been just Lawrence and the gravedigger present. The poem, written
in pencil on what is now yellowing parchment, is now in the
possession of Lawrence's great grandson Ian Friend, who lives near
Melbourne. Lawrence appears to have cared about his men on the
one hand and to have cared about his pocket on the other, for he
allowed his partners, Hayman and Smith, to commit to a extraordinary number of games after the Lord's match. He not only coached

the men at the game, but he became their mentor, their confidant, their friend.

He ought to have known how important it was that the players, these tribal men, attended King Cole's funeral.

For a few years after King Cole was buried in 1868 the gravesite was well cared for, but then the Victoria Park Cemetery became what was described as 'delapidated and of a deplorable condition'. The Tower Hamlets Borough records reveal that it became the stamping ground of the worst elements of the district — 'loafers and roughs, gamblers, razor-boys'.[1] They defaced gravestones, pulled down walls and railings, fought gang wars and generally became the running sore of the neighbourhood. In the process, some time between 1868 and 1885, the plaque at King Cole's grave was destroyed. In 1988 John McGuire's Aboriginal Australian cricket team visited King Cole's grave. There they planted a gum tree and placed a plaque at the head of the grave. The plaque was later vandalised. In 1996 a new plaque was placed at the grave, or what was thought to be the gravesite. It survives, as does the gum tree, which has grown to a good size. In 1996 Rikki Shields, an Indigenous Australian who lives in London, wrote a piece in the wake of the King Cole ceremony. Entitled 'The Last Over', it reads, in part:

> Legend of the Southern Cross Stars that light the night-sky over Australia. Seven Aboriginal women fetch the wood at sundown. Then they fly into the sky and make seven campfires, while they wait eternally for the lost warriors to return home.

> 1866 was a starry night as the women watched the wooden ship sailing from Botany Bay, inside the ship were twelve gallant warriors. They went as ambassadors in games and humanity, to play this strange sport ... cricket.

> Behind their land was ravaged and claimed in the name of fair play. Loyoranna the Wind blew the ship, across mountainous seas Then finally to the River Snake ... Thames.

> London Town where Clay People dwell, Who rule by class, stone hearts, Darkness, No Fire in the Sky.

The Cricket Warriors knew the dangers, if they failed on this mission.
Wonderous people did they meet, the old, the young, but not politicians.

Then tragedy struck off spinner bowler, Sugar. Died whereabouts unknown.
Chief King Cole passed away in white-fella death house at St Guy's.
No sacred ceremony, No weeping women, to help their bones and spirit
return to the beginning time.

Did the evil Clayface Doctor swap King Cole's bones for their own?
Does he sit in a Shoe Box or glass jar in Royal College of Surgeons
In central London Town … We'll never know.

Yet the seven Aboriginal Women's night fire shines brightly
The women still weeping, still hoping.

There is humanity in this hostile jungle city of London
The People of Tower Hamlets erected a stone for the journey
And memory of our Dusky Warrior of Cricket
Ambassador King Cole …   © Rikki Shields, London, 1996

Shields' piece is poignant, although there are some inaccuracies.
He writes '1866' when it should be 1868, and he talks of Sugar as if
he had died on tour, when in fact Sugar died before the team set sail
for England. Shields also writes of twelve Aboriginal players. There
were, in fact, thirteen 'warriors'.

We find it surprising today that the team-mates of King Cole did
not attend his funeral. But Europeans in 1868 were far less culturally
aware than Europeans are now. There was a general ignorance about
other cultures and perhaps what today can be regarded as dominant-
culture arrogance. As to King Cole's illness and subsequent death, it
is not known what information about his condition was provided to
the other Aboriginal players by Lawrence and the managers. It is not
known whether King Cole's team-mates knew that he had died until
after he was buried. The first public announcement King Cole's death
did not occur until three days after King Cole's death, when a small
article appeared in London's *Daily Telegraph*.

Cricketers will regret to hear that King Cole, one of the celebrated Black

Eleven now on a professional visit to this country, died last Wednesday even in Guy's Hospital. His death was caused by inflammation of the lung and his loss is severely mourned by his mates and all who knew him.[2]

Seventeen years after the 1868 tour, in 1885, Fred Gale, an old cricketer and writer, who played against the 1868 Aboriginal team, cast what some perceived as being 'new light' on King Cole's burial. He wrote:

King Cole died over here and the Surrey Secretary Mr [William] Burrup, offered, on behalf of the club, to bury him; but they [the Aboriginal cricketers] had no sympathy, and did not care what became of him.[3]

Gale's assertion that King Cole's brothers did not 'care' about him because of their non-appearance at the funeral reveals the ignorance of Aboriginal culture of the English public and the Europeans among the tour party itself. For if Lawrence, Hayman and Smith had had any idea of the traditional ceremonies of the Wimmera region's Indigenous people they would have put down any suggestion that King Cole's team-mates did not care about his fate. There is no evidence that the 1868 tour managers acted in such a manner. Lawrence, Hayman and Smith's major concern, it appears, was about image and perception at home. They would have been mindful of the outrage this news would bring in certain quarters in Victoria, especially among the group which lobbied so hard to stop the tour. The deaths of Jellico, Watty and Paddy after the ill-fated 1867 Sydney tour must have haunted them. When King Cole died, the nightmare became a reality. Perhaps this very tragic event hastened the enactment of the Aborigines' Protection Act, which became law in 1869.

In 2001 the Young Indigenous Australian Cricket Team took part in a ceremony at King Cole's grave. It was a very emotional experience. The team manager, Grant Sarra, stood at the head of the grave and said, in part:

Today we — the 2001 Australian Aboriginal and Torres Strait Islander youth cricket team — have gathered to pay our respects to King Cole. The 1868 team is already entrenched in Australian cricket folklore. In 1868 the team of 13 Aboriginal cricketers from the Wimmera district of Victoria sailed for England on the fully-rigged woolclipper, the

Parramatta, on February 8, 1868. Remarkably the team sneaked out of Victoria where the Victoria Protection Act was about to come into force. On the pretext of fishing, the players went to the small port of Queenscliffe. There they rowed out to a ship en-route from Melbourne to Sydney where they eventually boarded the *Parramatta*. Under the Protection Act — which in Victoria was enacted in 1869, one year after the historic tour — Aboriginal people were not considered citizens of Australia.

They were forcibly removed from their traditional lands and placed into missions where their lives were controlled by the Chief Protector. Under the Act they were not allowed to leave the mission, were not allowed to marry. Nor were they allowed to practise traditional cere-monies — including song and dance. They were not allowed to own land …

Sadly King Cole played only seven matches. But he played a match at Lord's and he experienced the joy of being treated as an equal in England. A courtesy he was never afforded in his home country … This makes today especially poignant for the 2001 team. This ceremony represents a culturally important and spiritually significant occasion. Sharing, caring and respect is paramount for people and the environment. In traditional society Aboriginal people believed — and we still do believe — that the land is our mother. We come from the land and we go back to the land. Through our birth we have a very special and unique place and will always remain connected to the land we call Australia. The Aboriginal belief is that the land and all things are part of a vast network of relationships — created by the great Ancestral beings of the Dreaming.

They created the rivers, the streams, the plants, the landscape and the animals and we the people. Before settling back into the land, the great Ancestral beings laid down the laws for our people to live by. The land is our mother.[4]

As team leader I was honoured to be asked to read the poem that Lawrence had read at King Cole's burial. It was an unforgettable experience. I found myself choking with emotion for I was now living the story. The ceremony was being monitored by a gaggle of television and radio crews. Journalists stood silently. The sun shone, but it was, as they say in Yorkshire, a watery sun, for clouds flooded the sun like a thin soup. The ceremony involved pieces of ochre, the substance used in traditional society for cave art and which continues to be used today. Indigenous artist Laurie Wilson of the Fire-Works Gallery in Brisbane supplied the ochre, which was carried to England in a small plastic phial by Aboriginal and Torres Strait Islander Commission (ATSIC) field officer and artist John Tatten, who performed the Invocation. John, a former rugby star who lost the use of his right arm, has learnt to paint left-handed. He dot-painted a number of cricket bats which were given to the clubs that hosted our matches, such as Broadwater in Guildford and the MCC at Lord's.

John Tatten spoke the words of the poet Oodgeroo, from the poem …:

> To our fathers' fathers the pain and sorrow
> To our children's children the glad tomorrow

The ochre had been crushed to powder by members of the 2001 team. John sprinkled the powder on King Cole's gravesite and the players, officials and guests were invited to do the same. Grant Sarra said: 'As a sign of respect today we bring part of the mother's spirit to lay with the spirit of her child — King Cole.' Grant also acknowledged the warmth and friendliness shown by the British people to the 2001 team, noting that it was similar to the experience of the 1868 side, for 'they experienced what we have experienced'.

At the end of the 1868 tour the team management and the press held a farewell reception for the side in Surrey. That 'Artful Dodger' Dick-a-Dick was the popular choice to speak on behalf of the team. 'Dick-a-Dick's words then in 1868 are our words now,' Grant Sarra said. ' "We thank you from our hearts." '[5]

The sprinkling of ochre was most appropriate, for the mother earth was symbolically brought to the son. Under different circumstances the Aboriginal community would have asked for the return to Australia of King Cole's remains. The repatriation of remains from foreign soil is inestimably important to Aboriginal Australians. Even though there is a gum tree and plaque to mark King Cole's grave site, the exact location of his body remains a mystery.

King Cole lies somewhere in the twelve and a half acres of Victoria Park Cemetery on land which was once part brick field and part market garden. According to estimates collated by the Tower Hamlets borough, some half a million people are buried within that tiny allotment. The first interment at Victoria Park Cemetery was that of Francis Holland, 70, of Trinity Street, Islington, who was buried in December 1845. The last interment was that of John Stroud who died on 28 May 1882. The soil was considered suitable for burial as its greatest consistency was dry gravel. Initially the graves could not be dug deeper than 3 metres before reaching water. After the main sewer was built nearby the depth of the graves increased to 5.5 metres. An ordinary grave held ten full-sized coffins, or as many as fifty children. Nearly all the bodies buried in this cemetery were placed in common deal coffins, although a few were interred in oak, and twenty were buried in lead coffins.

During the cholera epidemic of 1866 as many as 80 bodies were interred in one day at the Victoria Park Cemetery. Most people interred in paupers' graves were buried on the same day they died. Bodies are buried at varying heights in the plot and it would be impossible to be sure which remains belonged to King Cole without DNA tests on each one of the half million bodies. A certificate of burial at the cemetery in 1876 cost 2/7. In 1868 it would have been around 2/-, but there is no evidence of such a document being requested for King Cole by Lawrence or the other managers of the team.

King Cole's death exposed all too dramatically the vulnerability of these tribal men. Dying on foreign soil was particularly heart-rending for the players and King Cole's family, because for them the land is the mother and King Cole died nearly 20,000 kilometres from his mother land. The sadness continues, for King Cole's remains are likely to stay interred somewhere in that plot of earth.

The Great Ancestors, Bunjil and Mindeye, explained creation and the origin of social rules and customs. Surviving rock art and archaeological evidence of cremations and other burial rituals reveal the ancient and rich religious sense of Aboriginal Australians. Early European settlers recorded ceremonies of more than ten days' duration, complete with huge bark figures and bark panels covered in 'hieroglyphics'. Mortuary ceremonies aided the separation of the dead from the living. The ceremony performed at the old Victoria Park Cemetery on Wednesday, 29 May 2001 may have appeased the ancestral spirits and allowed King Cole to finally rest easy.

CHAPTER SEVEN

THE 1868 tour was a wonderful success, save for the tragic death of King Cole. Financially the tour did handsomely, although there was a huge disparity between the accounts of certain parties as to whether the tour made a good profit or a disastrous loss. Having had a close look at the Graham ledger, I am satisfied that the 1868 tour produced a better than reasonable profit. Losses were recorded in six of 47 match venues: the largest single loss was £86–16–0 for the match against the Press played over two days, 28–29 September 1868. A substantial part of that loss was the £57–15–0 that the tour management spent on a special farewell party in Surrey. There are some curious notations in the Graham ledger and I suspect that not all receipts found their way into the official records. Lieutenant-Colonel Pitt-Rivers was so engrossed with warfare and weaponry made by indigenous groups throughout the world that it is inconceivable that he did not make an offer for a number of items such as the players' spears and shields. Dick-a-Dick's killer boomerang turned up at Lord's in 1946. Where had it been for 78 years? According to the Graham ledger the 1868 tour recorded an overall profit of £2176–3–10. This profit came after all expenses had been accounted for, so the players, especially those who had 'signed' the Gurnett contract in 1867, could have reasonably expected some payment as a reward for their efforts on tour. They received not one halfpenny.

Right up until October Lawrence had hoped to take his men for a winter's 'rest' in the south of France and then bring them back to England for the 1869 summer. Lawrence would have known that the death of King Cole would have been the catalyst for the 'protectionists' and that it was highly unlikely he would ever again be able to take an Aboriginal cricket team out of Victoria, let alone to England. Having the players stay overseas for another year, away from their families and their beloved land, was unreasonable and it smacked of greed.

Although the Graham ledger recorded a profit, the umpire and sometimes stand-in player on the tour, William Shepherd, maintained that the 1868 tour lost more than £2000. Shepherd obviously had no access to Graham's books and may have been told a tale of financial woe if the tour administration was not of the mind to pay Shepherd a decent day's pay. Shepherd wrote of his claims in a book years later, but he had no evidence to back his assertion that a huge loss was made. The Graham ledger remains the source of the best financial record available.

The Graham ledger is a damning indictment of the motives of Messrs Lawrence, Graham, Smith and Hayman. Profit was their overriding concern. They were displeased because the profit was not a monumental one.

Arrangements were made to sail home in the *Dunbar Castle*. When I first sought the history of this ship my efforts drew a blank. Even Ian Nicholson's superb *Log of Logs* — a catalogue of logs, journals, shipboard diaries, letters and all forms of voyage narratives from 1788 to 1998 for Australia and New Zealand — makes no mention of the *Dunbar Castle*. I began to doubt that it was the ship aboard which the Aboriginal team sailed back to Australia. However, I eventually found out that the *Dunbar Castle* was a wooden, fully-rigged ship, built by James Laing in 1864. She weighed 925 tons, with 817 tons under the deck. The forecastle was 31 feet long and the poop 60 feet. She was equipped with iron beams and was rigged with double fore and main top-sails. In 1866 she was sold to Devitt & Moore, London, and began her employment in the Australian trade. Sailing ships on the Australian run usually made one voyage a year. On the *Dunbar Castle* 'one of the hardships of travelling [for third-class passengers] was the rule of staying down in the between decks from evening to morning. A few oil lamps gave enough light for seeing one's way but there were no facilities for reading after dark.'[1] The *Dunbar Castle* had a sad end. On 18 May 1879 she collided with the Swedish barque *Christina* off Start Point in the English Channel and in 1881 she was sold to Goldmeister & Reis, Bremen, and renamed *Singapore*, having been cut down to a barque rig. In 1892 she was sold to German owners for £1800 and in August 1899 she was broken up and scrapped.

Like the ships upon which they sailed to and from England, the 1868 Aboriginal tourists were soon to disappear from the public eye. Nothing has come to the fore regarding the team's trip back Australia. What we do know is that all the players returned home safely. The *Dunbar Castle* berthed at Sydney on 4 February 1869. The team had been away from Australia for almost a year. In England the Aboriginal players were feted and treated as equals by the English people, but they arrived home to a different world: Down Under prejudice ruled. This was a world where the black man either knew his place or paid the price.

A few games had been organised to wind down the tour. The Aborigines played New South Wales at Redfern, but bad weather had the final say. When the rains came the New South Wales score stood at 5/61. The team managers were keen to play extra matches to help swell the tour coffers, but Sydney's weather put paid to any boost in profits.

The team took a steamer to Melbourne. There were no officials to meet them and also no retribution from the protectionist lobbyists. The team was welcomed, slaps on backs all round. A three-day match had been organised against a strong Victoria team at the MCG. Victoria was led by the redoubtable Tom Wills. Victoria scored 237, of which Wills, still smarting from his omission as captain/coach of the Aboriginal team, scored an unconquered 26. The Aborigines struggled in reply with 141, of which Mullagh hit 31 and Twopenny 32. Lawrence's men held out for a draw. However, the Aboriginal players had done enough in this showing to impress some of their former critics. W. J. Hammersley, whose sobriquet was 'Longstop', was astonished by the Aborigines' improvement, especially in their batting. Longstop had roundly criticised the side before the England tour. The side suffered from the loss of Cuzens, who along with Peter was ill from the effects of the long voyage from England. Dick-a-Dick, as usual, thrilled the crowd with his brilliance in dodging.

In their next match they were to play against the Prince Alfred XI, the Duke of Edinburgh's personally selected team of officers from his ship, the *Galatea*. Lawrence called the side together to stress the importance of the match. No doubt he could see pound notes and half-crowns in his mind's eye. The match turned out to be the last played by the Aboriginal tourists. They scored an impressive 9/331. John Cuzens hit a breezy 63, Twopenny continued his amazing late-season form with a thunderous 56, and Redcap hit 36. That the side was able to score so well despite a rare failure by Mullagh spoke volumes for the team's improvement and perhaps its character. The men of the *Galatea* replied with 5/293 to end a high-scoring, if drawn, match. Prince Alfred took time out to reacquaint himself with all the players. He smiled when he was reminded that Tiger and Peter managed their usual duck apiece. The Royal visit to the match was a great tonic for the players and they responded with a welcoming war whoop and another collective cheer when the formalities were completed.

The cricket tour was now officially over. The players said their farewells and dispersed. In a normal society the tour would have paved the way for magnificent opportunities for the Aboriginal cricketers. But 1869 was the year in which the protectionists got their way. An Act to provide for the protection and management of Aboriginal natives of Victoria was passed in 1869. This effectively meant the end of pastoral cricket for Aboriginals in Victoria. The protectionist movement went back as far as 1860 when the Central Protection Board for the Protection of Aborigines was established. The Board expressed its concern about the mercenary manipulation of Aboriginal cricketers, and that concern became greater after the ill-fated 1867 Sydney tour, which resulted in the deaths of three of the Aboriginal cricketers. The Board wanted to stop the 1868 tour to England from going ahead, but it did not have the necessary statutory power. Now, in 1869, Victoria's Aborigines' Protection Act gave the colonial governor the power to control where an Aboriginal person lived, worked and conducted business. The governor also regulated how the money designated by Parliament for the benefit of Aboriginal people would be spent. Aboriginal children were to be entrusted to the Central Board for the Protection of Aborigines rather than to their parents. The Act allowed for penalties of up to 20 pounds or three months' imprisonment for any person or persons attempting to 'remove or instigate the removal of any Aboriginal from Victoria without the written consent of the Minister'. Effectively the Board was all-powerful and had total control over the lives of all Aboriginal people in the colony of Victoria.

From the time of European occupation, non-Aboriginal people had been encouraged to believe that the Aborigines were a dying race — that the 'full bloods' would die out and that 'part-Aboriginals' would eventually assimilate into white society. In 1861 the Central Board established a reserve for Aboriginal people at Framlingham. Four major church missions were established in Victoria: Ebenezer at Lake Hindmarsh in 1859, Ramahyuck at Lake Wellington in 1861, Lake Tyers in 1861 and Lake Condah in 1867.

Many of the local Aboriginal people continued to live independent lives until 1880, when the state government gave the Central Board greater control. The 1886 Aborigines Protection Act reversed the support for reserves. The Act stipulated that only 'full bloods', 'half-castes' over the age of 34 and children were allowed to live on the reserves. The remaining family members had to leave the reserves, fend for themselves and eventually assimilate into the general community. The Act proved an insensitive piece of legislation which effectively split families and removed the able-bodied from the family group.

The effect on the 1868 Aboriginal team was both immediate and, sadly, final. On tour these tribal men had cricket as their common bond. They all wore the same logo of a silver boomerang and a bat on their caps. Collectively they did well, but the team relied heavily on a core group of a few players who did most of the business of getting runs and taking wickets. The lion's share of the work fell into the capable hands of Johnny Mullagh, Charles Lawrence, Johnny Cuzens and Redcap. Others chipped in handy performances, like Twopenny, who had a sensational last couple of games. However, the team struggled whenever Mullagh, Lawrence and Cuzens had indifferent turns with the bat. The Aboriginal cricketers thought that to hit the ball was to hit the ball and run. They'd crash the ball straight to mid-off and tear down the track yelling excitedly. More than sixty run-outs were recorded on the tour.

The touring players brought great credit to their Aboriginal brothers at home, for they conducted themselves with dignity while abroad and they charmed the nation that first developed the game of cricket. Here is a brief look at their individual performances on the tour:

Johnny Mullagh (Unaarrimin)

Gifted right-hand batsman
Medium fast bowler
Matches 45
Runs 1698 at 23.65
Wickets 245 at 10.00

Johnny Mullagh was the all-round cricketing success of the tour. Considered by many to be the equal of any batsman in England, Mullagh possessed the style and the temperament of a top-flight first-class player.

On tour he hit 1698 runs at an average of 23.65, with his highest score, 94, being against Reading. However, Mullagh's most famous knock in 1868 was his faultless 75 against the MCC at Lord's. There he batted with courage and flair and earned a standing ovation. Mullagh possessed the understated, subtle power seen in later years by the Indian maestros Ranjhitsinjhgi, who challenged Victor Trumper as the premier batsman of cricket's so-called Golden Age (1894–1914), and the modern genius Sachin Tendulkar. Johnny Mullagh was an elegant batsman, wristy with deft glances and delicate cuts and the odd glorious cover drive. He often despaired of his team-mates' impetuousness. They lacked Johnny's patience for the task at hand, even allowing for the fact that they, like Mullagh himself, had by 1868 been playing the game for, at best, three years.

Mullagh's bowling was also a key factor in the team's success. He sent down 1877 overs, of which 831 were maidens, for a handsome return of 245 wickets for 2489 runs at an average of 10 runs apiece.

Mullagh was a confident, calm man, yet he seemed torn between two cultures. He idolised British women. During the English tour he collected photographs and pictures of English women and whenever he could he would bring out his stack of pictures and look adoringly at each one. Mullagh was besotted with the white man's world. His admission to Tom Hamilton that 'a white woman won't have me …

and I will never have a black one' reflected his melancholy attitude to his lot in life. Perhaps he was a realist. After all, a black man would never be accepted in most aspects of the white man's world.

Mullagh did not go to a reserve in 1869. Along with Johnny Cuzens, he was appointed to the Melbourne Cricket Club as a professional for the 1869–70 season. However, he played in only six matches before he decided to return to Harrow. It is not known whether Mullagh's departure from the Melbourne grade scene was because he was injured or sick, or whether he did not care for city life. In eight innings Mullagh scored 209 runs at an average of 34.5. He hit a highest score of 69 not out. And he collected 8 wickets for 300 runs. He was selected in the Victorian team to play New South Wales in an inter-colonial match that summer but sickness prevented him from playing. Mullagh was in the Victorian squad for the start of the 1870–71 season, but as the selectors did not hear from him his name was dropped from the list.

The sheer weight of runs for Harrow gave Mullagh a second chance. In 1879, eleven years after the 1868 tour, Mullagh was picked to play for Victoria against Lord Harris's England team. The *Age* cricket correspondent slammed the Victorian selectors for their 'boldness' in picking Mullagh and said that it was 'hardly justifed'. The match was played in March at the MCG. Mullagh batted at number nine in the first dig and he scored only 4, but in the second innings he top-scored with 36. The Melbourne *Argus* praised him for his 'long reach, his cool artistic style, his judicious treatment of dubious balls and his vigorous drives'. Johnny Mullagh so impressed the visitors that England batsman Albert (A.N.) Hornby, the great Lancashire opener, a scorer of 16,109 first-class runs, presented him with a bat. Also a collection was held and a sum of fifty guineas was raised by the former Premier of Victoria, J. G. Francis. It was indeed a fabulous sum for Mullagh, as in 1879 the average annual wage for a man was 100 pounds.

Strangely Mullagh was never again picked for Victoria. He went back to the stations and played for Harrow. In 1884 he was working as a shearer in Penola (South Australia) and at the end of the 1884–85 summer he visited Adelaide with a combined club team. He played on the Adelaide Oval, which had hosted its first Test match against

Arthur Shewsbury's England in December 1884, and he batted against the Test opening bowler George Giffen. Mullagh scored 43 not out against Giffen, negotiating the bowling with great skill. As a bowler Mullagh was said to have been of the old-fashioned type, fast and straight. He had a habit of rushing towards the batsman on his follow-through, rather like the old master of gamesmanship himself, W. G. Grace. WG would deliver, then trot habitually towards silly-mid-off. It was a ploy to get as close to the batsman as possible before he eyeballed him and let forth with the odd intimidating word. Against Maidstone at Mote Park in May 1868, Mullagh clean-bowled three batsmen in four balls.

Johnny Mullagh played cricket right up until a few months before his death on 14 August 1891. The *Sydney Mail* ran a small feature obituary in its 22 August edition:

> The Victorian Aboriginal cricketer, Johnny Mullagh, was found dead on the 14th instant at Harrow, in the Western District. Mullagh was the principal bat in the famous Aboriginal team which visited England in 1868. He had been the mainstay of the Harrow Cricket Club for many years, and although of late he became weak and stiff from age and exposure he was a keen batsman and lover of the game. The Western District will regret his death. He had been ailing for some weeks, but nothing serious was anticipated. Mullagh had often refused overtures made to him to provide him with a suitable home in his old age, and he chose to live near his old birthplace at Pine Hills, and to some extent after the custom of his forefathers. He was the last of his tribe. His funeral took place on Sunday, and representatives came from considerable distances to pay their token of respect to the deceased. On the veteran's coffin were placed the bat he used and a set of stumps tied together with Harrow colours and surrounded by numerous wreaths. The Anglican clergyman read the burial service and gave an address, pointing out that the world of cricket had lost a mighty man, and also dwelling on the virtues of the deceased, who was exemplary in his habits. He hoped that the cricketers of Victoria would erect a suitable monument to his memory. Much feeling was shown by all present.[2]

Johnny Mullagh was found dead, slumped on the ground at his bush camp, by James Edgar. As a schoolboy back in 1864, at about the time Mullagh began to play cricket, Edgar brought news from his school in Melbourne of the new-fangled over-arm bowling. To this day, the spot at Pine Hills where Mullagh's body was found is known as 'Johnny's Dam'. The *Hamilton Spectator*, still going strong in 2001, drove efforts to raise funds to establish a suitable memorial to Mullagh. Thanks to the newspaper's campaign a memorial was built at Harrow's Mullagh Oval. Each year a Victorian Aboriginal team travels to Harrow to play a local non-Aboriginal Glenelg XI for the Johnny Mullagh Memorial Trophy. Like many famous artists, Johnny Mullagh's fame and acknowledgment came long after his death. Johnny Mullagh can now rest easy. Lift your spirit, Unaarrimin.

Charles Lawrence

Right-hand batsman
Right-hand medium slow bowler
Matches 40
Runs 1156 at 20.16
Wickets 250 at 12.1

Charles Lawrence played in 40 matches on the 1868 tour. His all-round performance is testimony to his skill and stamina, for he hit 1156 runs at 20.16 and took 250 wickets at 12.1. Bullocky stumped 28 batsmen off Lawrence's bowling, which ranged from medium fast to slow, and Johnny Mullagh, when 'resting' from bowling, stumped a further four victims for Lawrence. Charles Lawrence holds a special place in Australian sporting history. He holds a unique record, for he toured Australia with H. H. Stephenson's trail-blazing 1861–62 England team and he led Australia's first touring team to England in 1868. His work with the Aboriginal team was the crowning glory of his sporting career. His taking of all ten wickets for Scotland against William Clarke's All England XI at Edinburgh in 1849 does not seem to rate a mention when the discussion turns to Charles Lawrence. He was a man of great courage and compassion, but there was a ruthless side to him as well. The first coach of the Aboriginal players, Tom Wills, was mercilessly shoved aside. Lawrence also saw the Aboriginal men not merely as cricketers. He saw cricket as the vehicle to get them to England, the 'excuse' if you like, so that he could make a financial killing on their brilliant spear and boomerang throwing, their athleticism and their value as 'curiosities' to the English public.

Lawrence did build an atmosphere of trust within the team environment. He empowered his players, although he depended largely on a small group of talented cricketers. Clearly several of the side merely made up the numbers, as their cricket ability was below par. The likes of Mullagh, Cuzens, Redcap and Bullocky were vital to the cause. Lawrence knew that a small band would have to play most of the games. He knew that Mullagh and himself needed to do most of the work with the ball.

On board the *Parramatta*, Lawrence was armed with exercise books and pencils. He wanted to teach the men to read and write during the voyage. In this he failed miserably for the players got bored with his teachings. They drew animals in the exercise books and they carved all manner of things — from combs to tatting shuttles. Lawrence also tried to woo them towards the teachings of Christianity. He probably meant well, as indeed did dozens of church men, but the move to 'convert' the Indigenous people of Australia had an underlying darkness for it was part of the push towards assimilation.

Charles Lawrence died on 20 December 1916, aged 88. At the age of 70 Lawrence played his final match at his beloved MCG. Tom Horan, who wrote so lovingly on the game for the *Australasian* under the pseudonym 'Felix', watched Lawrence's last match. He made the following observations:

Charlie Lawrence, in the prime of manhood, played with the first All England Eleven on the Melbourne Ground thirty-seven years ago, and now, in his seventieth year, he has played his last innings, and has said farewell to the green turf, and to the colts whom he has trained to such good purpose that, if time permitted, they would probably have beaten the Victorian Eleven pitted against them on Easter Saturday and Monday. The veteran played no small part in the early days of cricket in New South Wales in helping develop the game in that colony ...

He goes back to the days when eighteens and twenty-twos of Victoria were simply nowhere against the English team of which he was a member, or against the later and more formidable team brought out by the celebrated George Parr in 1863–64. In looking back to those days there is for Charlie a touch of sadness in the retrospect, for all, or nearly all, whom he then played with are 'vanished voices, all his steps are on the dead'. But the sadness is more than counterbalanced by a feeling of pleasure at the marvellous progress of cricket in Australia, a progress so pronounced that in this very season which witnesses his exit from the arena the picked men of Australia have defeated Mr A. E. Stoddart's Englishmen in every part of the British dominions.

It must, indeed, be gratifying to the veteran to observe this extraordinary improvement, seeing that he had a hand in laying the foundation on which has been reared, this splendid superstructure of skill; and, dropping metaphor and referring to solid bricks, it must be pleasing to him to note that the change from the primitive conditions of ground and appointments has been in keeping with our advancement as scientific exponents of cricket in all its departments.

While Old Lawrence stood in the field on Saturday and Monday, I could imagine him harking back to the days when the temporary wooden stand was erected for the first match against H. H. Stephenson's team. I could imagine him contrasting it and its surroundings with the magnificent grand-stand and pavilion of today, and I could also imagine him instituting a similar contrast between the old Albert Ground at Redfern, and the present beautiful enclosure in Moore Park [the Sydney Cricket Ground], with its handsome pavilion and stands, which cost, I believe, even more than our buildings on our MCC ground [MCG]. The aggregate outlay on these two grounds tots up to something like 100,000 pounds, and Lawrence, by his long career and associationship with the two colonies, is peculiarly fitted to bear testimony to the splendid results that have accrued.[3]

Lawrence played two matches for Surrey (1854–57), one match for Middlesex (1861), and five matches for New South Wales between 1862–63 and 1869–70. He also played in the one first-class match of H. H. Stephenson's historic first England tour of Australia in 1861–62. In nine matches Lawrence scored 227 runs at 15.13 with a top score of 78. He took 38 wickets at 10.94 with a best haul of 7/25. His cricket hero, Fuller Pilch, the best bat in England in the 1830s and 1840s, averaged only 18.61 in his career of 229 first-class matches. An average near 20 was exceptional, for games were played on rough tracks that saw balls rear at the head or shoot along the ground.

Lawrence's work with young cricketers helped lift Australian cricket to world standard in a few short years. Perhaps he more than any other person could claim the title of the Father of Australian Cricket.

Johnny Cuzens (Zellanach)

Hard-hitting right-hand batsman
Fast bowler with high arm action
Runs 1358 at 19.9
Wickets 114 at 11.3

Johnny Cuzens was the Jeff Thomson of his time. He was shortish, but strong like Thommo and Malcolm Marshall. He had explosive power and he bowled with a high arm action. He had a round, jolly face and was ever ready to exhibit his boyish grin. Batsmen found his body language disarming, for when he got to the top of his mark with a ball in his hand Cuzens was deadly serious. He charged in and let fly. Like Thommo there was nothing particularly scientific in his approach. He simply did it naturally.

Cuzens took 114 wickets in England at an average of 11.3 and he scored 1358 runs at 19.9. Nine times he hit scores in excess of 50 and he came third to Mullagh and Lawrence in the batting averages, and second to Mullagh in runs aggregate. But it was his express bowling which thrilled:

> Cuzens, when he likes — for they can bowl with the head as well as with the hand — can put the ball down faster than R. Lipscombe, of Kent, whose telling deliveries are well known to all who have ever faced them. Cuzens also takes full advantage of the unrestrained licence of the day regarding the elevation of the arm and has the knack of 'making her bump' even on the best wickets.[4]

This was high praise indeed given that Robert Lipscombe was a right-hand fast bowler who turned out for Kent in 60 first-class matches, taking 271 wickets at an average of 17. Three years after the Aboriginal tour Lipscombe took 9/88 for Kent against the MCC at Lord's, in the summer of 1871.

Cuzens was a stalwart of the side. He missed only one game, the first, against Surrey at The Oval. From then on he played every one of the matches, a testimony to his health and fitness and enthusiasm for the task. As with Mullagh, who hit a splendid 75 at Lord's, Cuzens turned on a great performance at headquarters, taking 6/65 off 25 overs straight in the MCC's second innings. He clean-bowled all of his victims and sent the stumps flying 'a good ten yards' when he bowled Colonel Bathurst and the brothers Fitzgerald. Cuzens also dismissed the Earl of Coventry (14) with a leg-cutter which took the off-stump and Captain Trevor (18). The team relied so heavily on Mullagh, Lawrence and Cuzens that if any one of them failed it meant that it was going to be a struggle. Consistency in batting was a key issue, and the team never achieved any semblance of consistency in that area throughout the 47-match tour. Cuzens adopted a higher arm action that most bowlers. He was able to achieve a greater degree of bounce than either Lawrence or Mullagh, but often his best balls beat the bat but also missed the stumps on their way through to the keeper, Bullocky.

Cuzens was the champion sprinter of the team. In the after-play sports, Cuzens beat all comers. At The Oval, in the 47th match, Cuzens hit a blistering 63 in the Australians' second innings. Surrey won the game comfortably, but afterwards Cuzens was challenged to a run by a mysterious character from 'the north':

Shepherd, who suspected some jiggery-pokery in the wager, was disposed to frown upon the challenge, but the tourists' London host happened to be William Holland, propietor of the Old Canterbury Music Hall, who was full of admiration for his guest [Cuzens]. Holland was a man of large ideas and was what we should now call public-minded. He once proposed to place an outsized carpet, valued at one thousand pounds, in the vestibule of his music hall and was undeterred by the suggestion that patrons would only spit on it.

'Fine,' said he, 'We'll advertise in the papers: "Come and spit on our £1000 carpet".'

Nothing could stop him from offering to put a fiver on Johnny Cuzens and almost before Shepherd could open his mouth in protest, the race had started. Cuzens sent his supporters' hearts into their mouths by being slow off the mark and subjected them to something near thrombosis when, half-way down the track, he kicked off one of his running pumps. But from that instant he moved like the wind and slipped past his rival. As he breasted the tape he was engulfed in the warm embrace of his chief backer who, true to the open-handed tradition of the music hall, pressed both stake and winnings into the runner's hand.[5]

After the tour Cuzens, along with Johnny Mullagh, was contracted to the Melbourne Cricket Club as a professional for the 1868–69 season. He was hired at the rate of one pound a week, for twenty weeks. His job was to bowl to the MCC members and to play for Melbourne at the weekend. He played a few matches, but his heart was not really in it. His contract with the MCC ran through the summer, but it was not renewed beyond March 1870. Cuzens returned to the bush, going to Framlingham Station in the Western District. Just three years after the 1868 tour Cuzens was dead. He is said to have died on 22 March 1871:

> He had developed a cold several weeks previously. After an apparent recovery, he accompanied Mosquito to the Warrnambool Highland Gathering. A soaking in the boisterous weather induced another cold which, aggravated by dysentery, proved fatal. A Warrnambool well-wisher notified his death to the Melbourne Cricket Club requesting a financial contribution for a 'decent burial'. However, as MCC evidently pleaded that the 'club funds will not permit', Cuzens was given a public funeral by the police. In the presence of the Framlingham Community he was buried at a service conducted by the station superintendent.[6]

The *Warrnambool Examiner* of 20 February 1875 features a cricket match between Aboriginal Players and Friendly Societies in which the scorecard lists a 'J. Cousins of Koongerong' who scored 30. The 'J. Cousins' was almost certainly Johnny Cuzens' brother Jimmy, who was known as Mosquito.

Cuzens played his early cricket at Edenhope. He developed quickly as was the case with most of the gifted Aboriginal players. With encouragement and guidance Cuzens may well have had the ability and the temperament to become a brilliant first-class cricketer. He didn't get that opportunity.

Bullocky (Bullchanach)

Right-hand batsman
Wicket-keeper
Matches 39

569 runs at 9.33
Wickets 4 at 11.5

Bullocky played 39 matches on the tour. He was the side's number one wicket-keeper. He showed his mettle standing up to the stumps, for he stumped 28 batsmen off the bowling of Charles Lawrence. Bullocky needed to be tough and resilient, as the pitches were all ridge and furrow. Few of the pitches got much of a decent cut and a roll, and they favoured the bowler. It was Bullocky's work up to the stumps, always the hallmark of a top-class glove-man, which endeared him to the enthusiasts: '… later on Lawrence tried some lobs, off which Jupp was cleverly stumped by Bullocky. The fielding was good, at times brilliant, and Bullocky at length stumped Mr Baggallay in a style worthy of Lockyer.'[7]

Bullocky played 61 completed innings on the 1868 tour, hitting a modest 569 runs at an average of 9.33. He came fourth in the batting averages, proof that the team relied heavily on a select few. Bullocky should have done better with the bat, but he had a huge workload as a keeper and he did that job exceedingly well:

> Bullocky was a courageous wicket-keeper with a granite frame and would have kept just as boldly unarmed by pads or gloves. He was also a stubborn bat, sometimes exasperatingly so, and had one heroic innings of 64 not out at Hastings which would have done credit to the last of the Saxons.[8]

There are various vague reports about Bullocky's doings and whereabouts after the 1868 tour. He never lived down the stigma of his being 'absent' for the second Australian innings of the MCC match at Lord's. No satisfactory explanation was ever provided for the absence of the team's opening batsman. It was assumed that he had succumbed to the demon drink the night before and simply was not in a fit state to get to the ground, let alone bat. The incident labelled Bullocky. Unsubstantiated reports that he was seen 'begging beer money' at the Coroma cricket ground in the 1870s fuelled the rumours.

After the 1868 tour Bullocky continued to work on various stations and play cricket. He opened the batting with Johnny Mullagh for Harrow against Apsley in 1872 and led the Lake Condah Mission team right up until 1890 when, at the age of 53, he died of congestion of the lungs.

Redcap (Brimbunyah)

Right-hand batsman
Right-arm medium-pace bowler
Matches 47
630 runs at 8.46
54 wickets at 10.7

Redcap bowled manfully on the 1868 tour, but he sent down only 366 overs and managed to grab 54 wickets at an average of 10.7. His strike-rate was outstanding. We can only surmise that he was of the slow medium-paced variety. As a batsman Redcap held the bat low. He appeared to apply the 'choke' grip, not the 'soft' hands that cricket coaches today tend to stress as being essential to survival at the top level. Redcap represented Australia in every one of the 47 matches of the 1868 tour. It was an incredible feat of endurance. He scored 630 runs on tour at 8.46, with a highest score of 56. His strike-rate with the ball was a wicket every 27.11 deliveries, second only to Twopenny, who was given lots of bowling, but only in the last few games. Redcap will always be remembered for his having helped Dick-a-Dick to locate the missing Duff children in 1864.

After the 1868 tour Redcap spent most his days on the Dergholm Reserve until about 1879 when he sought and received a grant of 40 acres of land. He built a stout log and mud hut for his wife, Caroline, and himself and he found regular work as a shearer. At Roseneath shed on 11 November 1881, Redcap shore 91 sheep, part of a season's total of 1274.

The date of Redcap's death is not known, although there have been suggestions that he died sometime between 1891 and 1894, having spent a period in the Hamilton Hospital in 1886. As with many of his 1868 team-mates, Redcap's life after 1868 is sketchy at best. Legend has it that he is buried under a wattle tree just outside the Dergholm Cemetery. He is remembered by Red Cap Creek and until a few years ago the local telephone exchange linking Pine Hills Station had the call sign 'Redcap One ...' We do not know what happened to Redcap's wife and whether the couple had children. 'Redcap' was the pseudonym adopted by *Sydney Morning Herald* cricket writer Phil Wilkins when he was writing for a now-defunct Australian cricket magazine. The writer achieved somewhat limited fame within the circle of his readership, but his choice of pen-name was significant in the context of Australian cricket history, as it rekindled memories of a fine cricketer.

Twopenny (Jarrawuk or, more commonly, Murrumgunarrimin)

Right-hand batsman
Explosive right-hand fast bowler
Matches 46
589 runs at 8.29
35 wickets at 6.9

Twopenny is generally acknowledged as being the first Aboriginal first-class cricketer. It is a matter of definition, because, although Bullocky represented Victoria in 1867, it was against a Tasmanian Sixteen and thus not deemed 'first-class'. Twopenny got his chance for New South Wales in 1870, two years after the tour to England. He was unheard of in the cricket world before November 1867 when he was listed to play for the International Aboriginals against Illawarra. However, although listed he did not appear in the 6–7 November match. Why he did not show up we do not know. Perhaps Lawrence wanted to keep Twopenny back, the surprise packet. Here was a strong man with an abundance of stamina and a man who could bowl with genuine speed.

It was later learnt that Twopenny's action was under a cloud. In 1864 the MCC had changed the law and allowed a bowler to deliver over-arm. Some cricketers were taking the new law to the extreme and chucking the ball. Some even suspected Tom Wills, the great Victorian all-rounder, of being a thrower. After 1864 any bowler of genuine pace was looked upon by batsmen and administrators, including umpires, with the William Clarke 'beady eye'. Some historians, including Bernard Whimpress of Adelaide, argue that Twopenny may have been used by Lawrence as a chucking response to Wills who he reckoned threw.

(Lawrence and Wills, of course, had a longstanding rivalry which went beyond Lawrence's successful lobbying to oust Wills from leading the 1868 tour of England. Wills presided over a powerful Victorian team in the 1860s. Victoria beat Lawrence's New South Wales team on eight out of ten occasions in the 1860s and Lawrence was keen to win more than his share in the new decade. The fierce rivalry between Lawrence and Wills reflected the combativeness of the rival States that existed then and continues today.)

Twopenny was believed to have been born in Ulladulla on the south coast of New South Wales.[9] The most extraordinary aspect of Twopenny's cricket is that he was given few chances to show his bowling form in 1868 in England until very late in the tour. Then he really turned it on and was the surprise packet of the tour, taking 35 wickets in 704 balls or a wicket every 20.11 balls. As a batsman Twopenny was a crude smiter of the ball. He slogged whatever the situation. He hit a tour total of 589 runs at an average of 8.29, with a highest score of 35.

Why did Lawrence hold Twopenny back from the bowling crease for so long on the 1868 tour? The most logical reason had to be that Lawrence was afraid that Twopenny might be called for throwing and that the stigma of one of his bowlers being 'called' would cast a cloud over the tour and place future matches in doubt. Messrs Lawrence, Smith, Graham and Hayman were not in England for the good of their health. They were there to make money, lots of it.

Twopenny was given free rein in the 43rd match of the tour, against East Hampshire at Southsea, when he bowled like the wind taking 9/9 and 6/7. Twopenny terrorised the batsmen and beat them with the sheer hostility of his approach and delivery. In the next match, against Hampshire at Southampton, Twopenny took 9/17 and 3/39, a similar story. In two matches Twopenny had taken 27 wickets.

Twopenny's only first-class match for New South Wales, against Victoria in 1870, was a disappointing game for him. He scored only 8 runs and failed to take a wicket (0/56) in his 30 overs. C. P. (Charles) Moody, a noted critic of the day, suggested that Twopenny's action was doubtful and he wrote that Lawrence's reluctance to use

Twopenny until such time as the England tour was almost completed was because he (Lawrence) also believed that Twopenny chucked the ball. Twopenny was never called for throwing, but he was never again invited to play for New South Wales. He died in Maitland in New South Wales in March 1883; apparently he suffered from 'dropsy'.[10]

Twopenny and so many of his kind did not have many advantages in life. The 1868 tour gave a small group of Aboriginal sportsmen a golden opportunity. They were all grateful for it, but when they came home the opportunities were no more. I wonder whether Charles Lawrence ever regretted not giving Twopenny the chance to bowl more early on in the tour. It is possible that with Twopenny in full flight the Australians' win ratio would have been far greater.

King Cole (Bripumyarrimin)

Right-hand batsman
Right-arm medium slow bowler
Matches 7
75 runs at 7.5
Wickets 1 at 34

King Cole's death was one of the saddest chapters in Australian sporting history. He suffered from a chest complaint, but he was among a number of the players to suffer in that way on the 1868 tour. The summer of 1868 was hot and dry. Hay fever abounded, so too chest complaints and a variety of minor lung infections. King Cole played every match leading up to and including the important fixture against the MCC at Lord's. He scored 75 runs in 10 completed innings for an average of 7.5. His top score was 18. King Cole took 1 wicket on tour, from 14 overs, at a cost of 34 runs and he took a number of brilliant catches in his specialist fielding position of backward point. Early in his cricket career King Cole was known as Charlie Rose. He was the brother of Harry Rose, one of boxer Lionel Rose's ancestors. King Cole was suffering from chest pains in the match against Lewisham at Ladywell (10–11 June 1868). He played at Lord's on 12–13 June, but within days of that match his chest complaint worsened. He developed a combination of tuberculosis and pneumonia and he died in his bed at Guy's Hospital, London on 24 June 1868.

Tiger (Bonnibarngeet)

Right hand batsman
Matches 47
431 runs at 6.17

Tiger was not one of the 'gun' players, but his fitness was unquestioned. He played in all 47 tour matches. He did not bowl a ball on tour, but he scored 431 runs at an average of 6.17 as a specialist batsman. These were not figures to make him jump for joy. Tiger was labelled as a man with a liking for a jar or two, and records show that he was involved in one incident on the tour — in Sheffield where he ended up in hospital after a scuffle with two policemen.

What became of Tiger after the tour is a mystery. A. A. Cowell of Brippick Station, Booroopki, was said to have helped a number of Aboriginal people and Tiger was believed to have been among them. Cowell and Hugh McLeod of Benayeo helped care for Aborigines who were infirm or displaced. It is believed that Tiger died sometime before 1884. During 1874 a Harry Tiger, described in a newspaper as 'one of the Aboriginal cricketers taken to England', was charged with being drunk and disorderly at Sunbury, near Melbourne. There is no record of Tiger's death.

Dick-a-Dick (Jumgumjenanuke)

Matches 45
356 runs at 5.26
5 wickets at 19.2

Dick-a-Dick was one of the great successes of the 1868 tour, yet his success was in relation to his dodging cricket balls off the pitch, not in doing anything startling with the bat or the ball. His skill in finding the Duff children, his generous nature, his gentleness, his quick wit and his unparalleled ability as a dodger endeared him to all.

Dick-a-Dick's health deteriorated almost from the time the team arrived back in Australia in February 1869. A lot of misinformation circulated about the returned Aboriginal cricketers. In Dick-a-Dick's case, he was reported to have been seen at the Mt Elgin races in 1884

— 14 years after he died. According to another source, Dick–a–Dick died in the mid 1890s.[11]

In fact, Dick–a–Dick died on 3 September 1870 at the Ebenezer Mission in Victoria. On his return from England Dick–a–Dick and his wife, Amelia, travelled to the mission. Dick–a–Dick's health was poor and he returned to the Wimmera in the hope of getting well again, but he soon returned to the mission. His health got worse. As he lay on his deathbed, Dick–a–Dick confessed his faith in Christianity. He was baptised at his sick-bed on 30 July 1870. Within a few weeks he was dead. Amelia died before Christmas in the same year.

Peter (Arrahmunyjarrimin)

Right hand batsman
Matches 42
284 runs at 4.48

For a specialist batsman Peter did hardly enough to warrant his name being mentioned in the newspapers. He played 42 matches, which reflects in his case the total lack of playing staff available. With only a handful of good players, Lawrence had his work cut out to form a reasonable outfit. The likes of Peter, Mosquito, Jim Crow and Sundown simply made up the numbers. However, Peter could crack the stockwhip almost as well as Mosquito. At Hastings Peter gave an exhibition with the stockwhip which was, as William Shepherd said, 'almost sleight-of-hand activity'. Many Aboriginal men of that time were called 'Peter' and nothing is known about him from the moment he arrived back in Australia. Perhaps he was the 'Peter' who lived under the care of Cowell at Brippick Station, described in 1881 as 'an old man'. He died unsung, whereabouts unknown.

Charley Dumas (Pripumuarraman)

Right-hand batsman
Matches 44
218 runs at 4.6

Charley Dumas wasn't the best of cricketers, but he was a master at throwing the boomerang. It was his forte and he delighted everyone with his skill throughout the England tour. As a specialised batsman he was a total failure, scoring just 218 runs in 44 matches at an average of 4.4. But as a boomerang thrower he had no peer.

After the team arrived home, Charley Dumas disappeared. There has been speculation that he may have returned to his native Sydney. His life post-tour, where he lived, where he worked and where he eventually died, remains a mystery.

Mosquito (Grongarrong)

Right-hand batsman
Matches 34
77 runs at 3.17

Mosquito was also known as James Cousins. While the spelling of the surname is different, he was in fact the brother of Cuzens. However, they were poles apart in cricketing ability and in wielding the stockwhip. As a cricketer Mosquito struggled. But with the whip he was the master. Charles Lawrence did not need to teach Mosquito to read and write, as he had already acquired these skills before the 1868 tour. In June 1876 Mosquito wrote a letter to an official of the Aborigines Protection Board:

> I write to you with the intention of bringing under your notice that I have been working on the Station this last six years. And never received any payment for the same doing Carpenter work. And I wish to let you know if they intend giving me any thing for my work I would prefer a double-bareled gun for the money. I have made a bullock dray wheel for the dray. Please write as soon as convenient.
>
> I remain your true servant
> James Cousins[12]

It is not known what the Board's response to the letter was. Mosquito married and had a child, Sarah, who died, aged 8, from tuberculosis in 1880. There is no documentary evidence of when and where Mosquito died, although it appears he died sometime between 1887 and 1890.

Jim Crow (Lytejerbillijun)

Right-hand batsman
Matches 13
37 runs at 2.7

Jim Crow (sometimes called Neddy) was said to have been a brother of Dick-a-Dick. Jim Crow had a terrible tour as a specialist batsman on the 1868 tour. He suffered ill-health and returned home on the *Parramatta* in August 1868, long before the main party left England. Little is known of what became of him after he got home. A lot of Indigenous Australian males were given the tag 'Jim Crow' and it has been suggested that the violent Jim Crow known to police at that time was not the Aboriginal cricketer. In 1876 a Jim Crow was listed as an 'absentee' from Ebenezer Station and there was a Jim Crow arrested at Swan Hill in 1875. It is believed that a Jim Crow was murdered by two Aboriginal men in about 1875 for violating marriage rules. Could this have been the fate of the 1868 cricketer?

Sundown (Ballrinjarrimin)

Right-hand batsman
Matches 2
1 run at 3

Sundown played in only a couple of matches, but it is said that the England tour gave him his best batting performance. He scored one run in three completed innings. But that one run was apparently the only run he ever scored in any form of cricket. With Jim Crow he was sent home early due to sickness. Sundown took a steamer from Sydney to Melbourne after the *Parramatta* berthed in Sydney. Arrangements had been made with Cobb & Co to take Sundown from Melbourne to Edenhope, with funds provided for him to find his own way to Hamilton. A 'gentleman' in Hamilton paid Cobb & Co for the journey. The coach stopped and the coachman pointed out to Sundown the 'gentleman's' house in Hamilton. Sundown swung his carpet-bag over his shoulder and walked off, beyond the reach of history.

CHAPTER EIGHT

SINCE the European occupation of Australia, Aboriginal people have rarely been in a position of power. In the 1860s they had no power whatsoever in this white-ruled society. Often they worked for no wages. Payment for work was payment in kind: a pouch of tobacco, a blanket, a bottle of grog: all part and parcel of a system which left the Aboriginal people totally dependent on the conscience or the whim of the white man. They did not have the vote and therefore had no political influence. Yet they were the victims of politics. While the White Australia policy held sway in Australia, the idea of a black man playing Test cricket for Australia was 'unthinkable'. Against this tide of prejudice, by the beginning of the 20th century some very good Aboriginal cricketers had begun to emerge. Queensland produced a fast bowler named Alec Henry and New South Wales produced a splendid bowler of the same type, Jack Marsh. Both suffered, as Eddie Gilbert suffered years later, the indignity of being branded unreliable and a chucker.

My research and my experience lead me to believe that any Aboriginal bowler at first-class level was considered a threat to the exclusive whiteness of the Australian Test team. So whenever an Aboriginal cricketer of Test potential turned up, officialdom stepped in. Umpires were considered to be people of such high standing that they were beyond reproach. If an umpire 'called' a bowler it came with the time-honoured knowledge that the umpire was doing his job without fear or favour. For years, umpires were never questioned about any decision. The stigma of being labelled a chucker was so great that anyone so branded was immediately struck from the selector's little black book. Henry was called, as was Marsh, and later on, during the days of Bradman at his zenith, so was Gilbert.

Albert 'Alec' Henry was born at Deebing Creek in 1880. He

became a regular player with the mission team. In addition to his cricketing skills and his natural inclination towards bowling fast, Henry was a good runner. He ran professionally and was a key member of the Deebing Creek Rugby team. Henry played cricket for South Brisbane and his name still adorns the honour board at the club. He was an outstanding success for South.

In 1902 Henry won the best average trophy for his 5.15 per wicket; in 1904 he again won the averages, with 59 wickets at 9.3 runs apiece. In 1903 Henry played two matches for the Metropolis against a combined country side. 'His pace was terrific and the length splendid,' as he took 5/5 in his first match, including four consecutive clean-bowleds, followed by seven batsmen clean-bowled in 13 overs in the second game. In other matches he was deemed 'practically unplayable.'[1]

After consistent wicket-hauls in Brisbane grade cricket, Henry was soon rushed into the Queensland team. He was described as a 'real speed merchant, but lacking in heart'[2] and 'fiery and unpredictable — a genuine character subject to moodiness'.[3] During a Queensland–New South Wales match in 1903, the newspaper the *Referee* carried the following description:

Henry was very fast … Henry's ubiquitous movements in the field were amusing to onlookers, he was everywhere and seemed inclined to chase the ball wherever it went after leaving his hand … He is tall and lath-like in build … He lacked direction and tired perceptively.[4]

Henry played first-class cricket for Queensland between the summers of 1901–02 and 1904–05. In 1904 he was called for throwing in a Brisbane grade match. The umpire, A. C. Crossart, was a long-serving member of the umpiring fraternity and well-respected. At the end of the over, the fiery Aboriginal fast man approached the umpire and said heatedly: 'You bastard! You no-ball my good balls and the ones I throw, you never! You know nothing about cricket!'[5]

Umpire Crossart alleged that throughout the tirade Henry continually waved his hand in the umpire's face. Henry played against Pelham Warner's 1903–04 England team and he impressed the visitors with his genuine pace and fire. Bernard Bosanquet, the man who invented the 'Bosie' or 'wrong' un' — the ball that spins from the off with the seeming leg-break action — wrote of his impressions of that tour Down Under in an article published in the 1905 edition of *Wisden Cricketers' Almanack*. Bosanquet quoted his England team-mate, Len Braund, who spoke of facing Henry's bowling:

> I took the first ball from the Aboriginal, Henry, who is supposed to be the fastest bowler in the world. Certainly I will say that the first three balls he gave me were indeed the fastest I have ever seen. I got him away for two on the leg side, but two balls later, in cutting him, I was splendidly caught at point.[6]

The great England wicket-keeper Herbert Strudwick added to Braund's impressions of Henry:

> Henry fairly had the wind up Braund and when Warner looked to him to open the second innings, Len replied: 'Not me, I'm not going to commit suicide, going out to be shot by that black devil!'[7]

Henry did not lack commitment to the cause, nor did he lack 'heart'. In fact, he was the very antithesis of a gutless player. Henry suffered bouts of overwhelming tiredness due to his suffering from a serious pulmonary disease.

> Like so many Aboriginal sports-people he was enmeshed in the rigid authoritarianism of the protection-segregation era. He was removed to Barambah (which was renamed Cherbourg in 1931) and imprisoned for a month for 'loafing, malingering and defying authority'. As with the Morgan brothers, he was isolated further afield, to inaccessible Yarrabah, to die there of tuberculosis aged 29 — defiant at the system, yet a certain victim of it.[8]

Jack Marsh was arguably the greatest Aboriginal fast bowler never to have played Test cricket for Australia. Super-talented, Marsh would most certainly have played at the highest level had the Australia of his day been a fairer society, one that embraced the cultures and traditions of all peoples. Sadly the Australia of the early 1900s was a racist, bigoted society, so the Jack Marshs of this world had not a chance in hell of realising their considerable potential. Jack Marsh was born to a 'full blood' Aboriginal woman at Yugilbar Station, the Ogilvie family estate at Baryulgie (near Grafton, New South Wales) on the Clarence River. It is thought that Ogilvie sent Jack and his brother, Larry, to Sydney where there would be more opportunities.[9]

Jack and Larry Marsh met up with the great Aboriginal sprinter Charlie Samuels at La Perouse. Samuels encouraged and inspired the brothers and between the years 1889 and 1895 they competed regularly in major races in Sydney and Melbourne. The 1868 Australians would have loved Jack Marsh. He had a sense of adventure and, like Dick-a-Dick, Mosquito, Charley Dumas and Cuzens, Marsh had a great belief in his own ability and loved a challenge.

Jack Marsh began playing cricket for West Sydney in 1895. Alf Dent watched Marsh throw a boomerang and he reckoned that the Aboriginal man might be able to bowl a ball with the same skill and flair that he displayed with the boomerang. Alf Dent's instincts proved correct. Only a talent that was outstanding could attract media attention in that era. In October 1896, Jack Marsh featured in *Australian Cricket: A Weekly Record*:

> We note with pleasure that J. Marsh has already taken 16 wickets for 44 runs for West Sydney in the second junior competition. For his club versus Adelphi ... he secured 6/12, an excellent performance.[10]

Marsh once clean-bowled the celebrated Australian captain Monty Noble for a duck, and in November 1900 he played for a Colts team against New South Wales — considered to have been an important trial match — and he knocked Victor Trumper's leg stump out of the ground with a magnificent, outswinging off-cutter. The ball swerved late and Trumper gathered himself to launch into a cover drive. Trumper was perfectly poised for a classic drive, but the ball changed course completely, veering late and dramatically like a runaway colt. Instead of the ball veering away from Trumper, or following a predictable course, it broke back from the off and found its way though a tiny gap between bat and pad, hitting the champion's leg-stump. Trumper had fallen for 1. Marsh could not have picked a better batsman to dismiss cheaply, for Trumper was the greatest batsman of cricket's Golden Age — the period from 1890 to 1914. However, umpire W. Curran announced that he would no-ball Marsh the next day. The *Sydney Morning Herald* ran this story after the second day's play:

> Marsh who was no-balled ... feels so confident that his delivery is fair, that he is prepared to have his arm so bandaged as to render it impossible

to bend or jerk the elbow — which is generally accepted as constituting a throw. As a matter of fact, he has already demonstrated to some of the principal members of the Sydney Cricket Club that his delivery is absolutely fair. He caused a piece of wood to be tightly fixed along the arm, and bowled as fast as ever. Orders have been given for a splint for the arm, which will keep it absolutely rigid, and, if completed in time, will be worn for the balance of the eleven's innings … if the splint be not ready something equally effective will be used.[11]

However, all of Marsh's attempts to prove beyond doubt that his action was legitimate did not turn a hair on the head of the man who most mattered when it came to clearing or condemning Marsh — the umpire — and Marsh decided to retire from the match.[12]

The mould was cast. In a clash with Victoria, umpire Bob Crockett, Australia's most senior umpire, called Marsh three times for throwing, then in a return clash he called him 19 times. Marsh had the crowd on his side, but not the umpire. Not that the umpires agreed about Marsh's deliveries. Umpire Curran called Marsh for his faster deliveries and Crockett found fault only with Marsh's slower ball. Warwick Armstrong, the Big Ship, had his off stump knocked out by a Marsh special, but he didn't have to leave the arena for the umpire had called no-ball. Umpire Crockett copped a continuous barrage of verbal abuse from the crowd but he remained as impassive as ever.

Most players and officials in Sydney grade cricket found Marsh to be an extremely gifted bowler, a natural with not a hint of a jerk in his action. In 1902 he took 58 grade wickets at 9.35 runs apiece. In 1916 J. C. Davis wrote:

Marsh possesses gifts like no other man in Australia — and probably no other bowler in the world — possesses: he curves the ball, he bowls a peculiar dropping ball which and his break back on a perfect wicket is phenomenal for a bowler of his pace. Marsh could make the ball do stranger things in the air than any other bowler I saw.[13]

In February 1902 the visiting England team agreed to play against a combined group of fifteen grade players at Bathurst, New South Wales. Archie MacLaren, the skipper, refused to play if Jack Marsh was in the grade team. He claimed that he did not 'care to risk injury to any of his men'. The professionals among the England party were prepared to play against Marsh, but not the amateurs. Some believed that Monty Noble, the New South Wales selector and Test all-rounder, had unduly influenced MacLaren and his men, for Noble reckoned Marsh was a 'chucker' and did not have 'class enough for representative matches: his bowling was erratic and could not be relied upon'. Noble's reference to 'class' was pertinent for Marsh was a great talent. That a black man could play for Australia and with such brilliance and flair that he might show up some if not all of the white men was something that officials and players of the day might not have found particularly palatable. Marsh didn't play against MacLaren's men, but he made his mark a couple of summers later in 1903–04 when Pelham Warner's England team played a Combined XV at Bathurst. Marsh bowled with all his old skill, taking 5/55, winning the visitors' lasting respect. Warner was most impressed with Marsh's effort and he echoed the England team's verdict, when he said that Marsh's 'action is perfectly legal and Marsh was the best bowler in the world'.

Jack Marsh was a very personable character. He was a much-liked member of the New South Wales Sheffield Shield team and he revelled in having fun and telling jokes. At a public reception in the Sydney Town Hall on the night of 12 December 1902, some 5000 people turned out to pay homage to the 1902 Test team and in particular Victor Trumper, the star of the side. The New South Wales team was also part of the throng and there grabbing the limelight was none other than Jack Marsh. The New South Wales thirteen was introduced to the crowd and a brief word said about each player. The players rose, politely acknowledged the crowd's acclaim and sat down. Not Jack Marsh. He nearly brought the house down when he bowed to each section of the crowded hall and waved his arms above his head. The people loved it.

There seems little doubt that both Alec Henry and Jack Marsh should have played Test cricket. While Henry was fiery and fast, Marsh had skills like no other of the time and he was unlucky not to have played Test cricket and gone on more than one England tour. Marsh was a favourite among some critics for the 1905 England tour, but he didn't win the selectors' vote. L. O. S. Poidevin said of Marsh at the time:

He is certainly a marvel with the ball. What a treasure, a gold-mine indeed he would be to an English county. But you will not see him because the absurd White Australia policy has touched or tainted the hearts of the rulers of cricket, as it has the political rulers: but this much is certain — if the Australian team were chosen by popular vote ... then the man to top the poll would most likely be Jack Marsh ...[14]

The great Australian left-handed opening bat, Warren Bardsley did not mince his words when it came to Jack Marsh. 'The reason Marsh was kept out of big cricket was his colour.'[15] J. C. Davis was the best cricket writer of the era in Australia. He knew the game and he knew Jack Marsh.

Of all the dark-skinned bowlers seen in this country the most remarkable was Jack Marsh. He had such command over the ball that it was simply unbelievable what he could do with it in the matter of curving, dropping and breaking and in variations of speed. If he had been a white man with a head for the game, there would have been no room for discussion as to who was the greatest bowler the world ever saw — Spofforth and Charlie (CTB) Turner, not withstanding.[16]

Marsh lived with a W. H. Watson for some eight years in Sydney. Watson described Marsh as being 'perfectly honest', the best-dressed man he had ever seen on a cricket ground, a man who acquired the 'fast twister' by watching baseballers at practice, a man possessed of plenty of brain and who knew what he was doing.

'I remember on one occasion on the eve of a match against Paddington he sketched a plan of the field, and pointed out the positions at which he hoped to have Noble, Trumper and Gregory caught off his bowling. Remarkably enough his prophecy proved correct, and I have his sketch to this day.'[17]

Jack Marsh may well have been one of the great Australian bowlers of all time. His 'problem' was that he happened to be an Aborigine, not 'a white man with a head for the game'.

Marsh ended his days sadly. At about the time of the 1905 Australian tour of England, a tour he should have been on, Marsh drifted out of the game. He joined a travelling Royal Hippodrome, appearing on the same star billing as strongmen, martial arts exponents and wrestlers. In 1909 he was charged with having attacked the owner of a grog shop. In 1916 he died in horrific circumstances, kicked to death by two men on a footpath in Orange, New South Wales.

The two men — John Hewitt and Walter Stone — were charged with manslaughter, although the evidence pointed to Marsh's skull being fractured by 'the toe of a boot'. Predictably the all-white jury acquitted Marsh's murderers without so much as leaving the box to consider their verdict. Judge Bevan then summed up with these chilling words: 'So far as the kicking [of Marsh as he lay prone on the footpath] was concerned, Marsh might have deserved it, because he had been offensive.'[18]

In 1929, a year significant in the world of economics because of the Wall Street crash which sparked the beginning of the Great Depression, Eddie Gilbert became, for a short, explosive time, almost as famous as the most famous cricketer of them all, Don Bradman. In that year Porteus Semple, superintendent of the Aboriginal reserve of Barambah (later Cherbourg), wrote a letter that was to change Gilbert's life for all time. Addressed to the Queensland Cricket Association, Semple outlined the great potential of Edward Gilbert and offered to send him to Brisbane for a trial. His batting average, as Semple explained, then stood at an almost Bradman-like 69, with a top-score of 217, but it was his extraordinary pace with the ball that Semple and others marvelled at. Statistically Gilbert had bowled 126 overs (33 maidens) for a return of 48 wickets for 291 runs. The trial was a success and within a year Gilbert was selected for the Queensland Country Colts against the Queensland Metropolitan Colts. Gilbert had the batsmen ducking and diving like startled rabbits and he finished with 6/29. (By an amazing coincidence Jack Pizzey, who later became Premier of Queensland after holding the portfolio of Minister for Aboriginal Affairs, took the other 4 wickets. When he became premier in 1968 Pizzey promised to bring Queensland into an 'age of enlightenment on matters Aboriginal'.[19]

Gilbert's bowling steadily improved. He developed superb rhythm and with the better rhythm came sustained pace — genuine pace. He took 6/82 for the Queensland Colts against New South Wales, a feat which quickly led to State selection. In his first Sheffield Shield summer Gilbert took 15 wickets for 502 runs. Against the West Indies in 1931–32, he took 5/69 off 19 fiery overs.

On 6 November 1931 Eddie Gilbert had a famous confrontation with Don Bradman. This clash has become part of the folklore of Australian cricket. Queensland was up against the powerful New South Wales side and was bundled out in the first innings for 169. The New South Wales opening bat, Wendell Bill, fell for a duck, then in strode the world's most brilliant bat, Don Bradman. He walked briskly, with his collar turned up, his head held high, a confident air about him, and if you looked closely you would swear there was a faint wisp of a smile on the lines that were Bradman's lips.

Eddie Gilbert was of wiry build, slim, yet deceptively strong. When he let the ball go it came with the force of a catapault. The first ball faced by Bradman reared viciously. The great batsman was caught off guard, but he reacted rapidly and managed to move swiftly to the off and the ball whizzed through to the keeper at chest height, the man with the gloves taking it on the 'up'. Gilbert smiled. He was at the very height of his pace powers and he sensed he had Bradman on the hop. His second ball was bang on line and it fairly flew at the little batting genius, who met the ball smack in the centre of his bat, but the ball struck with such force that it knocked the bat from Bradman's grasp. If was the first and only time Bradman experienced such a phenomenon. The crowd gasped, as did the man at the non-striker's end, Jack Fingleton. The next ball flew past Bradman's outside edge and the following ball, the fourth of the over, Bradman snicked to the keeper. He was out for a duck! Years later Bradman recalled his first encounter with Gilbert:

> That day [Gilbert] was even faster than Larwood at his peak. From the pavilion his bowling looked fair. But in the middle his action was suspect. He jerked the ball and only delivered it from a very short approach. It's very hard that way to generate such speed with a legitimate delivery.[20]

Four New South Wales players questioned the legitimacy of Gilbert's action. However, they all did so on the basis of their amazement that Gilbert could generate high speed from the few shuffling paces he took before he delivered the ball. That is something Bradman also questioned. That Gilbert actually threw the ball is in grave doubt. The New South Wales manager, Al Rose, was in no doubt. He reckoned Gilbert chucked the ball, yet Rose viewed Gilbert from the dressing shed at least 100 metres from the action. Bradman said that Gilbert's action from such a distance looked okay, but when you faced him from close range, say the length of a cricket pitch, it was not clear-cut. Rose stuck to his guns and said that Gilbert's bowling was a 'blot' on the game. At that time Gilbert had New South Wales reeling. He had captured 3 wickets for 12 runs, Alan Fairfax joining Bill and Bradman in the dressing shed. Stan McCabe, the man who later made one of the great scores in Test history, 187 at the SCG against Larwood at the height of Bodyline in 1932–33, hit an unconquered 229. He was in his element against the most ferocious of fast bowlers. Gilbert finished with 4/74 off 20.7 overs, but the explosive clash with Bradman was the talk of the nation. Racist politicians must have worked overtime to ensure that Gilbert would never take the next step and wear the baggy green Test cap.

Any bowler can be no-balled for throwing. The way the MCC law on throwing was framed, it depended entirely on the umpire's interpretation. Gilbert's bowling was explosive and dangerous. A black bowling hero was about to emerge in Australian cricket. For the first time since Jack Marsh, an Aboriginal fast bowler was about to take centre stage. If today's Australia is considered racist, think of an Australia in the 1930s when Aboriginal people had no rights at all. They could not drink, they could not vote, they were publicly humiliated in a myriad ways. If Gilbert were to have played Test cricket, it would have upset the status quo and boosted Aboriginal morale enormously.

Old footage of Gilbert's action exists, but it does not prove that he threw. In fact, it is no more evidence of a doubtful action than footage reduced to slow motion of Harold Larwood or Ray Lindwall. Almost every bowler who uses the wrist sometimes gives the impression that the ball has been 'jerked'. Bradman's immediate appraisal of Gilbert in the wake of his fourth-ball duck could now be construed as having had a damning impact on the Aboriginal player's career, for it tended to lend credence to any umpire who may have been thinking that Gilbert's action was not quite above board. Much later Bradman declared, 'If Gilbert did not actually throw the ball, he certainly did jerk it.'[21]

The phenomenon that was Bradman demanded public attention. A single sentence from him, no matter how off-the-cuff, light-hearted or serious, was placed under the public microscope. For him to cast doubt on Gilbert's action may well have sounded of the death knell for Gilbert's Test cricket aspirations. Only days after he got the champion out for a duck, Gilbert was no-balled for 'throwing'.

Gilbert was no-balled eleven times when bowling for Queensland in a match against Victoria at the MCG. Umpire Andy Barlow was a well-respected official who stood in 86 first-class matches, including 11 Tests. Barlow was the headline-grabbing personality that we might associate with some of the modern umpires. He called a number of notable bowlers, including Ron Halcombe, the Western Australian speedster, whom he called for chucking before Gilbert, in the 1929–30 season. After Gilbert, Barlow called Harold Cotton in 1936–37 and again in 1940–41 and Western Australian off-spinner Ron Frankish. Barlow was the only umpire to 'call' Eddie Gilbert. Slow-motion footage of Gilbert's action proved inconclusive. Many, including Bradman, thought it impossible for a bowler to generate express pace from a short, shuffling approach to the wicket. (Jeff Thomson, surely the fastest bowler to draw breath, achieved his great pace after only an eight-pace run-up.) I am convinced that Gilbert was discriminated against in an Australia that was decidedly racist. We were a land of apartheid, but here the whites outnumbered the blacks and here our form of apartheid was not on the statute books. Aboriginal people were discriminated against alright — blatantly, openly and cruelly — but it was done unofficially.

At the beginning of the 1936–37 season the Queensland Cricket Association, which had employed Gilbert as a member of the ground staff, along with other State players including Don Tallon, wrote an amazing letter to John Bleakley, the Queensland Protector of Aborigines. Fate decreed that this letter would become Eddie Gilbert's cricketing 'death warrant':

At the meeting of the Executive Committee held last evening the matter of Eddie Gilbert was fully discussed and as it was unlikely that he would be chosen for a representative team this season, it was decided with your concurrence, to arrange for Gilbert to return to the settlement next week. With regard to the cricketing clothes bought for Gilbert, it is asked that arrangements be made for these to be laundered at the Association's expense and delivery of the laundered clothes to be made to this office.[22]

Eddie Gilbert was sent home to the Aboriginal settlement at Cherbourg and in 1949 was incarcerated in a mental institution in Brisbane, Wolston Park, where he spent an extraordinary 30 years. The (white) authorities in Brisbane said that Gilbert was suffering from alcoholism and syphilis.

> There was ill-treatment because he was black, the only Aborigine in a ward of ninety meant to house fifty. He was not altogether incapable of speech as some writers have it; he died there, not at Cherbourg, in 1978; his cause of death was a degenerative brain disorder, not syphilis. He is buried at Cherbourg, in company with other great sportsmen, Jerry Jerome and Charlie Samuels.[23]

Some years before Eddie Gilbert died, David Frith, then editor of the British cricket magazine *Wisden Cricket Monthly* and a prolific author, decided to visit Brisbane to do some research on an old fast bowler.

> While in Queensland I thought I'd establish once and for all when it was that the legendary Aborigine fast bowler of the 1930s, Eddie Gilbert, had died. Questions dropped all around the Brisbane suburb where he was last seen pointed me back towards Ipswich, to Goodna, where Eddie had been in care. When I asked the superintendent about the cricketer's date of death, he staggered me by talking of Eddie Gilbert in the present tense. He was still alive! And right here! ... Soon, by the door stood a white-haired Aborigine, long arms hanging limply, black shorts, T-shirt, eyes, when they finally lifted, bloodshot and nervous. There was the man who had put a thunderbolt or two through Bradman, who had made the ball generate smoke when he bowled on the concrete pitches back home in Barambah ... 'Shake hands, Eddie,' the superintendent requested, and he complied. But, as we had been forewarned, there was no conversation. Eddie was under sedation, having been violent in years past ... He wouldn't talk despite all manner of persuasion. When a cricket ball was placed in his hand he stared at it then let it drop to the ground ... So this was the popular little chap who had been denied a Test cap either

because of racial prejudice or his bowling action. When the superintendent was looking away, I took a photograph and tried to convey with a smile all the warmth felt by cricket-lovers who knew — or half-knew — the tragi-romantic story of Eddie Gilbert. I could only finish the article I put together that evening as follows: 'Eddie walked off, still breathing his wheezy monotone; he wandered through the meal hall, and the last I saw of him was as he drifted, a desolate individual, across the parched grass.'[24]

Alec Henry, Jack Marsh and Eddie Gilbert were denied greater cricket honours because they were black. They were treated badly by some individuals, but far worse by the collective attitude of an intolerant, racist Australia. They deserved a fair go. They deserved the chance to wear the baggy green cap.

CHAPTER NINE

JASON GILLESPIE is the first acknowledged Aboriginal (male) Test player. The word 'acknowledged' is significant here for I suspect there have been a number of players before Gillespie who have had an Aboriginal heritage and who played Test cricket for Australia. Jason Gillespie is a warrior fast bowler if ever there was one. Strong and fearless, Gillespie is at his best when he leads an attack.

While the White Australia policy was in force, a cricketer who acknowledged his Aboriginality would not have played Test cricket. The New South Wales batsman Graeme Thomas toured South Africa in 1965–66 and there was some conjecture that he had an Aboriginal background. Certainly had he been so 'classified', John Vorster, the then South African prime minister, might have denied him entry to the Republic. Vorster had refused to allow an England tour of South Africa to go ahead in 1969 because the England selectors had picked a coloured man, Basil d'Oliveria, (originally from South Africa but at that time an English resident), thus beginning the 21-year sporting boycott and widespread international condemnation of South Africa. D'Oliveria hit 158 in The Oval final Test match in August 1968 and was not picked in the original England squad for the South African tour. However, 'Dolly' eventually won a place in the England tour squad when Tom Cartwright withdrew through injury. The Australian cricket authorities encouraged the line that Graeme Thomas was of Native American origin. Apparently that was okay for Vorster.

It has been said that there are other current Australian players beyond Jason Gillespie who are of Aboriginal descent. As recently as August 2001 I met a young man who hails from Tasmania and plays league cricket in the United Kingdom each winter, and who claims to have an Aborignal heritage. He insists that he is a cousin of a well-known former Test batsman, which means the high-profile ex-player has an Aboriginal heritage. Just how many Australians with Aboriginal blood have donned the baggy green? We may never learn the full truth because so many Australians are genuinely ignorant of their heritage and others have lived in denial. In Australia, from 1788 right up until very recent times, to be Aboriginal meant discrimination in a variety of forms, most of which were of the insidious, unspoken sort. No wonder there has been, and still is, denial among some who discover they have Aboriginal blood. There are also people of the Stolen Generation who were never told of their background.

Jason Gillespie is the role model Aboriginal cricket needed so badly. As with almost every living Australian, Gillespie's heritage is a mixture, but his paternal great grandfather was a warrior of the Kamilaroi. The Kamilaroi are one of the largest groups of Aboriginal people in Eastern Australia.

> The early ethnologist A. W. Howitt called them [the Kamilaroi] a 'large nation consisting of many tribes under the same designation', while his one-time collaborator Lorimer Fison held that 'strictly speaking Kamilaroi is the name of a language, not a tribe'. Under this term, he added, 'are included quite a number of tribes'.[1]

The Kamilaroi managed a vast tract of land. According to Norman Tindale, the territory embraced some 75,000 square kilometres. Only the Wiradjuri, 'who spread across to the Lachlan down through the Riverina and back over to the upper Murray', inhabited a larger area in New South Wales, 'some 97,000 square kilometres'.[2] The pronunciation of 'Kamilaroi' differs depending on who is uttering it. There are a number of derivations, the name being spelt in English in these ways: Gamilaroi, Gummilray, Cammealroy, Cummeroy, C'amilarai, Koomilroi, Kamularoi and Kaamee'larai.

Academics have worked out that the Kamilaroi people said 'Kamil', which means 'no'. So they are the people who said 'no'. The Kamilaroi language embraced a host of various tribes in a vast area as far south as the Hunter River, west to Walgett, north to Goondiwindi and east to just beyond Tamworth. Before the white invasion, an estimated 15,000 Kamilaroi lived in the region. A resourceful people, they were superb hunters and gatherers. They skilfully harvested the seeds of wild grasses (Panicum Coevinode). They ground the seed with stone mortar and pestle and the flour was baked into cakes. The process was described thus:

> The burnt seeds were piled on possum skin rugs for the men to thresh them by trampling them in a rectangular hole in the ground. After winnowing in bark dishes, the grain was stored in skin bags until needed, being prepared for eating by wet-grinding on millstones called Dayoorl and made into flat cakes cooked in the ashes of a fire.[3]

They also dug for yams and gathered fruit. Gum was extracted from the acacia and kurrajong trees. It was worked into a paste in a wooden bowl, then rolled into a lump and carried from camp to camp, good tucker for the winter months. The Kamilaroi warriors stalked game: kangaroo and wallaby, iguana, native bear, parrot, scrub and plain turkey, swan, duck and snake. They used stone fish traps and huge nets in the river. Water fowl and emu, especially, were considered great delicacies.

Charles Greenway, son of the famous early convict architect Francis Greenway, spoke of the Kamilaroi's impressive physique. He said they were 'a well-formed, agile and enduring race ... many of the men six feet in height'.

Gillespie's success has come amid a myriad injuries and mishaps. His most famous mishap occurred a couple of years ago in Sri Lanka. He was running in to complete another Test match outfield catch and captain Steve Waugh was running towards him, hell-bent on making the catch. There was a sickening collision of bodies, resulting in a broken leg for Jason and less serious but painful facial injuries for Steve.

When Gillespie was playing third grade for Adelaide his then captain told him that he would never make it as a bowler, but that he might go up a peg or two if he improved his batting. But the teenager believed that he would be playing State cricket within a couple of years and Test cricket by the age of 21. Perhaps others have made like statements. I was a State selector at the time Gillespie made his State debut. He was then raw but fast and he possessed an ability to build pressure on his opponents by his pace and unerring accuracy. Often

Gillespie would pitch just outside off and the batsman would shoulder arms, only to watch in horror as the ball cut back alarmingly to take the off stump or trap the unwary player lbw. It was a case of: if the batsman missed, Gillespie struck. He has been a veritable thorn in the side of every opposing Test team. There is something relentlessly old-fashioned about his bowling. He storms in and delivers with an explosive fluency, wearing the expression of a man on a mission. There is nothing tear-away or flighty about this bowler. So long as he maintains his fitness, Gillespie is a fast bowler here for the long haul. During that remarkable series in India in March–April 2001, Gillespie bowled his heart out on largely unresponsive tracks (unresponsive, that is, if you happen to be an out and out fast bowler and not a spinner such as Harbhajan Singh). He out-thought the master Tendulkar when he came around the wicket at Madras to bowl with a ferocity no other fast bowler could show on that placid track.

Gillespie has two brothers, Rob, aged 23, and Luke, 13. His father, Neil, is of Scottish, German and Kamilaroi heritage, while his mother, Vicki, has a Greek and Irish background. Neil Gillespie says that Jason, while proud of his Kamilaroi heritage, is totally focused on his cricket and prefers not to discuss his heritage publicly. But the family's Aboriginal link is strong. Neil is CEO for the Aboriginal Legal Rights Movement in Adelaide. He was a member of the ACT Chief Minister's Aboriginal and Torres Strait Islander Consultative Council, a member of the National Museum ACT Cultural Centre Advisory Committee, a member of a committee to elect an Indigenous person to the national parliament, and he made a submission to the national parliament's Standing Committee on electoral matters for the 1998 election on the inconsistencies in the treatment of Indigenous elected officials and other elected officials and Indigenous officials and public servants. Neil has worked for the Australian Tax Office, presenting GST workshops to Indigenous artists and art organisations. He has also worked for the ACT Electricity and Water Authority (now ACTEW Corporation Ltd) and praised the organisation's indigenous scholarship program, open to all ACT Indigenous public servants.

Neil and Vicki Gillespie drove to Canberra for the reconciliation match between the ATSIC Chairman's XI and the Prime Minister's XI in April 2001. It was there that I first met them. When I first spoke to Neil about Jason and the Gillespie Kamilaroi heritage, he asked, 'Are you sure Jason is the first male Aboriginal Test player?'

Denial of Aboriginal heritage has been a part of the story of the clash of cultures between white and black in this country since the Union Jack was first raised at Botany Bay more than 200 years ago. All we know for sure is that Jason Gilliespie is the first *acknowledged* Aboriginal male Test player. Aboriginal women have had an even more difficult time gaining acceptance. Women's cricket began in Australia in the 1920s. In the 1934–35 summer a visiting English women's team played a Queensland XI which included two Aboriginal women — Mabel Campbell and Edna Crouch. Edna's niece, Thelma Crouch, became a prominent player and represented Australian juniors against the English women in 1949.

But the player who achieved most for Aboriginal women's cricket was Faith Thomas (nee Coulthard). Born at Nepabunna Aboriginal Mission via Copley (in the Flinders Ranges, South Australia), Faith was the daughter of an Adnyamathana woman. Faith was a babe in arms when she went to the Colebrook Home in Quorn. 'Mum did not abandon me. There was no support for her at that time. Mum was single. She just had a baby and her only way of earning a living was working in pub kitchens. Mum reckoned a pub kitchen was not the sort of place for a baby, so she turned to Colebrook,' Faith recalled. 'You know, it was only two years ago that I first met my father. He had just celebrated his 100th birthday in the Ceduna Nursing Home.'[4]

How did she track her father down? 'Persistence,' she says. Her mother kept in contact with her through the years and she has never considered herself to be a 'stolen child'. Faith thought of Colebrook as 'home' and the people with whom she grew up were (and are) her extended family. The Colebrook Home was established in May 1927. Miss Ruby Hyde brought twelve Aboriginal children from Oodnadatta to establish the Home, which was named after T. E. Colebrook, the first Australian president of the United Aborigines Mission. Among Faith's Colebrook 'family' is well-known Aboriginal leader Lois O'Donohue. In 1943 fate changed the Colebrook family. The children were brought to Adelaide for a holiday, since Quorn was in the middle of a drought and water was scarce. Although it was the capital city of the driest state in the driest continent on earth, Adelaide had a reasonable supply of fresh water.

A new Colebrook Home was established in Adelaide on Shepherd's Hill Road, Eden Hills. Some thirty years later my wife, Christine, and I built a home just down the road from the old Colebrook Home site, which by then was vacant land, just a few fragments of masonry lying in mute testimony of what had been a historic building.

Faith says that many children were saddened by their separation from their families and their culture. She vividly recalls praying for fresh water and food. The mission relied on faith and on help from the generous few. Governments provided little or no support in those days, sometimes actively making life tougher for Colebrook by hindering its activities.

Faith remembers playing with sticks and stones at the Home in Quorn. The stick doubled for a 'bat' and the stone was a 'ball'. The children played a game which embraced roughly a combination of cricket and rounders. And they had fun chucking stones at electricity poles. When they moved to Eden Hills, they played the same games, but equipment was provided, so the bat was a real bat and the ball a real ball. Dick-a-Dick would have been proud of those forty-five kids at Colebrook Home in Eden Hills when Faith was there, for they used to throw stones at one another, with a tin to defend themselves. This was far from a parrying shield and leangle, but the skill and the principle were much the same. The kids emulated cricketers who played in the Blackwood area of Adelaide, about twenty minutes' drive to the south-east of the city.

Faith's interest in competitive cricket was kindled while she was a night-duty trainee nurse at Royal Adelaide Hospital. One night, at the handover shift, the girl replacing Faith expressed her disappointment at having to miss cricket practice that night. Faith said she would like to have a go at cricket and the following week she was invited to train with the Windsor Cricket Club. She took a hat-trick in her second match, on Saturday, 2 February 1956, the year of the Melbourne Olympics.

Women's cricket has come a long way since those days in the Adelaide Parklands, when Faith and her team-mates would shoo away the cows, spread matting over the pitch, peg it down and sprinkle ant powder to kill the ants. 'They gave me the ball and I did what came naturally to me — I bowled fast,' said Faith. Some said that Faith bowled with an action not unlike Keith Miller's, and if this is so, she had an action which must have been something to behold. Others say that Jeff Thomson's action reminded them of Keith Miller, so Faith Thomas may have been a bit like Thommo, just a few shuffling steps and then hurling herself into the fray, bowling as fast as she could, every ball. South Australia's great all-round sportsman Vic Richardson, who won State honours in cricket, football, baseball and tennis, advised Faith to add a few paces to her approach. He felt she needed to create better rhythm and balance to her craft. She took Vic's advice. 'The change was better, a smoother action rather than just letting it rip from the shoulder.' Faith went on to play two Tests for Australia. She also played State hockey.

Faith said that she didn't experience much racism on the field during her cricket days, although she once endured calls of 'Freight train, freight train, goes so fast …' by some opposing women in a club match in Adelaide, a rendition of a hit song which she perceived as racist given that a freight train was 'big and black'. However, Faith reckoned they soon stopped singing their ditty for the song made her bowl all the faster. As Faith Coulthard, she once took 6/0 in a club match. She was picked to go to England with the Australian women's side but withdrew because she wanted to complete her midwifery studies. She was about three-quarters of the way through the year and she was told that if she toured England she would have to do the full year of study again when she returned. She couldn't bear the thought of repeating the year, but now she looks back and regrets her decision, for she could easily have done the course again. The chance to tour England … It was a lost opportunity. Now Faith plays golf. Noted sports historian Bernard Whimpress interviewed Faith some years ago. He stayed at her house in Quorn and, in appreciation of her hospitality, he gave her a few golfing tips. Today she regularly enjoys a round of golf and plays with the same enthusiasm and passion she has for life.

Cricket has two wonderful Indigenous role models in their two Test players, Faith Thomas and Jason Gillespie. The bond between the two players was enhanced in Canberra on 19 April 2001 when Faith Thomas presented Jason Gillespie with the Johnny Mullagh Cup. Gillespie was the winning ATSIC Chairman's XI captain. His side beat Steve Waugh's Prime Minister's XI by one run in a historic reconciliation game of cricket which was far more than just a game. It was a positive step forward in Australian race relations. That Faith Thomas presented the Johnny Mullagh Cup to Jason Gillespie has inextricably linked the Test pair to the 1868 Australians.

CHAPTER TEN

T HE 1868 tour proved a moderate financial success, but, as history shows, not one penny went to any of the Aboriginal performers. To this day no evidence has emerged about an 1868 tour contract. Yet some of the 1868 tourists were among those who allegedly signed the 1867 contract conceived by the dubious Edward Gurnett. On 8 January 1867, sixteen Aborigines and William Hayman became party to a contract which was signed (albeit there was a surprising sameness about the cross against every one of the player's names, suggesting that someone else other than the player himself may have signed the document), sealed and delivered by William Edward Broughton Gurnett in the presence of Melbourne solicitor Thomas Pavey and his clerk, Johnathan D. Lynch. David Simpson, who wrote a paper about the contract, reported that:

> On February 11, 1867 Gurnett forwarded his contract, written in a beautiful copperplate hand, to Sir Redmond Barry, senior judge of the Supreme Court of Victoria. Sir Redmond was perceived as being the unofficial standing counsel for the Aborigines.[1]

His paper examined the incongruities between legal rights that are read literally, and the inequalities that existed between different races and classes of people. He says:

> Resulting from an unsuccessful initial attempt to launch the famous 1868 Aboriginal tour of England, its primary functions were two-fold. In the face of powerful government and philanthropic opposition, it was an attempt to convince an influential legal advocate for Aborigines of the propriety of the tour. Furthermore it bound the potentially lucrative Aborigines by contracting not only them but their familiar 'manager', Hayman, to the entrepreneur, Gurnett.[2]

Seven Aboriginal cricketers — Jellico, Tarpot, Lake Billy, Watty,

Harry Rose and Paddy — allegedly "signed" the Gurnett contract, but none of these men actually went on the 1868 England tour. Three of the men — Jellico, Watty and Paddy — were already dead by the time the tourists set sail for England. Tarpot, a good athlete and good cricketer, fell ill as the players were boarding the *Parramatta* on 7 February 1868, the day before the wool-clipper sailed, and was forced to withdraw from the tour. Tarpot was not only a good all-round cricketer but he could run 100 yards backwards in 14 seconds and would have been a sensation on the track. The tragic deaths of Jellico, Paddy and Watty in the wake of the ill-fated 1866–67 Sydney tour gave the protectionists fuel for their rhetoric against another tour of any description. Of the men named on the 1867 contract only Johnny Mullagh, Johnny Cuzens, Peter, Sundown, Dick-a-Dick, Redcap and Charlie Dumas went to England.

There is every likelihood that the 1867 Gurnett contract was a sham, because many Aboriginal people of the area could read and write at that time. As we have noted, Jimmy Cousins (Mosquito) wrote a letter at Framlingham, dated 2 June 1876, a copy of which is at the Victorian State Archives, revealing a good hand and excellent sentence construction. Johnny Mullagh and Johnny Cuzens were also likely to have been able to read and write, so the cross marked against every player's name on the Gurnett contract would seem to indicate that either Gurnett or Hayman "signed" for the players, or perhaps it was done by the solicitor, Pavey, or his assistant, Lynch. The contract lacked credence and would be unacceptable today and probably legally unenforceable.

The terms of the contract included a clause stating that William Hayman, manager, was to receive the sum of 1000 pounds upon the return of the side to Victoria. This sum was quite apart from his other entitlements — travelling expenses, suitable board and lodging for the length of the agreement, and 'five per cent on the net profits' from the matches. Gurnett's contract afforded the Aborigines far less. On their return to Victoria each of the players was to receive the sum of 50 pounds, which amounted to 5 per cent of Hayman's fee. And they were each to be provided with the sum of 7/6 per week for pocket money. Their lodgings would not be quite the star quality that Hayman was contracted to expect; rather they would be "suitable to their condition in life". This was a less than subtle reference to race rather than class.

Gurnett's contract stipulated that the players were "to behave with such sobriety and regularity as shall be necessary to the proper and effectual carrying out and performance of all matches". Some of the players drank, but not to the extent that the contract inferred. In England in 1868 only Tiger got into trouble as a result of the demon drink. Bullocky was absent from the Australian second innings at Lord's, but there is no evidence, only inference and innuendo, that he was the worse for wear after a night on the grog. The MCC won that famous match by a margin of just 55 runs.

The promised payments to the players were effectively safe for the shrewd and miserly Gurnett.

He could easily have, as Sampson suggested, found pretexts to avoid payment to the players by way of claiming any of a myriad of things — from laziness to drunkenness, from alleged illness to apathy. Sampson also noted that the Aborigines being party to a legal contract was in itself highly unusual and 'could be construed as assigning the Aborigines to a higher status than was customary at that time'.[3]

In the 1860s there had been considerable debate about whether Aboriginal people were capable of entering into legal agreements; some considered them childlike. Until the control of the Aboriginal people was vested in the Victorian statutes in 1869, one year after the famous tour, contractual requirements for Aborigines were *ad hoc*. The Gurnett contract might have comforted Hayman and others, but it appears that there was no follow-up contract or the original one was altered to take into account the new players to replace the seven signatories who did not make the 1868 England tour. If the original one was altered, the new or revamped contract has never come into the public spotlight.. In 1868 there were gathering storm clouds in a legal sense for all Aboriginal people living in Victoria, for the Natives Protection Act of 1869 made it an offence to 'remove or attempt to remove or instigate any other person to remove any Aboriginal from Victoria without the written consent of the Minister'.

Had this piece of legislation been enacted a year earlier there is no doubt that the 1868 Aboriginal Australian Cricket Tour of England would never have taken place. The Gurnett contract ran for just one year and it lapsed on 8 January 1868. One month later the team, having slipped secretly out of Victoria, sailed from Sydney Harbour.

Tom Wills, the original coach of the team, had been shoved aside, although William Hayman remained as manager. That no contract covering the 1868 tour has come to light is not the mystery it was first thought to be. One might surmise that such a contract would have threatened the tour simply because of the growing concern about the welfare of the Aboriginal people. To draw up a new contract would have alerted the authorities who wanted to prevent any such tour. Without a contract, the players were able to maintain a relatively low profile, thus allowing their escape to Sydney after rowing out to a Sydney-bound cutter which waited a few hundreds metres offshore at Queenscliff. There was no call for protection in Sydney; once there the team was legally free to do as it pleased.

The 1868 Australians were generally well cared for and they stayed in good, clean accommodation. Some might argue that they were exploited, given that they were used as 'curiosities' before and after play and during breaks in the cricket, throwing spears and boomerangs, dodging cricket balls and cracking the stockwhip like exotic circus performers. Yet by almost every account the players genuinely enjoyed the sports. They were certainly exploited financially. Apart from their lodging and travelling expenses, the players received nothing in the way of payment on tour and not a single penny for their efforts upon their return to Australia. In addition, the travel arrangements were hopeless, given that they criss-crossed the country, with venues vast distances apart. They would, for instance, take the train from Rochdale (in the north of England) to Swansea (in South Wales) then from Swansea back to Bradford in the north. Apart from being tiring, a better-planned itinerary would have saved considerable travel expenses.

It was suggested that George Parr, the great Nottingham and England batsman, would have been best qualified to organise the travel. Parr led the first England team abroad, to North America in 1859. He also led the second England team to Australia in 1863–64 and was the long-time captain–manager of the All England XI, the wandering team of professionals that travelled the English countryside each year. William Hayman would have argued that the itinerary virtually 'evolved' after the Lord's match. Most of the games were arranged after the side played the MCC at Lord's, on 12 and 13 June, and games were then arranged on a first-come, first-served basis.

The extraordinary number of games led to injury and illness and three Englishmen filled in from time to time. William Norton led the team at Hastings when Lawrence was with King Cole at Guy's Hospital; G. H. Shum-Story, a Tynemouth Club man, replaced Johnny Mullagh at Northumberland after Mullagh fell sick; and William Shepherd, who umpired many of the matches, also played seven matches. Shepherd, who was convinced (or conned into believing) that the team lost 2000 pounds on the 1868 exercise, wrote some interesting observations about the players and his thoughts were published 51 years later, in *Ayres Cricket Companion*, under the title of 'The Tour of Australian Aborigines in the year of 1919'. The following are his descriptions:

Johnny Mullagh: A first-class bat, splendid forward player, with a strong and brilliant defence, also a very fine fast (right-hand) straight bowler. He played no mid-wicket-on to his bowling, but fielded the ball himself, being on it like a flash, and his aim at the wicket was unerring, to the astonishment of many unwary batsmen. He scored well over 1500 runs during the tour and was undoubtedly the best all-rounder of the team. I recollect the late Fred Gale (the 'Old Buffer') saying that Mullagh's innings of 87 at The Oval in the Aboriginals' first match of the tour was as fine an innings as he has ever seen, Mullagh's forward play putting him in mind of that of Fuller Pilch.

Johnny Cuzens: Another brilliant bat, proved generally a fast scorer, hitting hard all round the wicket and making well over 1400 runs. He was a remarkably fast bowler with a high action, also a fine field and very fast on his feet. Johnny was a 'flyer', his alleged native record being something phenomenal: 100 yards in 9 seconds! Be that as it may, I can vouch for the fact that while he was here in this country, he took on all comers, and, although he was invariably very slow 'off the mark', was never once defeated. He used to run in bare feet, but when we were at Sheffield I called on a nephew of old Fuller Pilch. He was a boot and shoe maker, specially noted for 'running pumps'. I got him to make a special pair for Johnny Cuzens and after that our champion ran better than ever.

Bullocky: The wicket-keeper proved himself highly efficient; he was a good bat with a strong defence, bowlers invariably finding it difficult to secure his wicket.

Tiger: Another fair bat, with a good defence, he was also most reliable in the field.

Dick-a-Dick: Fair bat and bowler and a good field. He was brought over to give an exhibition of a native sport practised among the tribes, and of which Dick was the champion. He was also a splendid hurdler, never being beaten 'over the sticks' in his contests here.

King Cole: Would have undoubtedly developed into a highly satisfactorily all-round member of the team, as he was very keen for the game. He was also a good sprinter.

Twopenny: A good hard hitter without, however, much style, fair field. Very effective bowler, especially towards the latter end of the tour, but his delivery was somewhat doubtful.

Jim Crow: Could play better on the violin than with a cricket bat, but his specialty was spear and boomerang throwing.

Charley Dumas: A very fair and improving bat, and fair field. Brought over to display his remarkable skill in boomerang throwing, he being the acknowledged champion before leaving Australia.

Peter: A good, sound bat and field. He was, too, an expert spear thrower.

Jimmy Mosquito: A fair bat and splendid field. He was an exceptional jumper, being able to walk the horizontal bar and then jump over it. Also specialised with the stock whip.

Redcap: A good, useful bat. Having a weakness, however, to use his legs unduly, lbw often figured against his name. Umpires were more particular than they are now, at least I think so. He was a hard-working field.

Sundown: A very fair bat and field, but did not often play his health here being indifferent. Clever with the spear and boomerang, 'Sundown' was a cricketing 'curiosity': he came over with the reputation of never having made a run in any match at home, he certainly never made one here and in several matches played after they went back I learnt that he never made a run there.

On 7 May 1908 an article appeared in *Cricket: A Weekly Record of the Game*, written by David Scott, whose nom de plume 'The

Almanack' was conferred upon him by John Conway, manager of the 1878 Australian touring team, by virtue of his wide knowledge of the history of cricket and cricketers. Perhaps Scott was considered the 'Walking Wisden Almanack':

> The novelty of the black team caused many a rhymster an opportunity to indulge his fancy and this is one of the best –

Your swarthy brows and raven locks
Most gratify your tonsors,
But by the name of Dick-a-Dick,
Who are your doughty sponsors?

Arrayed in skin of kangaroo
And decked with lanky feather,
How well you fling the fragile spear
Along the sunny heather.

And though you cannot hope to beat
The Britishers at cricket,
You have a batter, bold and brave,
In Mullagh, at the wicket.

Mullagh was an outstanding player, a man of great dignity. He should have captained the 1868 Aboriginal team when Lawrence was unavailable, but English 'stand-ins' such as William Shepherd and William Norton led the team in Lawrence's absence. We glean from this that no Aboriginal player was to be given any sort of responsibility or authority on the tour. Shepherd and Norton were cricketers of very ordinary standard and being passed over as a replacement captain would not have pleased Mullagh.

The great sadness in all this is that the players never received payment from the tour. They came home to an initial round of back-slapping and good cheer, but the 'protectionists' got their way. Australia was a hard place, with a racist view of the world, as shown by the treatment of the likes of Alec Henry, Jack Marsh and Eddie Gilbert long after the 1868 tour. The 1868 tourists were exploited, there is no doubt. Some of the players played all or almost all of the matches. There was a plethora of matches — 47 matches in 115 days.

(The New Zealand All Blacks who toured England in 1905 played some 80 matches in a visit of similar or equal physical and travel stress to the 1868 Australian tour.) Some of the 1868 Aboriginal cricketers were simply not good enough to match it with their English opposition. The likes of Tiger (431 runs at 6.17), Peter (284 runs at 4.48), Charley Dumas (218 runs at 4.6), Mosquito (77 runs at 3.17), Jim Crow (37 runs at 2.7) and Sundown (1 run at .33) were clearly not up to the required standard. Their inclusion and Lawrence's idea that he could make big money by exhibiting the spear throwing and other skills of his players smacks of exploitation by the team managers. Among the virtual 'non-performers' Peter was good with the stock-whip, Charley Dumas was a magician with the boomerang, Mosquito was even better than Peter with the stockwhip, while Jim Crow and Sundown weren't really expert at anything in particular and it seems that this pair 'made up the numbers' in the wake of the deaths of Jellico, Paddy and Watty and Tarpot and Harry Rose not making the tour. Harry Rose, the brother of King Cole, who also went by the handle "C. Rose", almost made the England tour. He reached Geelong with Lawrence's men, but in January 1868 he was sentenced to jail for drunkenness by the Hamilton Court.

Poor cricket by a good many of the team led to the likes of Mullagh, Cuzens, Redcap, Bullocky and Lawrence having to work near mir-acles to get the side up for a win. In the circumstances the side performed remarkably well. The Aboriginal players thrilled crowds throughout England with their athleticism and demonstrations of traditional games and war strategies.

Aboriginal cricketers had to wait 120 years before another tour of England was made. The part re-enactment tour of England by an all-Aboriginal team was the brainchild of the then prime minister, Bob Hawke. It was timed to coincide with the 1988 Bicentenary. It is ironic that a celebration of Aborigines in cricket should be brought to the fore in the year that marked the 200th anniversary of the European invasion of their land. The team was captained by John McGuire and managed by rugby great Mark Ella, but, as with the 1868 Australians, when the players returned to Australia their progress was not monitored and their abilities were allowed to dwindle. There proved to be no opportunities for the players upon their return.

After months of research and writing the 1868 story, my involvement took a new twist in April 2001 when I played for the Prime Minister's XI against the ATSIC Chairman's XI. I wanted to be at this match, played at Canberra's Manuka Oval, because the game was a re-enactment of the 1868 Australians, the ATSIC players all wore distinctive maroon shirts with a white sash and they played for the Johnny Mullagh Cup. There was also talk of another part re-enactment tour of England. Steve Waugh left the field with a migraine and the Finance Minister Joe Hockey pulled a hamstring, so I found myself in the field for 28 overs. I swear I missed four balls at mid-on by twenty-five years, but the game was played in the right spirit.

Soon after, I was being considered for coach of the 2001 Indigenous Youth Team to England and I found myself lobbying the Prime Minister, John Howard and ATSIC chairman, Geoff Clarke. There was enthusiasm all round, but it proved difficult to get the tour off the ground. We had a consultant to help get the tour together, but I realised that nothing would be accomplished unless I organised a squad of players. I contacted all the Indigenous directors of cricket in the various states. We got a squad of twenty players, which was pruned to fourteen, and the tour got under way, leaving Brisbane on 14 August. We played 10 matches, winning 5, losing 3 and having the better of the two drawn games. Unlike the 1868 side, we played only one-day matches. The match at Lord's was a highlight, and the game against an all-black United States team from Los Angeles was a fabulous experience.

Some of the squad looked every bit the part and are potential first-class players. But they need monitoring and encouragement and ongoing help, something the 1868 players and the 1988 re-enactment side did not receive.

Among our team executive were Grant Sarra (team manager) and ATSIC field officer John Tatten. A number of John's specially dot-painted bats were presented to some of the teams we played, especially the 're-enactment' matches such as the MCC match at Lord's. A bat was presented to Michael L'Estrange, the Australian High Commissioner, during a reception for the squad at Australia House. Our 2001 Aboriginal Australian Youth Team consisted of Barry Firebrace (captain), Joel Liddle and Adam Walker from Victoria; Barry Weare, Jacob

Sarra, Kieren Gibbs and Glen Martin from Queensland; Ryan Bulger and Kevin Thomas from South Australia; Paul Holland, Jaydon Bennell, Marsh Jackson and Baden Richer from Western Australia; and Aiden Jones from Tasmania. Four players — Barry Firebrace, a left-hand bat with a touch of Brian Lara class about him, Barry Weare, Kevin Thomas and Marsh Jackson — were nominated for the 8th National Aboriginal and Torres Strait Islander Sports Awards for 2001. Barry Firebrace won the State award in that event.

At the end of the tour the players presented me with a small dot-painted bat. It features the names of each player in the team and dots signifying their state of origin and their age and other coloured dots indicating continuity and friendship. On the face of the bat, near the bottom, is fastened the coin used to toss in the MCC match at Lord's. I had become a brother of this touring family.

The 1868 Australians were more than a collective 'curiosity'. There was widespread sympathy for the American negro given the overt racism and discrimination which led to Lincoln's vision to free the black slaves. The American Civil War (1861–65) was barely three years past when the Aboriginal players arrived in England. *Uncle Tom's Cabin* was fresh in the minds of thousands of English readers.

In those stern Victorian days, many Englishmen wore a holier-than-thou face. They considered cricket to be a highly desirous recreational sport for the 'lower orders', believing that it would help provide for these unfortunates the virtue of team-work and unquestionable obedience to the umpire's authority. They saw cricket as a noble pursuit: the game of the upstanding, the pure, the Christian and the gentleman. Some suggested that the game of cricket would replace the corroboree in Aboriginal culture. The protectionists and discriminatory men of the cloth saw cricket as a fine 'muscular Christian pursuit'. The racist principles of Charles Darwin's theories became manifestly indoctrinated into society in 1859 with his *Origin of Species*. Darwin's theory was that there was an unbridgeable distance between the white man, who had developed what Europeans might call civilisation and the black man who had remained naked and close to the ape. They shared fundamental physical attributes, but they had nothing in common in terms of reason and intellect. If it all began as a naïve view, it would soon degenerate into hate-based ideology which would effectively sanction genocide.

There were many well-meaning individuals determined to help the Aborigines and to right the wrongs of the past, but they were the minority. In 1814, just 26 years into the occupation of Australia, Governor Lachlan Macquarie wrote in a letter to Westminster that it seemed 'only to require the fostering hand of time, gentle means and conciliatory manners to bring these poor unenlightened people into an important degree of civilisation'. There was no official sanctioning of genocide, but that is exactly what is was, albeit in a slow and insidious way, for the Aborigines had been hounded off their lands. They fled deeper into the bush. They fell victim to a range of diseases the white man brought to their land, including the dreaded syphilis. They had little or no resistance to such diseases. A heavy cold often developed, as it did with King Cole, into pneumonia, which, in those days before the advent of antibiotics, meant almost certain death.

The Aboriginal people of Australia do not deserve better treatment than any other Australians. What they do deserve is a fair and equal chance. The story of the 1868 Australians was the most fascinating literary journey of my writing experience. And it all began for me with my offer to loan my baggy green Australian Test cap to the Aboriginal community. Then came the documentary film with James McCaughey, the idea of writing the book, the ATSIC cricket match in Canberra and the 2001 Aboriginal Youth Cricket Tour of England. From the outside looking in, I suddenly had become part of this story. Today when I look into the face of an Indigenous elder, I see a mix of pain and joy. ATSIC's John Tatten has such eyes. He is a calm man who taught himself to paint left-handed after losing the use of his right arm through bungled surgery. Painting has helped John cope with the never-ending pain. But he doesn't harbor grudges about the misfortunes he has had to suffer, for he is a man who dwells on the positives. He gets on with life. His art is integral to his Dreaming. John will tell you that in traditional Aboriginal society everyone is an artist. Art is part of the training of Aboriginal songs and dancing. Art is the essence of daily life and every artist's Dreaming.

My Dreaming, my secret side
I must hold on to it
It makes me feel good
Happy in heart and spirit
Our story is in the land
It is written in our paintings
On sand, bark and cave
It is our Dreaming

John's words evoke the power of the King Cole ceremony at London's Meath Gardens that Wednesday of 29 August 2001. His specially painted cricket bats now adorn such places as Lord's Cricket Ground and Australia House in London, plus a handful of English clubs, including the Reading Cricket Club. It was against Reading in 1868 that Johnny Mullagh scored the highest individual knock of the tour, 94. John's painting on the bats depicts his people's relationship to the game of cricket. Two large circles represent two distinct meeting places. The track down the centre of the bat connects two circles, 'our pathways'. The U shape represents Indigenous Australians and the different colours are the different nations which comprise the Aboriginal nation.

At the top of the bat footprints show us the bowler's approach. The circle represents the stumps and the track joining the two circles is the pitch. The U shapes are the different fielding positions. While the different shapes and colours are similar, none are the same, and that is representative of the diversity of the Indigenous people. John's paintings are called 'It's just not cricket'.

Similarly, this story of the 1868 tour and beyond is not just a cricket book. It is a journey into the heartland of a nation's conscience. When I look at Adam Walker and Barry Firebrace, cricketing relatives of Johnny Cuzens, I see more than great skill. I can sense their pride in their history and place of origin.

Meantime, out in the backblocks of Australia, Aboriginal kids play a dangerous game called 'hook'. This is the game where one kid stands about twelve paces away and throws a rock at his mate, who is armed with a stick or club. The stone is aimed at the head of the kid with the stick, who proceeds to hook the stone just as the missile is about to crash into his temple; shades of Viv Richards cutting loose at a bumper from Dennis Lillee. Dick-a-Dick, that Artful Dodger of the 1868 tour, would be rapt watching the skill of these kids. Who knows, they may one day find themselves hooking for real at Lord's and Barbados and the SCG. The Australian Cricket Board is working towards giving every youngster in this land an equal chance to make the top in cricket. Maybe this story will help in some small way towards that end. Certainly I have learnt that there is an enduring power in the human spirit.

NOTES

Introduction

1. A. G. Steele in 'Badminton Cricket', reproduced in *Lord's 1787–1945* by Sir Pelham Warner, George G. Harrap & Co., London, 1946, pp. 59–60.

Chapter 1

1. H. G. Bennett, extracts from a letter to Earl Bathurst, Secretary of State for the Colonial Department, on the condition of the colonies in NSW and Van Dieman's Land, London, 1820. Reproduced in Rupert Christiansen's *The Visitors: Culture Shock in Nineteenth Century Britain*, Chatto and Windus, London, 2000, p. 170.
2. Gib Wettenhall, *The People of Gariwerd: the Grampians' Aboriginal Heritage*, Aboriginal Affairs, Victoria, 1999, p. 18.
3. ibid., p. 19.
4. John Mulvaney and Rex Harcourt, *Cricket Walkabout*, Macmillan, 1988, p. 28.
5. Gib Wettenhall, *The People of the Gariwerd: the Grampians Aboriginal Heritage*, Aboriginal Affairs Victoria, 1999, p. 30.

Chapter 2

1. Colin Tatz, *Genocide in Australia*, Aboriginal Studies Press, Canberra, 1999, p. 15.
2. ibid.
3. John Mulvaney and Rex Harcourt, *Cricket Walkabout*, Macmillan, South Melbourne, 1988, p. 38.
4. Martin Flanagan, *The Call*, 1998.
5. Contemporary newspaper report, source unknown.
6. John Mulvaney and Rex Harcourt, *Cricket Walkabout*, Macmillan, 1988, p. 46.
7. ibid., pp. 50–51.
8. ibid., p. 56.
9. Bernard Whimpress, *Passport to Nowhere, Aborigines in Australian Cricket 1850–1939*, Walla Walla Press, Sydney, p. 25.
10. Mulvaney and Harcourt, op. cit., p. 58.
11. *Australasian* newspaper, March 1867.
12. Newspaper, March 1867, source unknown, probably the *Australasian*.
13. Charles Lawrence Journal, p. 54.
14. ibid.

15. *Australasian*, September 1867.
16. Charles Lawrence Journal, p. 58.
17. ibid.

Chapter 3

1. Frederick Lillywhite, *Cricket Scores and Biographies*, Vol. I (facsimile edition of 1862 original), 1799–1827, Roger Heavens, Cambridgeshire, England, 1997.
2. Charles Dickens, *Pickwick Papers*, 1836, p. 130.
3. *Image MCC 1787–1937*, The Times Publishing Co. London, 1937, p. 120.
4. ibid., p. 36.
5. Derek Birley, *A Social History of English Cricket*, Aurum, London, 1999, p. 80.
6. ibid., p. 81.
7. ibid., p. 81.
8. ibid., p. 82.
9. Frederick Lillywhite, *Cricket Scores and Biographies*, Vol. II, 1827–1840, p. 200.
10. ibid., p. 179.
11. ibid., p. 311.
12. Peter Vansittart, *London: A Literary Companion*, John Murray Publishers, London, 1992, reprinted 1994.
13. Charles Lawrence, journal, pp. 8–9.
14. Vansittart, op. cit., p. 53.
15. ibid., p. 54.
16. Birley, op. cit., p. 88.
17. Charles Lawrence Journal, p. 10.
18. ibid., pp. 10–11.
19. Frederick Lillywhite, *Cricket Scores and Biographies*, Vol. II, p. 434.
20. Tony Lewis, *Double Century*, MCC, Pelham Books, 1997, p. 86.
21. John Marshall, *Lord's*, Pelham Books, London, 1969.
22. ibid., p. 14.
23. Frederick Lillywhite, *Cricket Scores and Biographies*, Vol. II, 1827–1840, pp. 413, 414.
24. ibid., p. 414.
25. *MCC 1787–1937*, The Times Publishing, London, 1937, pp. 25–26.
26. Charles Lawrence Journal, p. 4.
27. ibid., p. 5.
28. ibid., p. 6.
29. ibid., p. 14.
30. ibid., p. 14–15.
31. ibid., pp. 17–18.
32. ibid., p. 21.
33. ibid., p. 23.
34. ibid., p. 33.
35. ibid., p. 36.

36. A. A. Thomson, *Odd Men In: A Gallery of Cricket Eccentrics*, Museum Press, London, 1958, p. 19.
37. ibid., p. 21.
38. ibid., p. 21.
39. Charles Lawrence Journal, p. 39.
40. John Forster, *The Life of Dickens*, Chapman & Hall and Henry Frowde, London, 1880, p. 756.
41. Charles Lawrence Journal, p. 50.
42. ibid., p. 51.
43. ibid., p. 51.
44. Keith Dunstan, *The Paddock that Grew, The Story of the Melbourne Cricket Club*, Hutchinson, Australia, 1988, p. 31.
45. ibid., p. 32.
46. Bernard Whimpress, *Passport to Nowhere: Aborigines in Australian Cricket 1850–1939*, Walla Walla Press, Sydney, 1999, p. 74.
47. *Bell's Life in London & Sporting Chronicle 1822–1886*.

Chapter 4

1. Reverend Henry Nisbett's Journal, p. 246, Mitchell Library, Sydney, NSW Vols ML MSS 3093/11–12.s.
2. Charles Lawrence Journal, p. 63.
3. Rev. Henry Nisbett's Journal, p. 247, op. cit.
4. John Mulvanny and Rex Harcourt, *Cricket Walkabout: The Australian Aborigines in England*, Macmillan, Melbourne, 1988, p. 163.
5. A. G. 'Johnny' Moyes, *Australian Cricket: A History*, Angus & Robertson, Sydney–London, 1959, p. 152.
6. Russel Ward, *Finding Australia: The History of Australia to 1821*, Heinemann Educational Australia, 1987, pp. 62–63.
7. Adapted from M. F. Christie, *Aborigines in Colonial Victoria 1835–86*, Sydney University Press, 1979, reproduced in *The People of the Gariwerd*, Gib Wettenhall, Aboriginal Affairs Victoria, 1999, p. 48.
8. Reverend Nisbett Journal.
9. Charles Lawrence Journal, pp. 64–65.
10. ibid., p. 65.

Chapter 5

1. Reverend Henry Nisbett journal.
2. John Mulvanney and Rex Harcourt, *Cricket Walkabout*, Macmillan, South Melbourne, 1988, p. 94.
3. Newspaper report, possibly *The Cricket Field*, May 1868.
4. *Bell's Life in London*, 23 May 1868.
5. Mulvaney and Harcourt, op. cit., p. 121.
6. W. B. Tegetrmeier, *The Cricket Field*, May 1868.

7. ibid., May 1868.

8. *Bell's Life in London*, 30 May 1868.

9. Alverstone and Alcock's Surrey Cricket: Its History and Association 1895.

10. Newspaper cutting, Gravesend (source unknown), 1868.

11. Newspaper report, *Eastbourne Gazette*, October 1868.

12. *Brighton Gazette*, 10 June 1868.

13. 1868 Scorebook.

14. *The Old Buffer, American Cricketer, A Journal of the Cricket Field*, Philadelphia, 18 June 1885, front page. His contribution to the journal was by way of a letter to the editor written from London, dated 24 May 1885.

15. Debrett research for E. Gordon Mallett, December 1983.

16. *Yorkshire Gazette*, 18 July 1868.

17. *Yorkshire Gazette*, 18 July 1868.

18. *York Herald*, 19 July 1868.

19. Letter to editor of the *Yorkshire Gazette*, published 25 July 1868.

20. Longsight newspaper cutting 18 July 1868, author and publisher unknown.

21. *Bury Times*, 25 July 1868.

22. Ibid.

23. *Norwich Mercury*, 29 July 1868.

24. Bootle newspaper, 2 August 1868, unknown.

25. Bootle newspaper, 2 August 1868, unknown newspaper.

26. Ibid.

27. *Sheffield Independent*, 12 August 1868.

28. *Sheffield Independent*, 13 August 1868.

29. ibid.

30. Newspaper report, Dewsbury, 15 August 1868, source unknown.

31. *Lincoln Standard*, 8 September 1868.

32. English newspaper cutting, author/publisher unknown, published 9 September 1868.

Chapter 6

1. Tower Hamlets records, Mulberry Place, London, pp. 52 of Our Fascinating Borough.

2. *Daily Telegraph*, London, 27 June 1868.

3. The Old Buffer, *American Cricketer*, Philadelphia, 18 June 1885.

4. Part of speech by Grant Sarra, Team Manager, 2001 Aboriginal Youth Cricket Tour of England, Meath Gardens Cemetery, 29 August 2001.

5. ibid.

Chapter 7

1. A. G. Course, *Painted Ports: The Story of Ships*, Devitta Moore.

2. *Sydney Mail*, 22 August 1891.

3. Felix, alias Tom Horan, *Australasian,* summer of 1898–99, actual date of article uncertain.

4. Major C. H. B. Pridham, *The Charm of Cricket — Past and Present*, Herbert Jenkins Ltd, London, 1949, p. 39.

5. A. A. Thomson, *Odd Men In: A Gallery of Cricket Eccentrics*, Museum Press Limited, London, 1958, pp. 75–77.

6. John Mulvaney and Rex Harcourt, *Cricket Walkabout: The Australian Aborigines in England*, Macmillan, 1988, p. 154.

7. Excerpt from article in newspaper on first match of the tour against Surrey at The Oval and reproduced in *The Cricketer Spring Annual*, 1930. The Cricketer article was written by Major C. H. B. Pridham).

8. Thomson, op. cit., p. 76.

9. There is a contradictory claim of where Twopenny was born by Colin Tatz, in *Obstacle Race: Aborigines in Sport* (University of NSW Press, 1996, p. 68) Tatz writes that Twopenny was born in Bathurst, NSW, in 1845 and that he was the only non-Victorian Aboriginal player in the team. What we do know is that Twopenny hailed from NSW. Lawrence spotted this strong young man who possessed raw power and invited him into the fold.

10. Mulvaney and Harcourt, op. cit., p. 188.

11. ibid., p. 159.

12. Mulvaney and Harcourt, op. cit., p. 155.

Chapter 8

1. Colin Tatz, *Obstacle Race: Aborigines in Sport*, University of NSW Press, 1996, p. 70.

2. ibid., p. 70.

3. ibid.

4. ibid.

5. ibid.

6. ibid.

7. ibid., p. 72.

8. ibid.

9. ibid., p. 92.

10. ibid., p. 72.

11. ibid., pp. 72–73.

12. ibid., p. 73.

13. Wrote J. C. Davis in 1916, Colin Tatz, op. cit., p. 73.

14. L.O.S. Poidevin, quoted in Colin Tatz, op. cit., p. 74.

15. ibid., p. 74.

16. J. C. Davis of the *Referee,* quoted in Colin Tatz, op. cit., p. 74.

17. ibid.

18. ibid.

19. ibid., p. 76.

20. Excerps from a widely circulated newspaper report (circa 1950) which has also been used in stories in magazines and books about the Aboriginal fast bowler Eddie Gilbert.
21. Michael Page, *Bradman: The Illustrated Biography*, MacMillan, South Melbourne, 1983, p. 133.
22. Excerpts from a letter from Queensland Cricket Association to Queensland Protector of Aborigines, October 1936.
23. Colin Tatz, op. cit., p. 80.
24. David Frith, *Caught England Bowled Australia*, Eva Press, London, 1997, pp. 173–74.

Chapter 9

1. Roger Milliss, *Waterloo Creek*, McPhee Gribble, Ringwood, Victoria, 1992, p. 21.
2. ibid.
3. ibid.
4. Personal comment, telephone conversation 11 April 2001.

Chapter 10

1. David Sampson, 'The Nature and Effects Thereof Were ... by Each of Them Understood: Aborigines, Agency, Law and Power in the 1867 Gurnett Contract, Labour History', *A Journal of Labour and Social History*, no. 74, May 1998, pp. 53–70.
2. ibid., p. 53.

BIBLIOGRAPHY

Aboriginal Australians 1868 England tour scorebook.

Aboriginal Australian 1868 England tour ledger (George Graham's ledger, now at MCG Museum).

The *Age*, various 1867, 1868.

Keith Andrew, *The Handbook of Cricket*, Penguin Group, London.

The *Argus*, 5 January 1867.

The *Australasian*, 1898–99.

Australians, to 1788 and 1838, Syme & Weldon Associates, 1987.

Bell's Life in London & Sporting Chronicle 1822–1886.

Bendigo Advertiser, 23 January 1867.

Derek Birley, *A Social History of English Cricket*, Aurum, London, 1949.

Genevieve Blades, Australian Aborigines Cricket and Pedestrianism, Culture and conflict, 1880–1910, BHMS Thesis.

Duncan Brown, Journal, 5 September 1868 to 19 May 1869.

Peter Carey, *Jack Maggs*, University of Queensland Press, Brisbane, 1997.

M. F. Christie, *Aboriginals in Colonial Victoria 1835–86*, Sydney University Press, 1979.

Wayne Coolwell, *My Kind of People: Achievements, Identity and Aboriginality*, University of Queensland Press, 1993.

A Daft, *Kings of Cricket*, Bristol, 1893.

Charles Dickens, *Pickwick Papers*, Chapman & Hall, London, 1880.

Keith Dunstan, *The Paddock that Grew: the Story of the Melbourne Cricket Ground*, Hutchinson, Australia, 1988.

Eastbourne Gazette, October 1868.

David Frith, *The Pageant of Cricket*, Macmillan, 1987.

David Frith, *Caught England Bowled Australia: A Cricket Slave's Complex Story*, Eva Press, 1997.

John Forster, *The Life of Charles Dickens*, Chapman & Hall and Henry Frowde, London, 1880.

S. T. Gill, *Australian Sketchbook*, 1864.

Janet Gyford, *Witham Park: 100 Years Old*, Witham Town Council, 2000.

Hamilton Spectator, 1868, 1869, 1891.

Les R. Hill, *Australian Cricketers on Tour, 1868–1974*, Lynton Publications, Blackwood, 1974.

Charles Lawrence Journal — recollections of his cricketing days, written at the age of 83 in 1911.

Tony Lewis, *Double Century*, MCC Lord's, Pelham Books, 1997.

Frederick Lillywhite, *Cricket Scores and Biographies of Celebrated Cricketers*, Vol. I, 1799–1827, and Vol. II, 1827–1840.

Lincoln Standard, 8 September 1868.

London Illustrated News.

Colleen McCullough, *Morgan's Run*, Century, London, 2000.

Lord's: The Home of Cricket, MCC Museum, Lord's, London.

Ashley Mallett, *Bradman's Band*, University of Queensland Press, Brisbane, 2000.

Ashley Mallett, *Evonne Cawley (Goolagong)*, Master Sportsman Series, Hutchinson, Melbourne, 1983.

MCC (Melbourne Cricket Club) annual report, 1867.

MCC 1787–1937, The Times Publishing Company, London, 1937.

A. G. 'Johnny' Moyes, *Australian Cricket: A History*, Angus & Robertson, Sydney–London, 1959.

John Mulvaney & Rex Harcourt, *Cricket Walkabout*, Macmillan, South Melbourne, 1988.

Norwich Mercury, 29 July 1868.

Nottingham Cricket

Nottingham Guardian, 5 August 1868

The Old Buffer, *American Cricketer: A Journal of the Cricket Field*, Philadelphia, 18 June 1885.

Lt-Gen Pitt-Rivers, Pitt-Rivers Museum, University of Oxford, England.

Jack Pollard, *Australian Cricket: The Game and the Players*, Hodder & Stoughton & the ABC, 1982.

Major C. H. B. Pridham, 'The First Australians: The Pioneer Colonial Touring Team, *The Cricketer Spring Annual*, 1930.

Major C. H. B. Pridham, *The Charm of Cricket — Past and Present*, Herbert Jenkins, London, 1949.

Punch

Reverend Bill Edwards, Australian Aboriginal Studies, 1999, The fate of an Aboriginal cricketer: when and where did Dick-a-Dick die?

Reverend Henry Nisbett's Journal (on board the *Parramatta*, February–May 1868), Mitchell Library, Sydney, NSW. Vols MLMSS 3093/11–12S.

Reynolds News.

Victor Richardson, *The Victor Richardson Story*, Rigby, Adelaide, 1967.

Rochdale Observer, 27 June 1868.

David Sampson, ' "The Nature and Effects Thereof Were ... by Each of Them Understood": Aborigines, Agency, Law and Power in the 1867 Gurnett Contract', Labour History, *A Journal of Labour and Social History*, Number 74, May 1998.

Sheffield Independent, 12 August 1868.

Six and Out: The Legend of Australian and New Zealand Cricket, Jack Pollard Publishing, 1964.

Sporting Life, London, 28 October 1868.

Colin Tatz, *Black Diamonds*, NSW Press, Sydney, 1996.

Colin Tatz, *Genocide in Australia*, Aboriginal Studies Press, Canberra, 1999.

Colin Tatz, *Obstacle Race: Aborigines in Sport*, UNSW Press, Sydney 1995.

W. B. Tegetrmeir, *The Cricket Field*, May 1868.

The Bury Times, 25 July 1868.

The Illustrated Australian News, 1864.

The Sydney Mail, 22 August 1891.

The Times, June 1868 and 12 June 2000.

The Yorkshire Gazette, 18 July 1868.

A. A. Thompson, *Odd Men In: A Gallery of Cricket Eccentrics*, Museum Press, London, 1958.

Peter Vansittart, *London: A Literary Companion*, John Murray Publishers, London, 1992.

Russel Ward, *Finding Australia: The History of Australia to 1821*, Heinemann Educational Australia, 1987.

Roy Webber, *The Phoenix History of Cricket*, Phoenix Sports Books, London, 1960.

Gib Wettenhall, *The People of the Gariwerd: The Grampians' Aboriginal Heritage*, Aboriginal Affairs, Victoria, 1999.

Bernard Whimpress, *Passport to Nowhere: Aborigines in Australian Cricket, 1850–1939*, Walla Walla Press, Sydney, 1999.

Wisden Cricketers Almanacks (various) including 1869, 1916.

Wisden on Bradman, Hardie Books, 1998.

INDEX